C N AMERICA

THE TRIAL OF CAPTAIN AMERICA

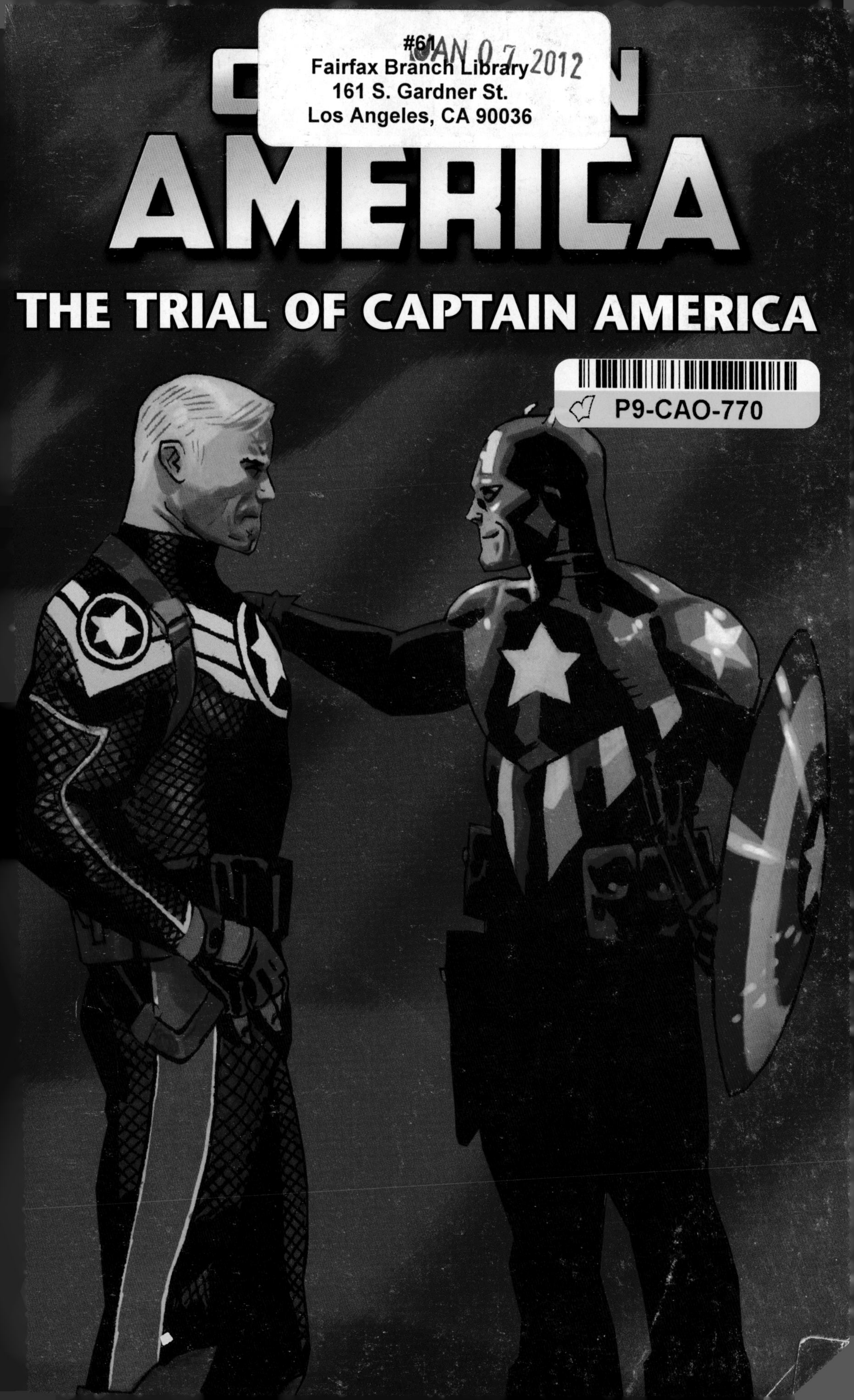

CAPTAIN AMERICA

THE TRIAL OF CAPTAIN AMERICA

WRITER: Ed Brubaker

ART & COLORS, ISSUE #611: **Daniel Acuña**

PENCILS, ISSUES #612-615: **Butch Guice**

INKS, ISSUES #612-615:

Butch Guice & Stefano Gaudiano
with **Rick Magyar, Mark Morales,
Tom Palmer & Mike Perkins**

COLORS, ISSUES #612-615: **Bettie Breitweiser**
with **Frank Martin, Chris Sotomayor & Jay David Ramos**

ART & COLORS, ISSUE #615.1: **Mitch Breitweiser**

COLORS, ISSUES #612-615: **Bettie Breitweiser**

LETTERER: VC's Joe Caramagna

COVER ART: Marko Djurdjevic & Daniel Acuña (Issue #615.1)

ASSOCIATE EDITOR: Lauren Sankovitch

EDITOR: Tom Brevoort

Captain America created by **Joe Simon & Jack Kirby**

Collection Editor: **Jennifer Grünwald**
Editorial Assistants: **James Emmett & Joe Hochstein**
Assistant Editors: **Alex Starbuck & Nelson Ribeiro**
Editor, Special Projects: **Mark D. Beazley**
Senior Editor, Special Projects: **Jeff Youngquist**
Senior Vice President of Sales: **David Gabriel**

Editor in Chief: **Axel Alonso** • Chief Creative Officer: **Joe Quesada**
Publisher: **Dan Buckley** • Executive Producer: **Alan Fine**

TAIN AMERICA: THE TRIAL OF CAPTAIN AMERICA. Contains material originally published in magazine form as CAPTAIN AMERICA #611-615 and #615.1. First printing 2011. Hardcover ISBN# 978-0-7851-5119-7. Softcover # 978-0-7851-5120-3. Published by MARVEL WORLDWIDE, INC., a subsidiary of MARVEL ENTERTAINMENT, LLC. OFFICE OF PUBLICATION: 135 West 50th Street, New York, NY 10020. Copyright © 2010 and 2011 Marvel racters, Inc. All rights reserved. Hardcover: $24.99 per copy in the U.S. and $27.99 in Canada (GST #R127032852). Softcover: $19.99 per copy in the U.S. and $21.99 in Canada (GST #R127032852). Canadian Agreement 668537. All characters featured in this issue and the distinctive names and likenesses thereof, and all related indicia are trademarks of Marvel Characters, Inc. No similarity between any of the names, characters, persons, and/ stitutions in this magazine with those of any living or dead person or institution is intended, and any such similarity which may exist is purely coincidental. **Printed in the U.S.A.** ALAN FINE, EVP - Office of the President, Marvel dwide, Inc. and EVP & CMO Marvel Characters B.V.; DAN BUCKLEY, Publisher & President - Print, Animation & Digital Divisions; JOE QUESADA, Chief Creative Officer; JIM SOKOLOWSKI, Chief Operating Officer; DAVID BOGART, of Business Affairs & Talent Management; TOM BREVOORT, SVP of Publishing; C.B. CEBULSKI, SVP of Creator & Content Development; DAVID GABRIEL, SVP of Publishing Sales & Circulation; MICHAEL PASCIULLO, SVP of Brand ining & Communications; JIM O'KEEFE, VP of Operations & Logistics; DAN CARR, Executive Director of Publishing Technology; JUSTIN F. GABRIE, Director of Publishing & Editorial Operations; SUSAN CRESPI, Editorial Operations ager; ALEX MORALES, Publishing Operations Manager; STAN LEE, Chairman Emeritus. For information regarding advertising in Marvel Comics or on Marvel.com, please contact Ron Stern, VP of Business Development, at rstern@ vel.com. For Marvel subscription inquiries, please call 800-217-9158. **Manufactured between 3/14/2011 and 4/11/2011 (hardcover), and 3/14/2011 and 10/10/2011 (softcover), by R.R. DONNELLEY, INC., SALEM, VA, USA.**

87654321

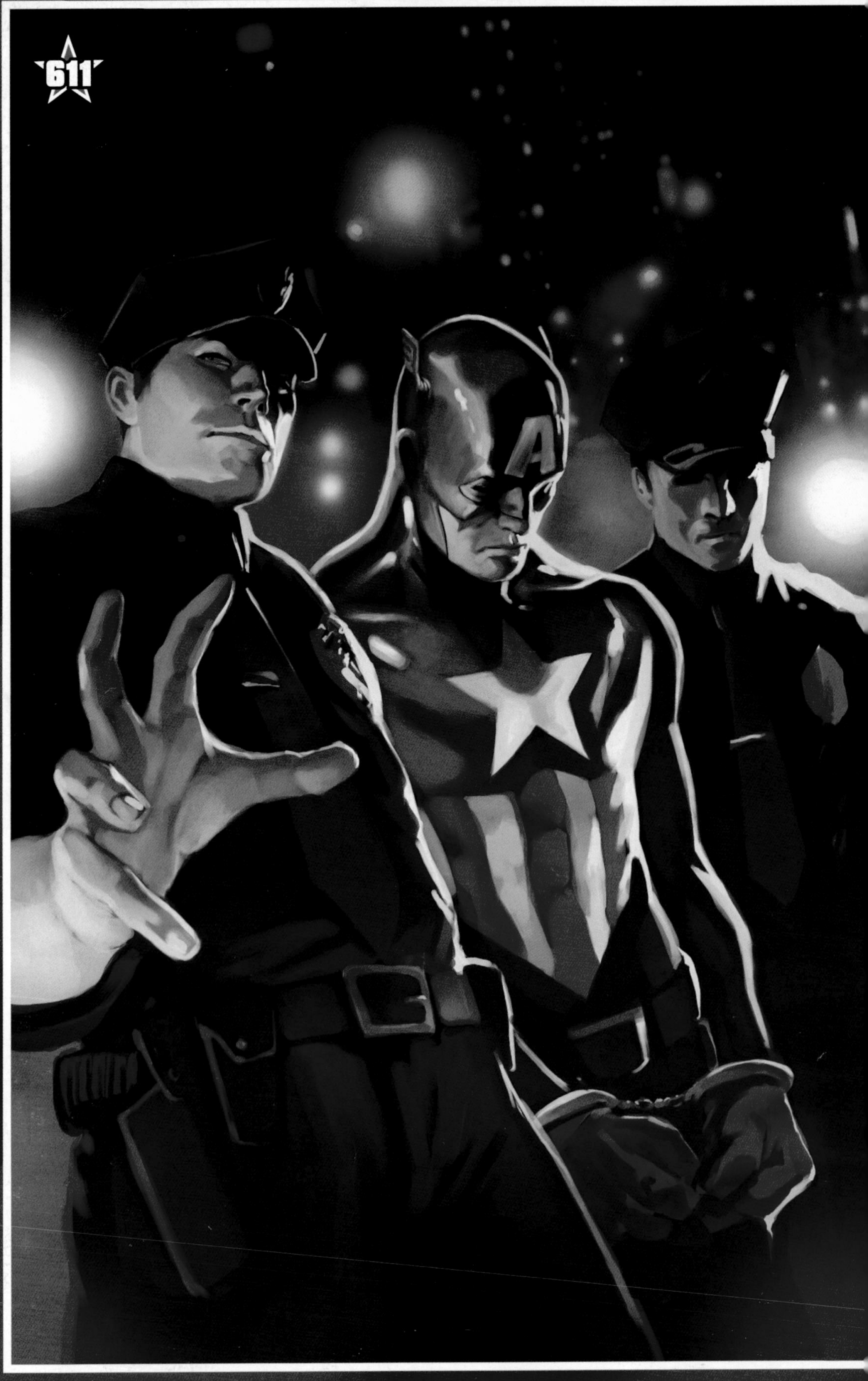
611

THE TRIAL OF CAPTAIN AMERICA PART 1

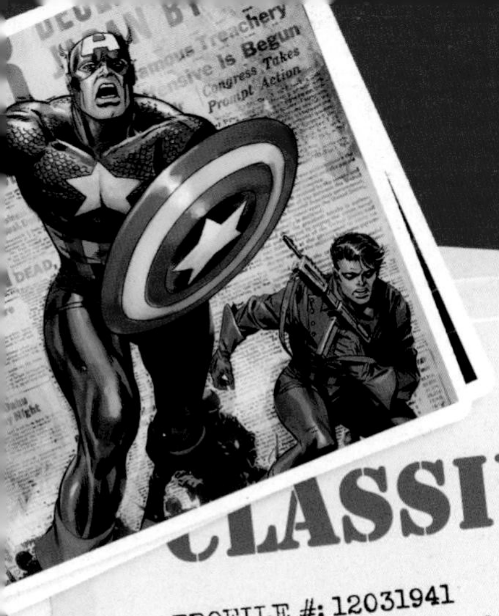
Congress Takes
Prompt Action

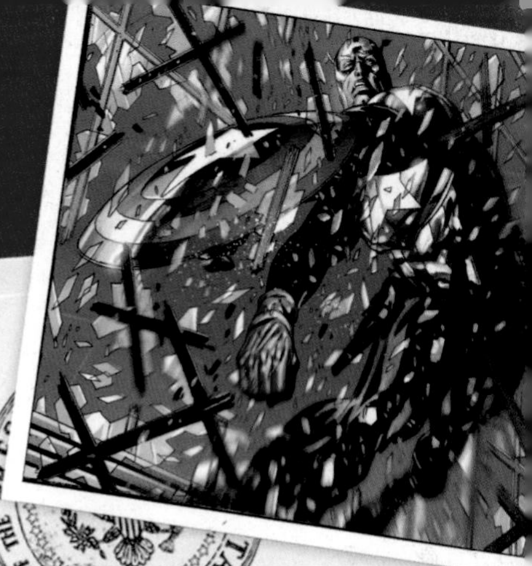

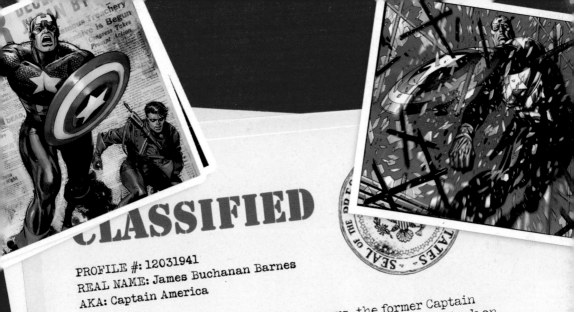

CLASSIFIED

PROFILE #: 12031941
REAL NAME: James Buchanan Barnes
AKA: Captain America

After the apparent murder of Steve Rogers, the former Captain America, Cap's partner from WWII, James "Bucky" Barnes, took on Steve's mantle and his mission. Even now that Steve Rogers has returned from the grave, Bucky continues to wield the shield as Captain America.

But there are some who are not happy that Bucky, thought killed towards the end of the war, is still alive. The son of the original Baron Zemo, Baron Helmut Zemo, recently discovered that his father failed to kill Bucky in World War II. Determined to destroy Bucky's life, believing Bucky has not properly earned it, Zemo revealed to the world media Bucky's dark tenure as the Soviet assassin, The Winter Soldier.

With the media frenzy building, it's only a matter of time before Bucky is called to account for his actions...

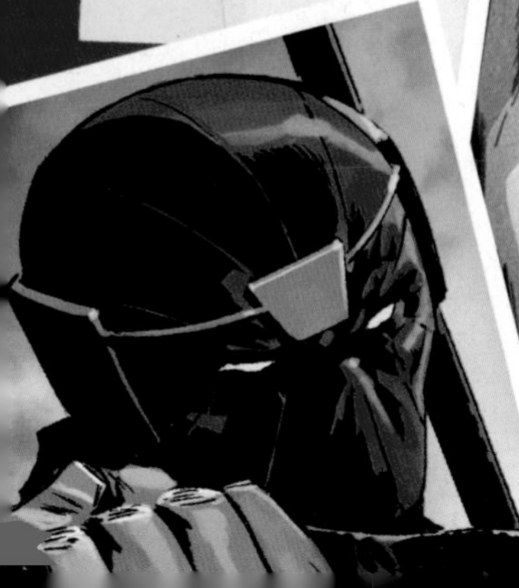

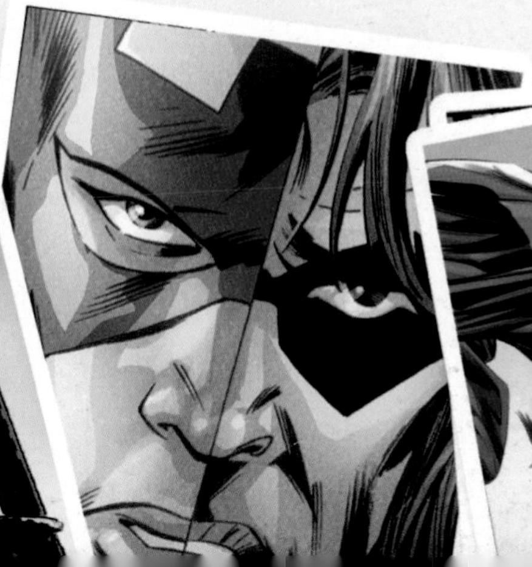

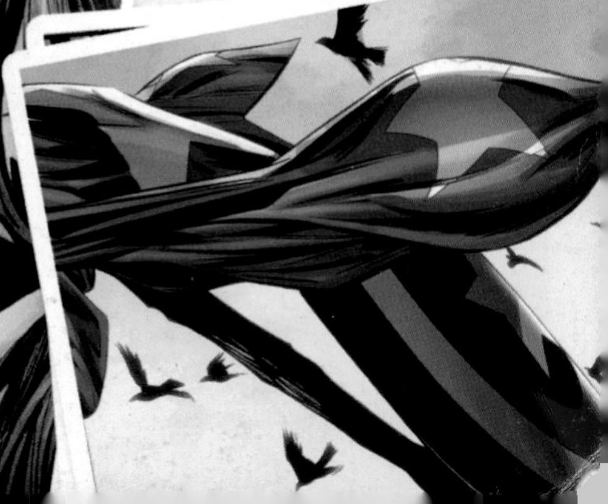

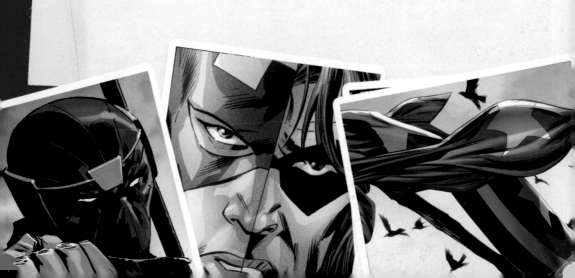

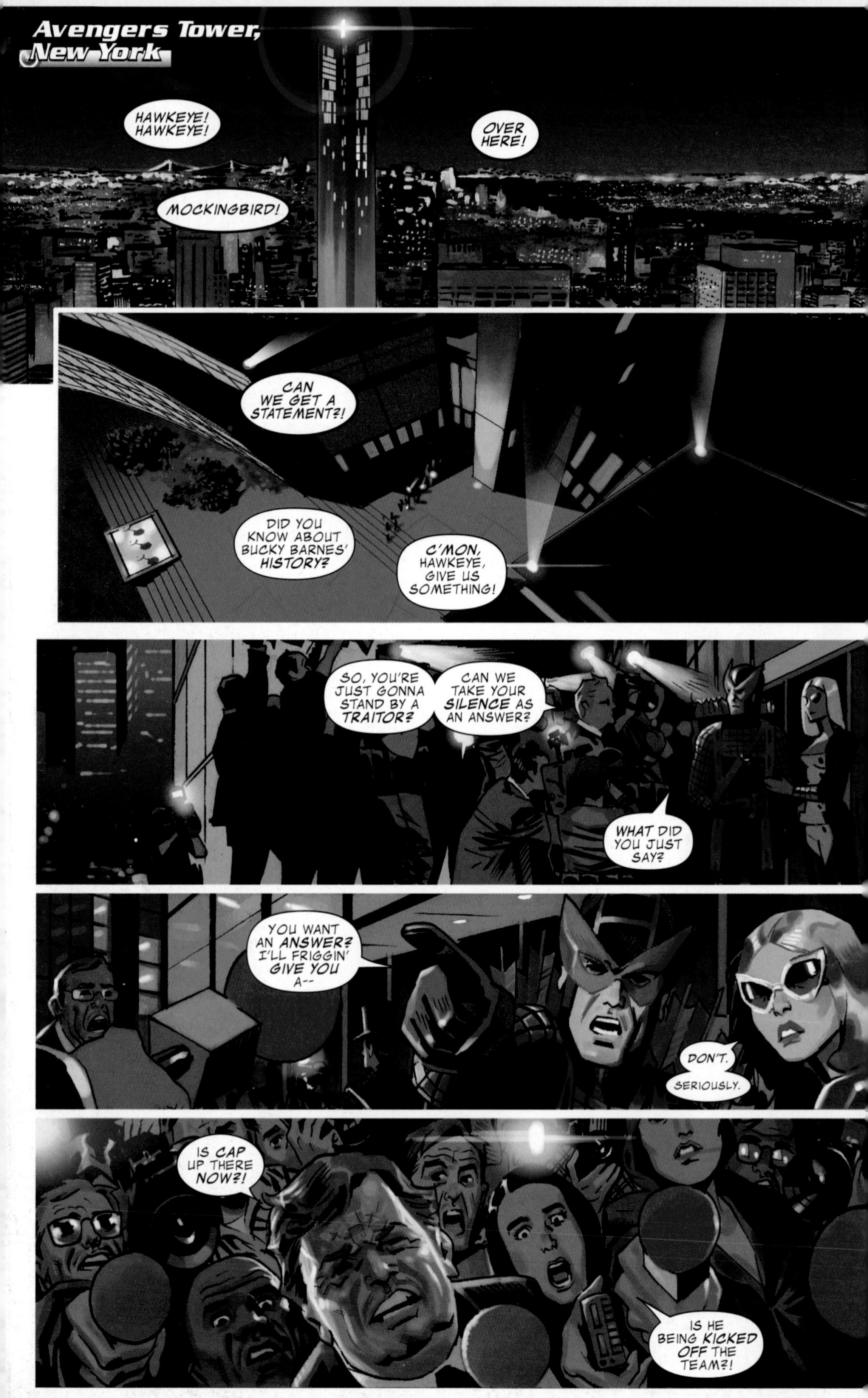
Avengers Tower, New York
HAWKEYE! HAWKEYE!
OVER HERE!
MOCKINGBIRD!
CAN WE GET A STATEMENT?!
DID YOU KNOW ABOUT BUCKY BARNES' HISTORY?
C'MON, HAWKEYE, GIVE US SOMETHING!
SO, YOU'RE JUST GONNA STAND BY A TRAITOR?
CAN WE TAKE YOUR SILENCE AS AN ANSWER?
WHAT DID YOU JUST SAY?
YOU WANT AN ANSWER? I'LL FRIGGIN' GIVE YOU A--
DON'T.
SERIOUSLY.
IS CAP UP THERE NOW?!
IS HE BEING KICKED OFF THE TEAM?!

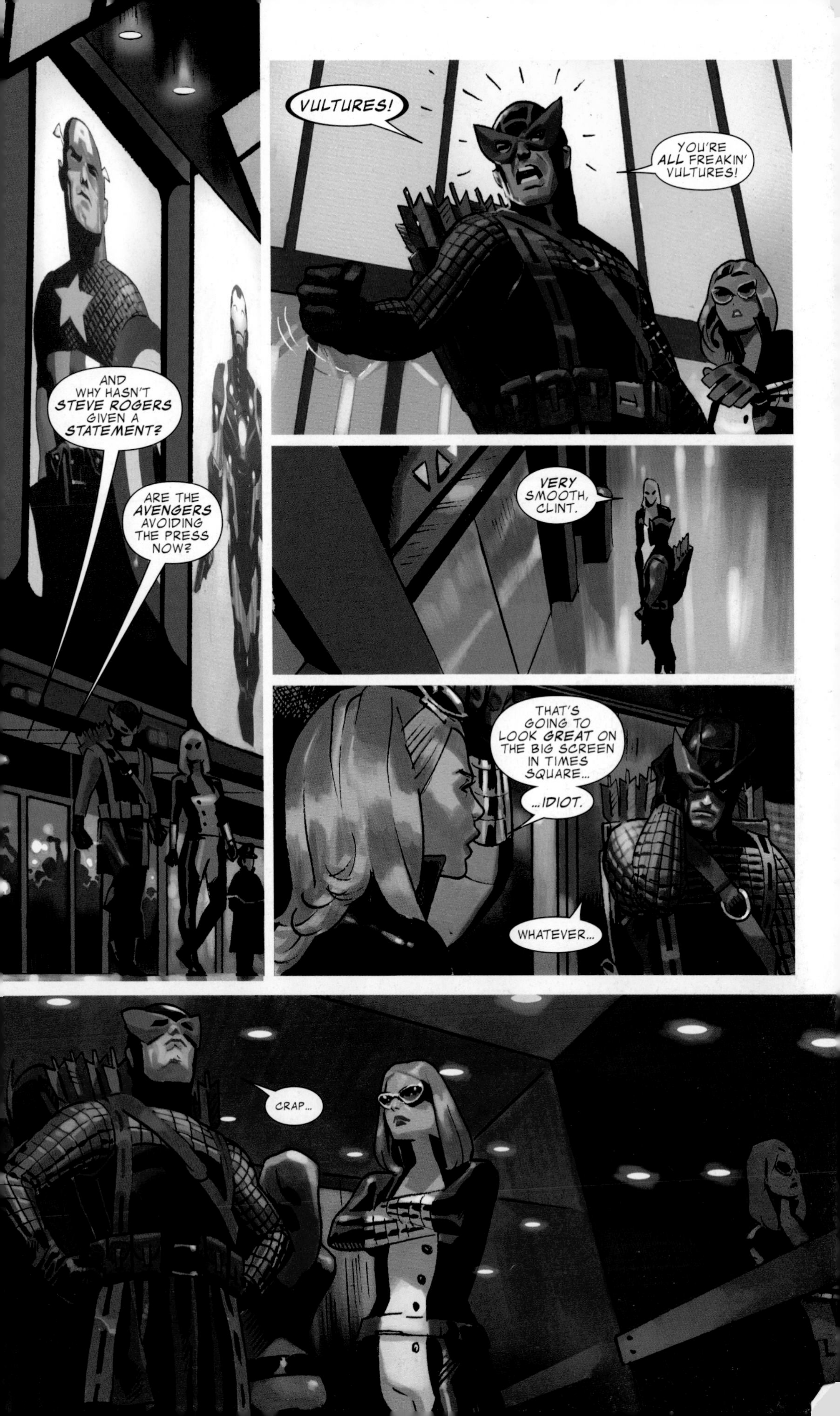
AND WHY HASN'T STEVE ROGERS GIVEN A STATEMENT?
ARE THE AVENGERS AVOIDING THE PRESS NOW?
VULTURES!
YOU'RE ALL FREAKIN' VULTURES!
VERY SMOOTH, CLINT.
THAT'S GOING TO LOOK GREAT ON THE BIG SCREEN IN TIMES SQUARE...
...IDIOT.
WHATEVER...
CRAP...

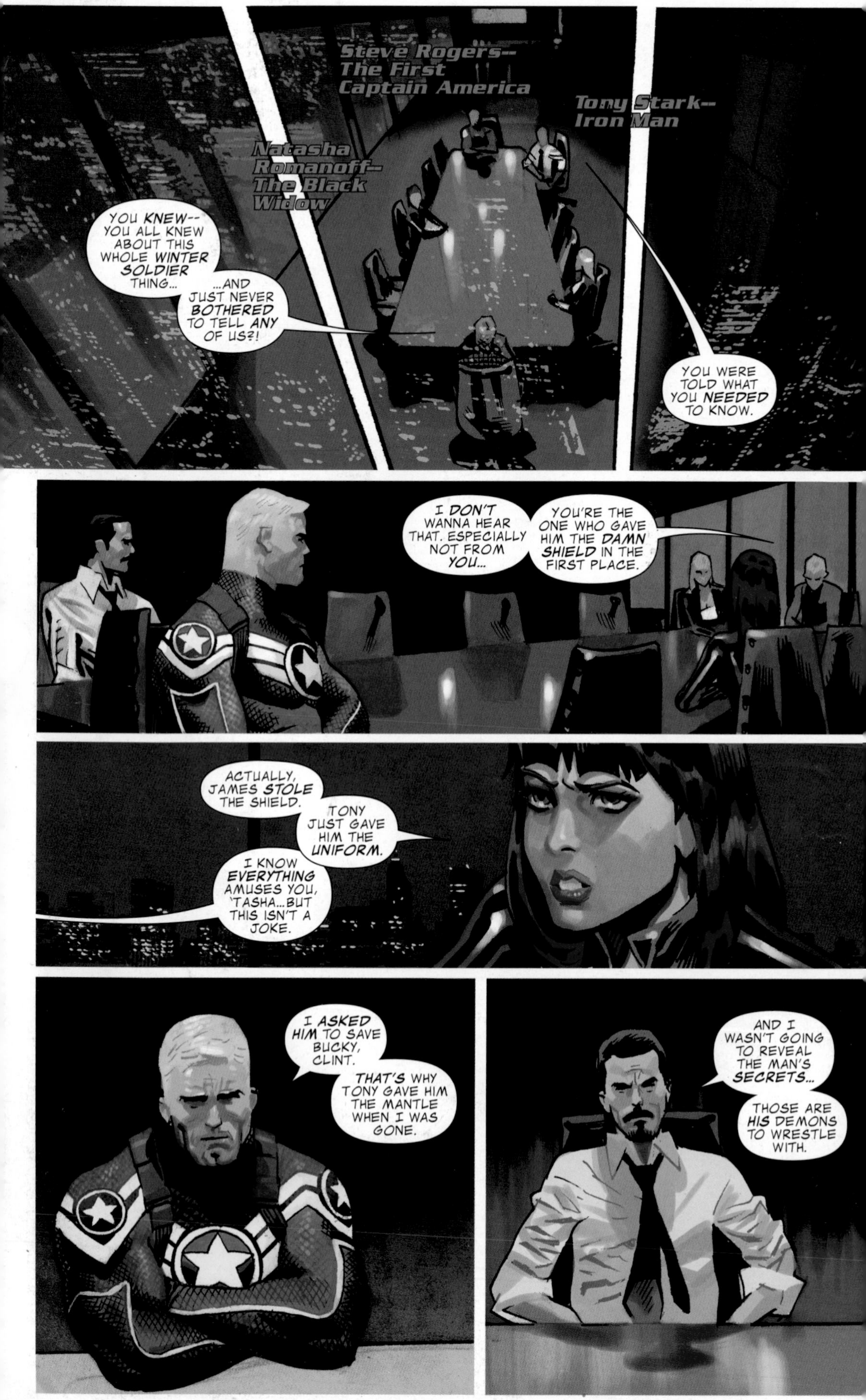
Steve Rogers-- The First Captain America
Tony Stark-- Iron Man
Natasha Romanoff-- The Black Widow
YOU KNEW-- YOU ALL KNEW ABOUT THIS WHOLE WINTER SOLDIER THING...
...AND JUST NEVER BOTHERED TO TELL ANY OF US?!
YOU WERE TOLD WHAT YOU NEEDED TO KNOW.
I DON'T WANNA HEAR THAT. ESPECIALLY NOT FROM YOU...
YOU'RE THE ONE WHO GAVE HIM THE DAMN SHIELD IN THE FIRST PLACE.
ACTUALLY, JAMES STOLE THE SHIELD.
TONY JUST GAVE HIM THE UNIFORM.
I KNOW EVERYTHING AMUSES YOU, 'TASHA...BUT THIS ISN'T A JOKE.
I ASKED HIM TO SAVE BUCKY, CLINT.
THAT'S WHY TONY GAVE HIM THE MANTLE WHEN I WAS GONE.
AND I WASN'T GOING TO REVEAL THE MAN'S SECRETS...
THOSE ARE HIS DEMONS TO WRESTLE WITH.

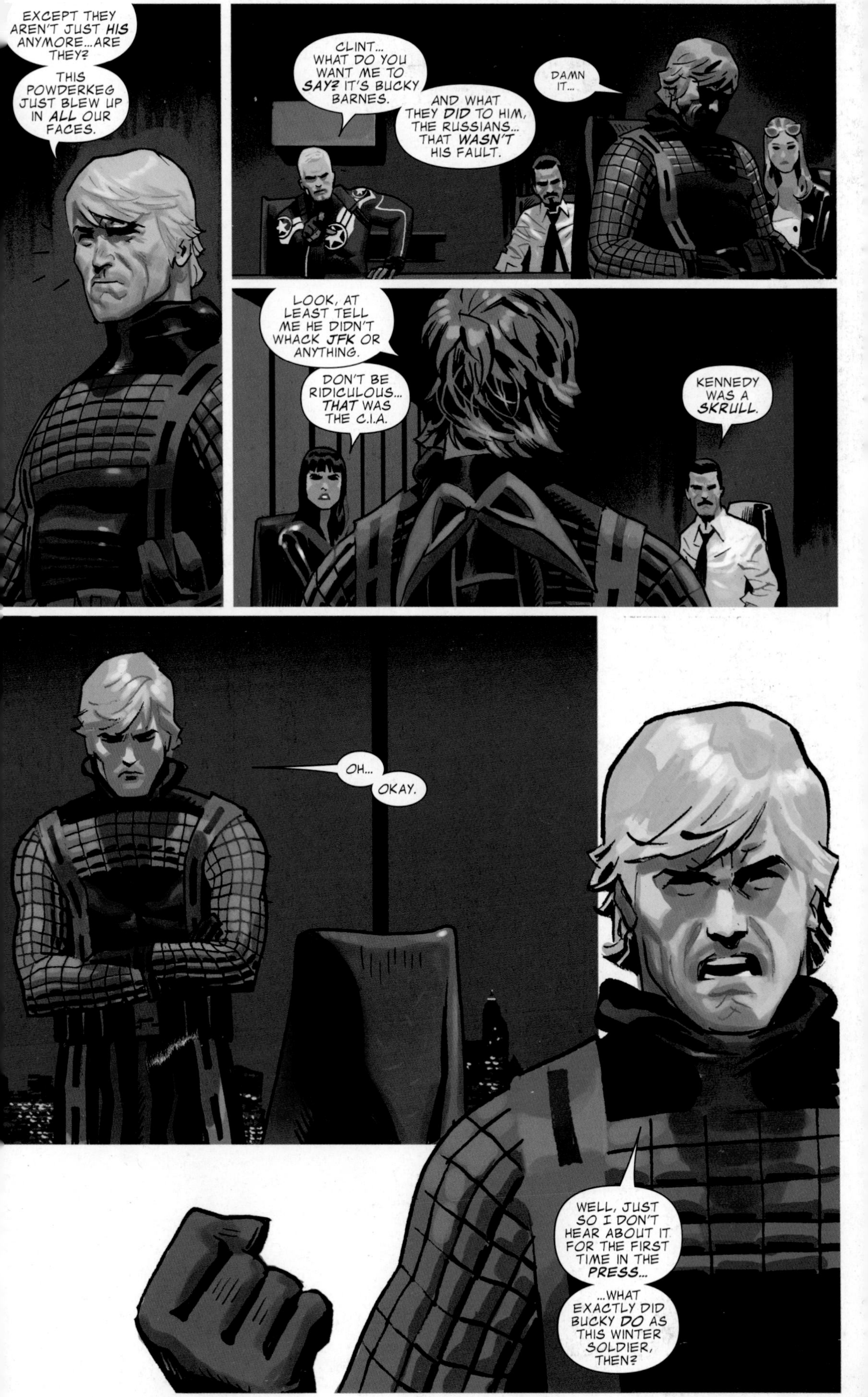

EXCEPT THEY AREN'T JUST HIS ANYMORE...ARE THEY?
THIS POWDERKEG JUST BLEW UP IN ALL OUR FACES.
CLINT... WHAT DO YOU WANT ME TO SAY? IT'S BUCKY BARNES.
AND WHAT THEY DID TO HIM, THE RUSSIANS... THAT WASN'T HIS FAULT.
DAMN IT...
LOOK, AT LEAST TELL ME HE DIDN'T WHACK JFK OR ANYTHING.
DON'T BE RIDICULOUS... THAT WAS THE C.I.A.
KENNEDY WAS A SKRULL.
OH... OKAY.
WELL, JUST SO I DON'T HEAR ABOUT IT FOR THE FIRST TIME IN THE PRESS...
...WHAT EXACTLY DID BUCKY DO AS THIS WINTER SOLDIER, THEN?

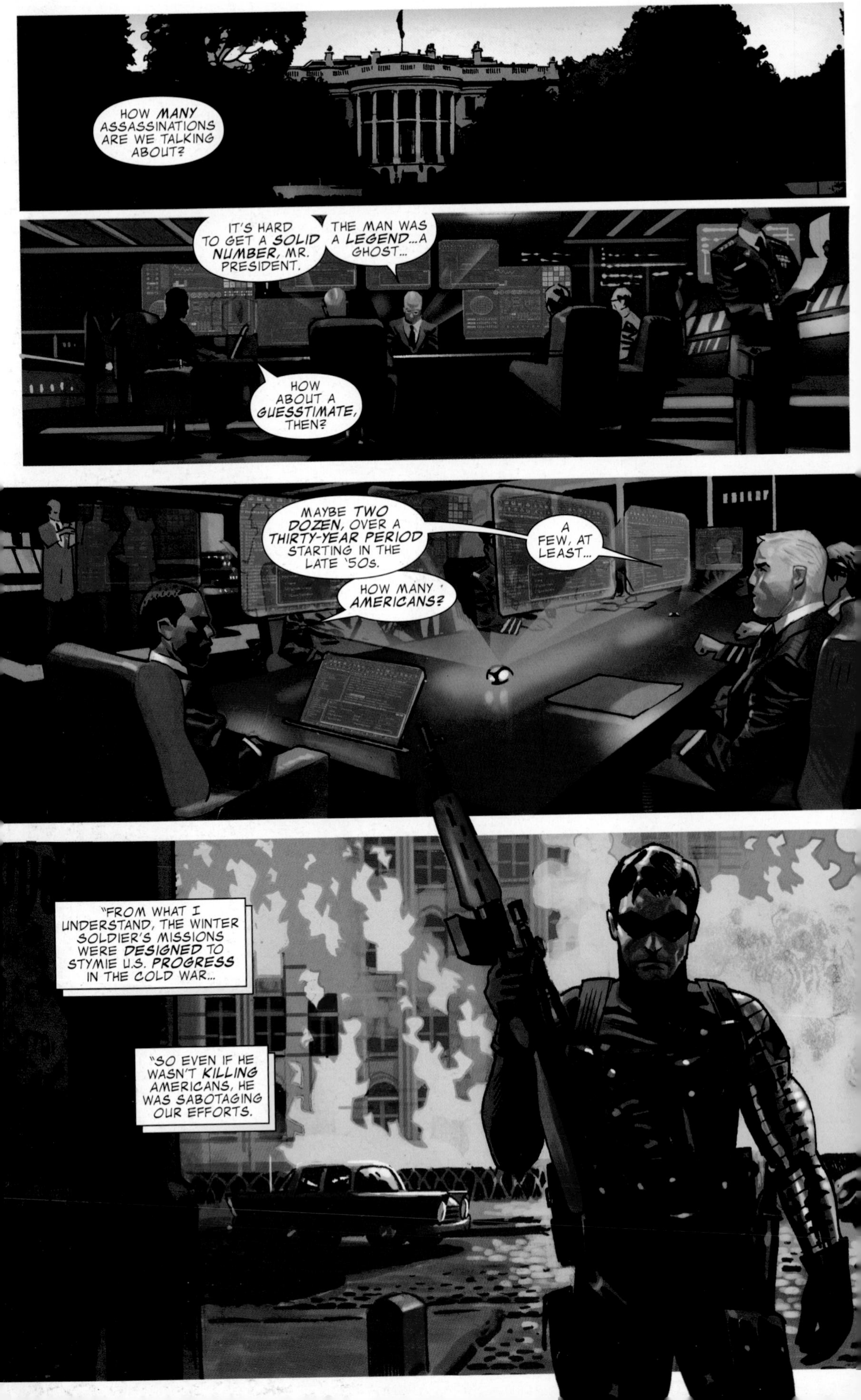
HOW MANY ASSASSINATIONS ARE WE TALKING ABOUT?
IT'S HARD TO GET A SOLID NUMBER, MR. PRESIDENT.
THE MAN WAS A LEGEND... A GHOST...
HOW ABOUT A GUESSTIMATE, THEN?
MAYBE TWO DOZEN, OVER A THIRTY-YEAR PERIOD STARTING IN THE LATE '50s.
HOW MANY AMERICANS?
A FEW, AT LEAST...
"FROM WHAT I UNDERSTAND, THE WINTER SOLDIER'S MISSIONS WERE DESIGNED TO STYMIE U.S. PROGRESS IN THE COLD WAR...
"SO EVEN IF HE WASN'T KILLING AMERICANS, HE WAS SABOTAGING OUR EFFORTS.

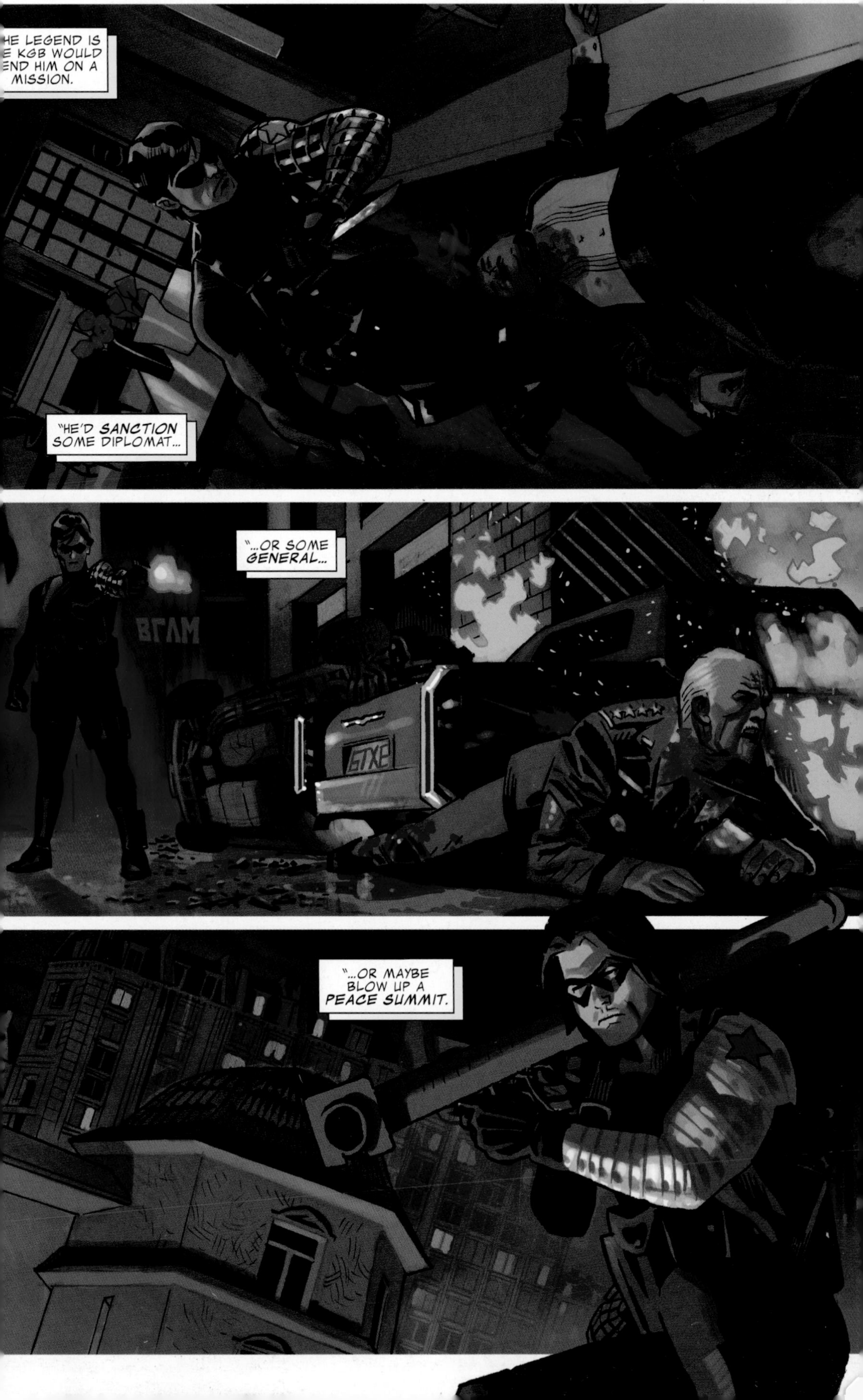
HE LEGEND IS
E KGB WOULD
END HIM ON A
MISSION.
"HE'D SANCTION SOME DIPLOMAT...
"...OR SOME GENERAL...
BГΛM
"...OR MAYBE BLOW UP A PEACE SUMMIT.

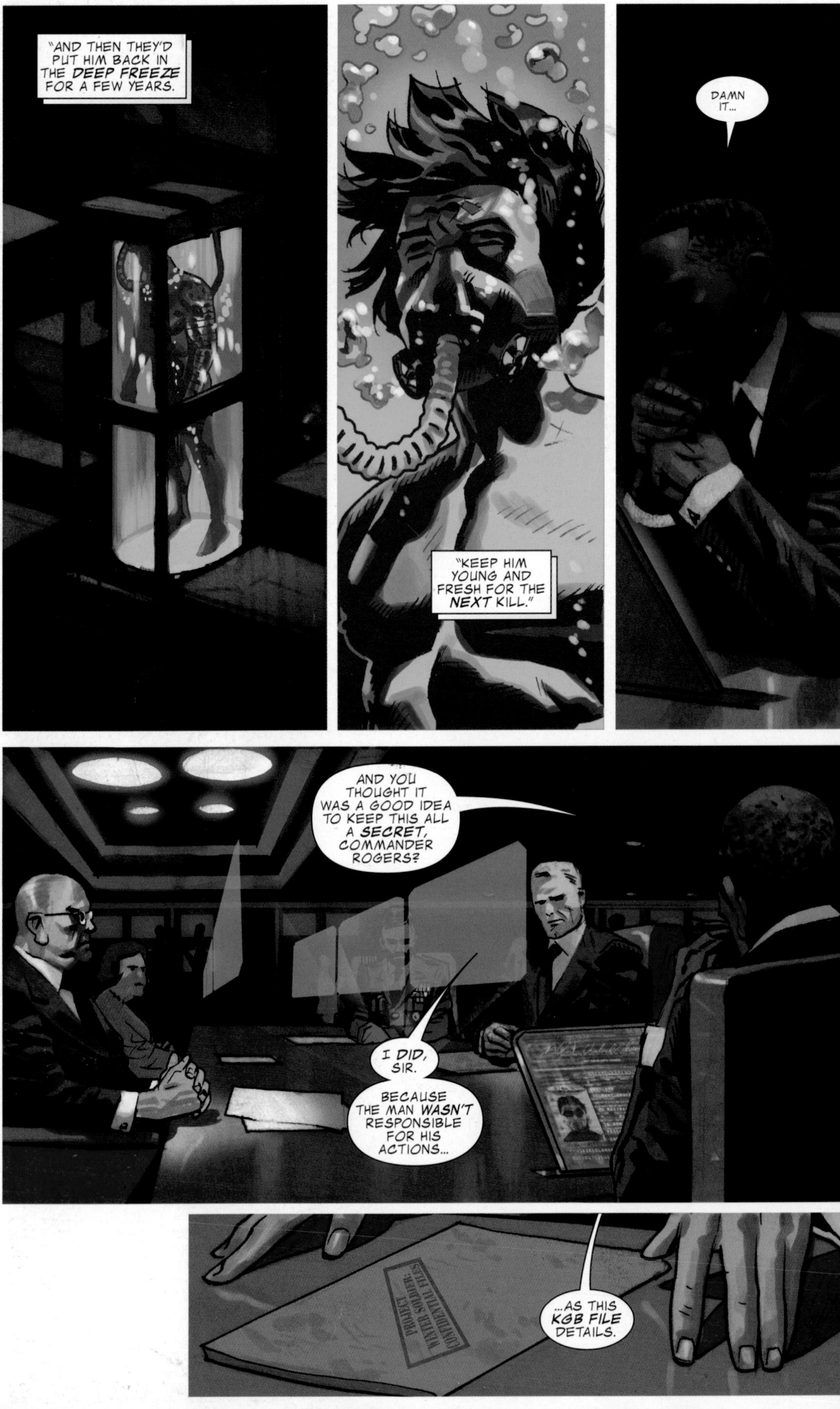
"AND THEN THEY'D PUT HIM BACK IN THE DEEP FREEZE FOR A FEW YEARS.
"KEEP HIM YOUNG AND FRESH FOR THE NEXT KILL."
DAMN IT...
AND YOU THOUGHT IT WAS A GOOD IDEA TO KEEP THIS ALL A SECRET, COMMANDER ROGERS?
I DID, SIR.
BECAUSE THE MAN WASN'T RESPONSIBLE FOR HIS ACTIONS...
PROJECT WINTER SOLDIER: CONFIDENTIAL FILES
...AS THIS KGB FILE DETAILS.

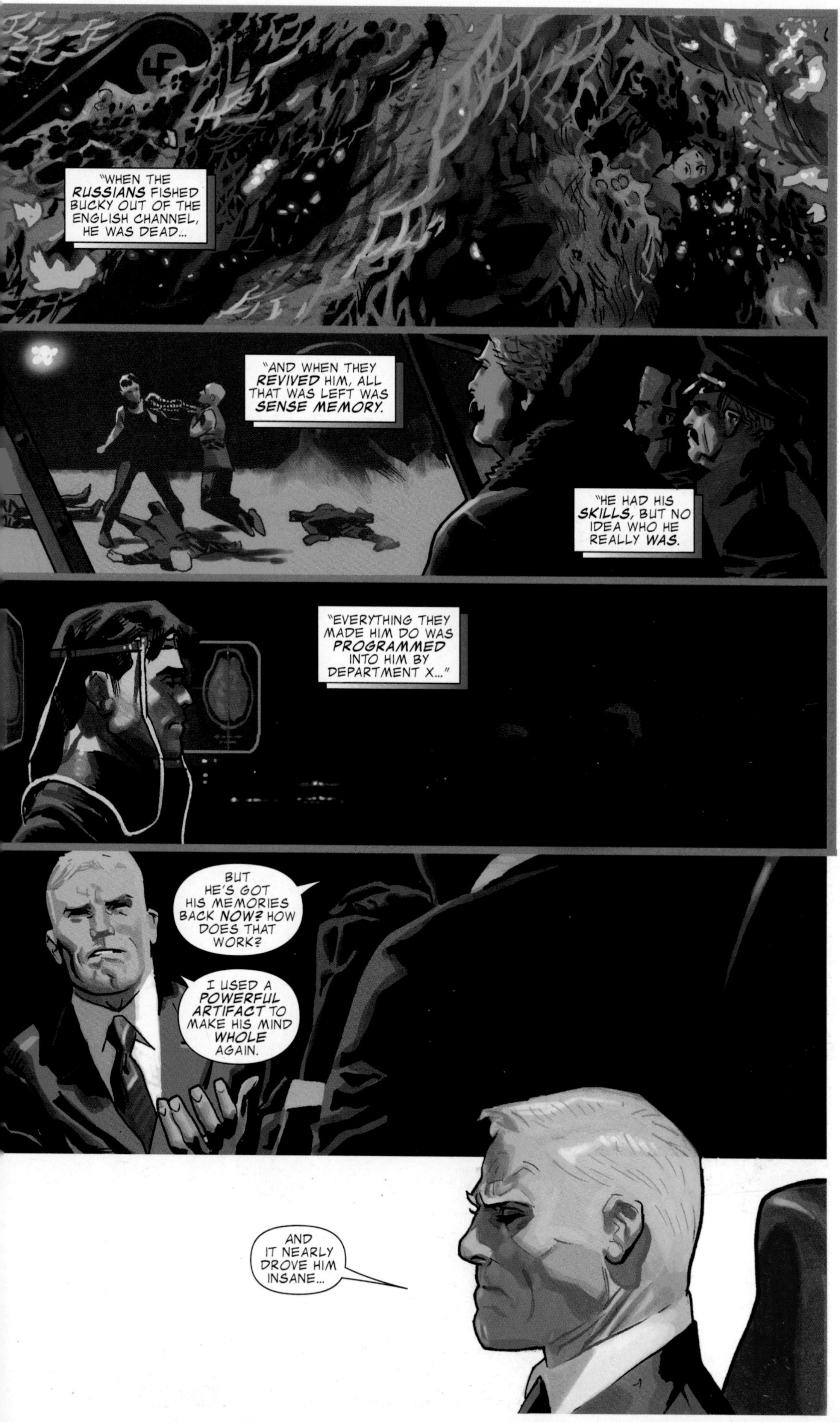
"WHEN THE RUSSIANS FISHED BUCKY OUT OF THE ENGLISH CHANNEL, HE WAS DEAD...
"AND WHEN THEY REVIVED HIM, ALL THAT WAS LEFT WAS SENSE MEMORY.
"HE HAD HIS SKILLS, BUT NO IDEA WHO HE REALLY WAS.
"EVERYTHING THEY MADE HIM DO WAS PROGRAMMED INTO HIM BY DEPARTMENT X..."
BUT HE'S GOT HIS MEMORIES BACK NOW? HOW DOES THAT WORK?
I USED A POWERFUL ARTIFACT TO MAKE HIS MIND WHOLE AGAIN.
AND IT NEARLY DROVE HIM INSANE...

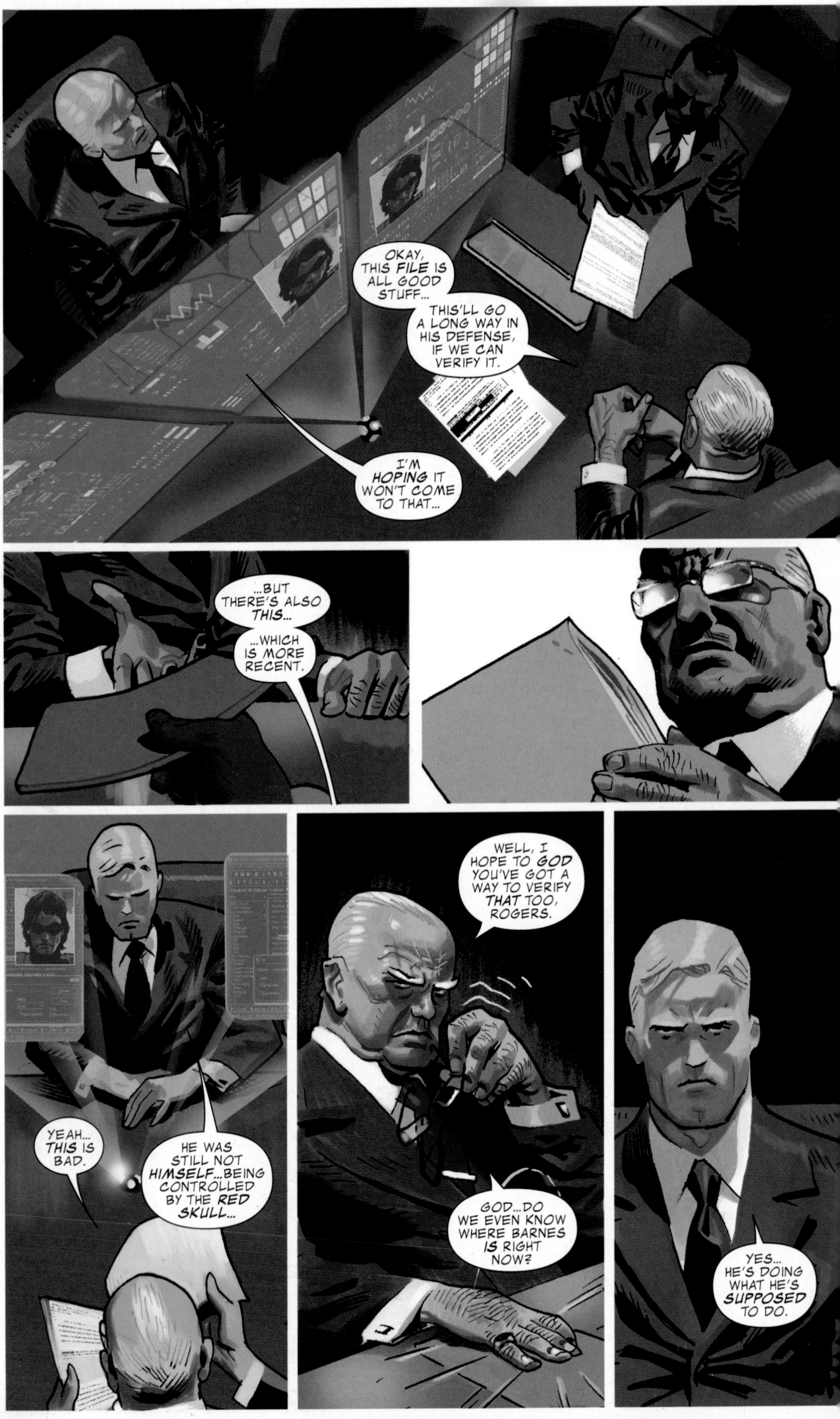

OKAY, THIS FILE IS ALL GOOD STUFF...
THIS'LL GO A LONG WAY IN HIS DEFENSE, IF WE CAN VERIFY IT.
I'M HOPING IT WON'T COME TO THAT...
...BUT THERE'S ALSO THIS...
...WHICH IS MORE RECENT.
YEAH... THIS IS BAD.
HE WAS STILL NOT HIMSELF...BEING CONTROLLED BY THE RED SKULL...
WELL, I HOPE TO GOD YOU'VE GOT A WAY TO VERIFY THAT TOO, ROGERS.
GOD...DO WE EVEN KNOW WHERE BARNES IS RIGHT NOW?
YES... HE'S DOING WHAT HE'S SUPPOSED TO DO.

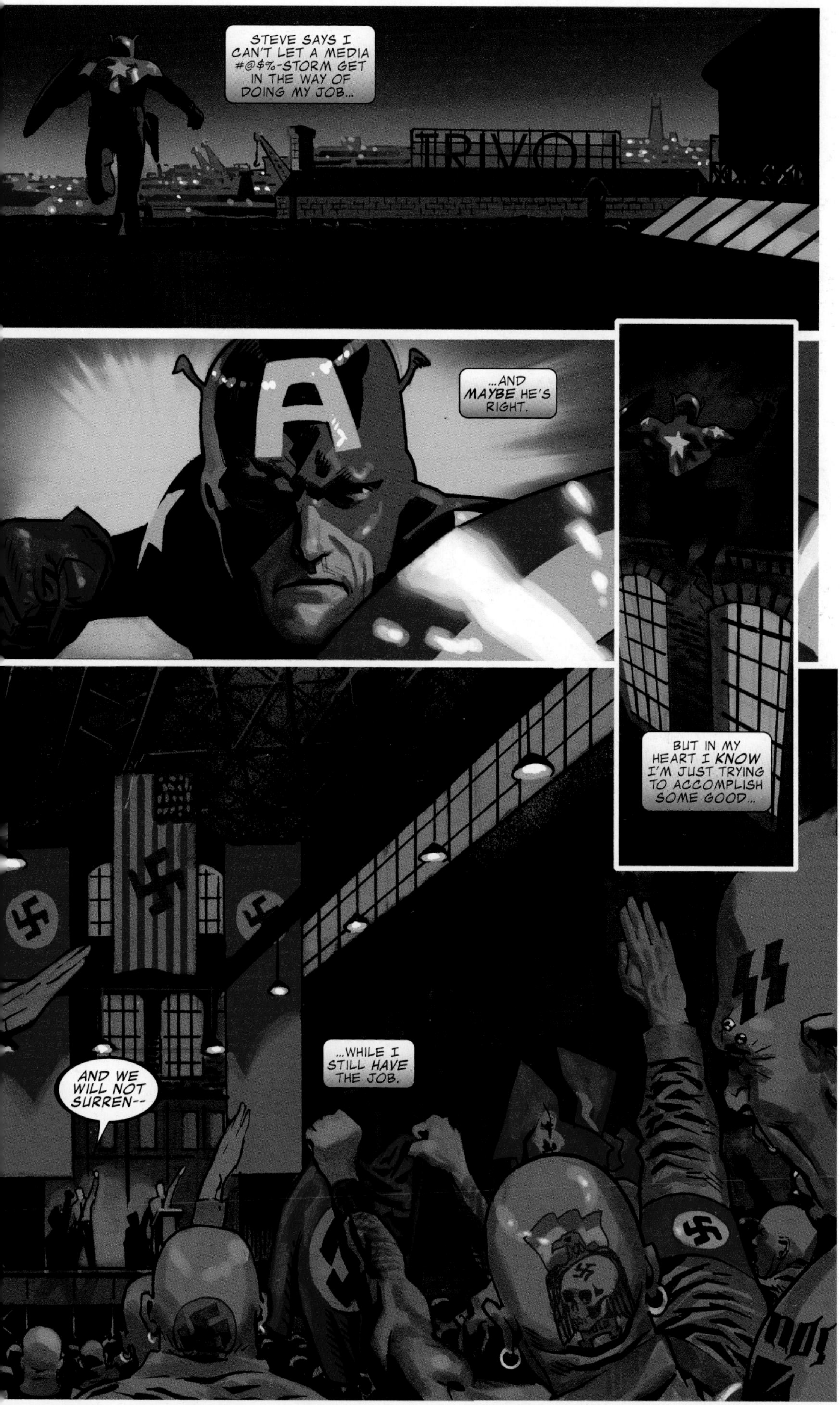

TRIVOLI
STEVE SAYS I CAN'T LET A MEDIA #@$%-STORM GET IN THE WAY OF DOING MY JOB...
...AND MAYBE HE'S RIGHT.
BUT IN MY HEART I KNOW I'M JUST TRYING TO ACCOMPLISH SOME GOOD...
...WHILE I STILL HAVE THE JOB.
AND WE WILL NOT SURREN--

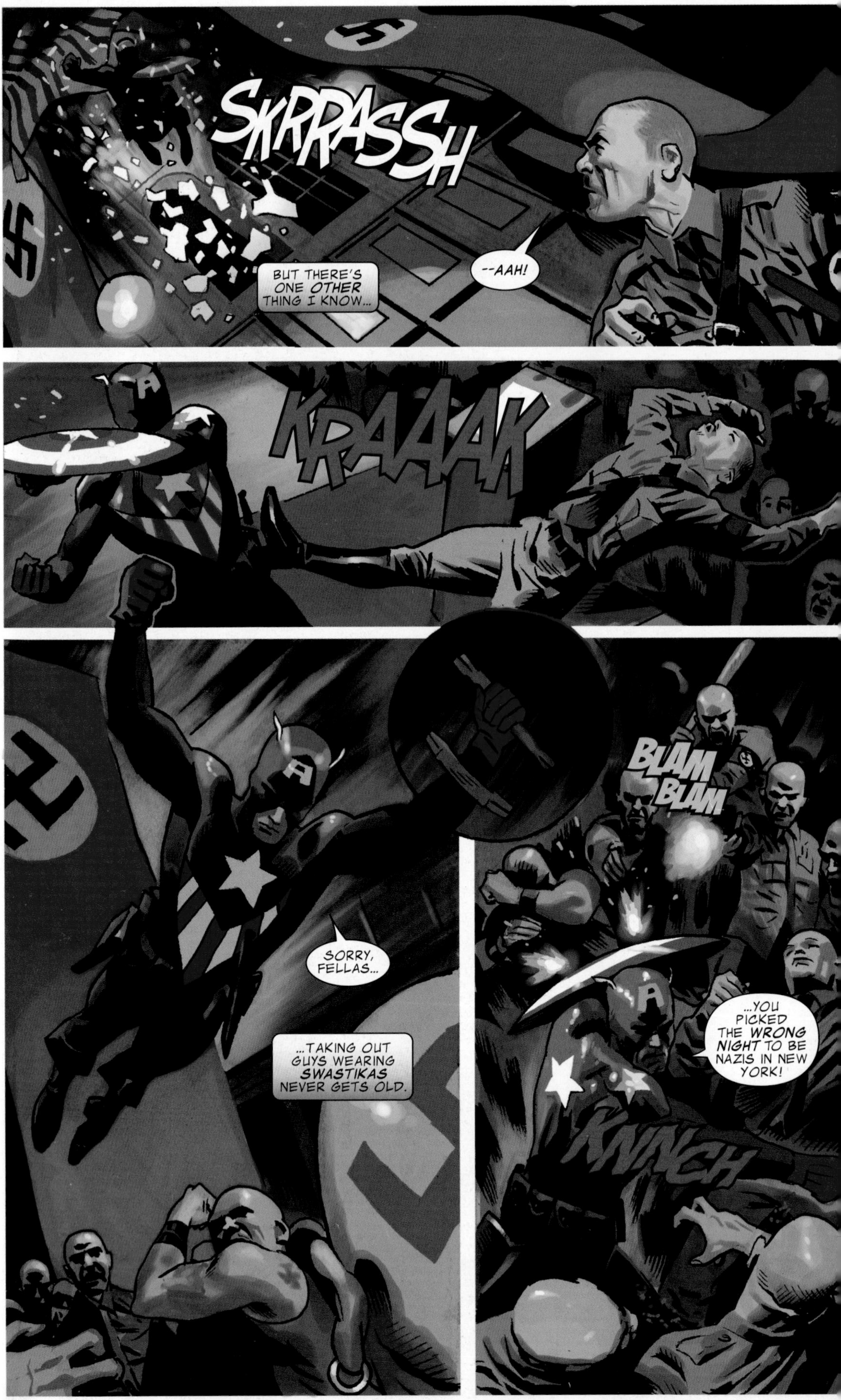
SKRRASSH
BUT THERE'S ONE OTHER THING I KNOW...
--AAH!
KRAAAAK
BLAM BLAM
SORRY, FELLAS...
...TAKING OUT GUYS WEARING SWASTIKAS NEVER GETS OLD.
...YOU PICKED THE WRONG NIGHT TO BE NAZIS IN NEW YORK!
KNNCH

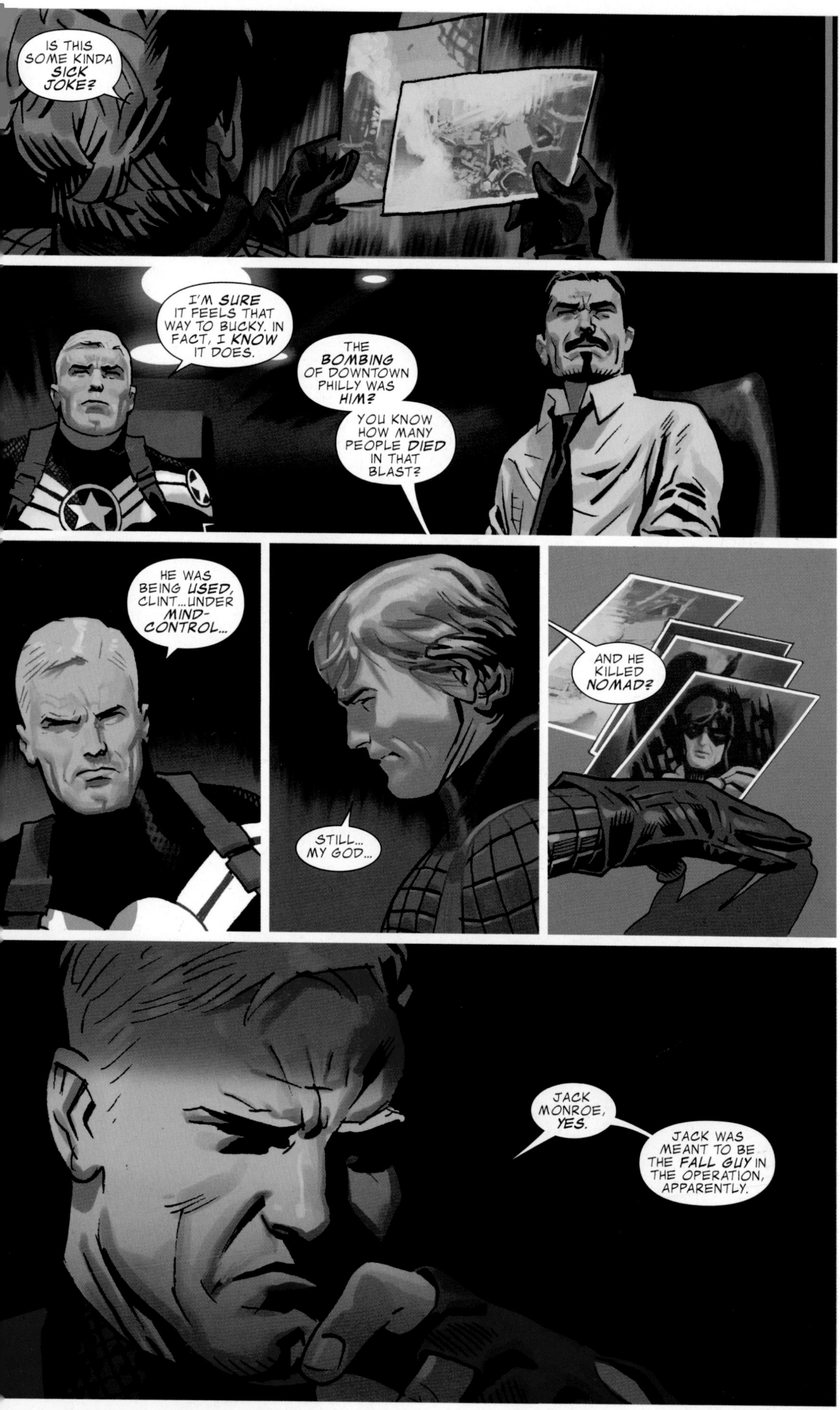

IS THIS SOME KINDA SICK JOKE?
I'M SURE IT FEELS THAT WAY TO BUCKY. IN FACT, I KNOW IT DOES.
THE BOMBING OF DOWNTOWN PHILLY WAS HIM?
YOU KNOW HOW MANY PEOPLE DIED IN THAT BLAST?
HE WAS BEING USED, CLINT...UNDER MIND-CONTROL...
STILL... MY GOD...
AND HE KILLED NOMAD?
JACK MONROE, YES.
JACK WAS MEANT TO BE THE FALL GUY IN THE OPERATION, APPARENTLY.

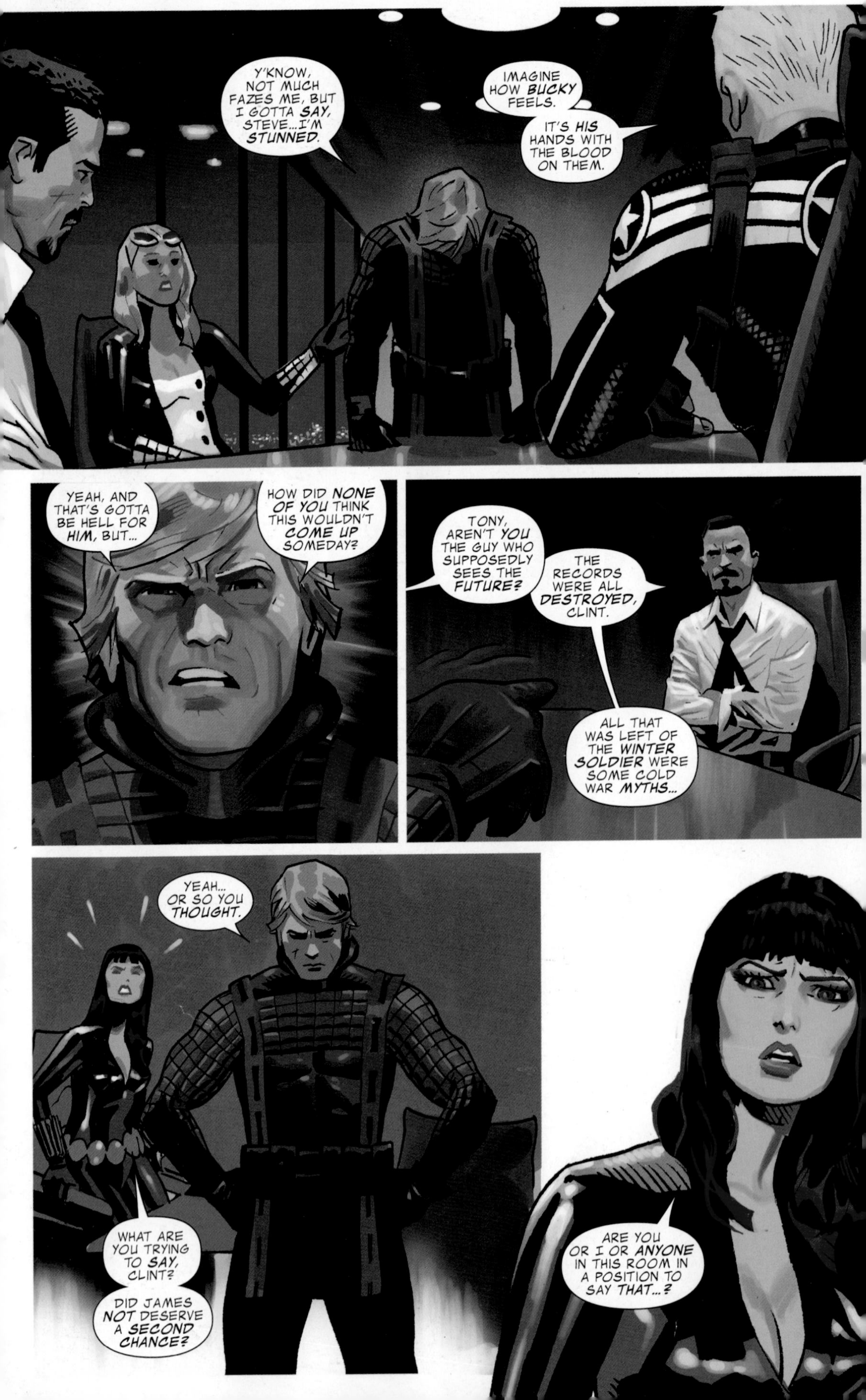
Y'KNOW, NOT MUCH FAZES ME, BUT I GOTTA SAY, STEVE...I'M STUNNED.
IMAGINE HOW BUCKY FEELS.
IT'S HIS HANDS WITH THE BLOOD ON THEM.
YEAH, AND THAT'S GOTTA BE HELL FOR HIM, BUT...
HOW DID NONE OF YOU THINK THIS WOULDN'T COME UP SOMEDAY?
TONY, AREN'T YOU THE GUY WHO SUPPOSEDLY SEES THE FUTURE?
THE RECORDS WERE ALL DESTROYED, CLINT.
ALL THAT WAS LEFT OF THE WINTER SOLDIER WERE SOME COLD WAR MYTHS...
YEAH... OR SO YOU THOUGHT.
WHAT ARE YOU TRYING TO SAY, CLINT?
DID JAMES NOT DESERVE A SECOND CHANCE?
ARE YOU OR I OR ANYONE IN THIS ROOM IN A POSITION TO SAY THAT...?

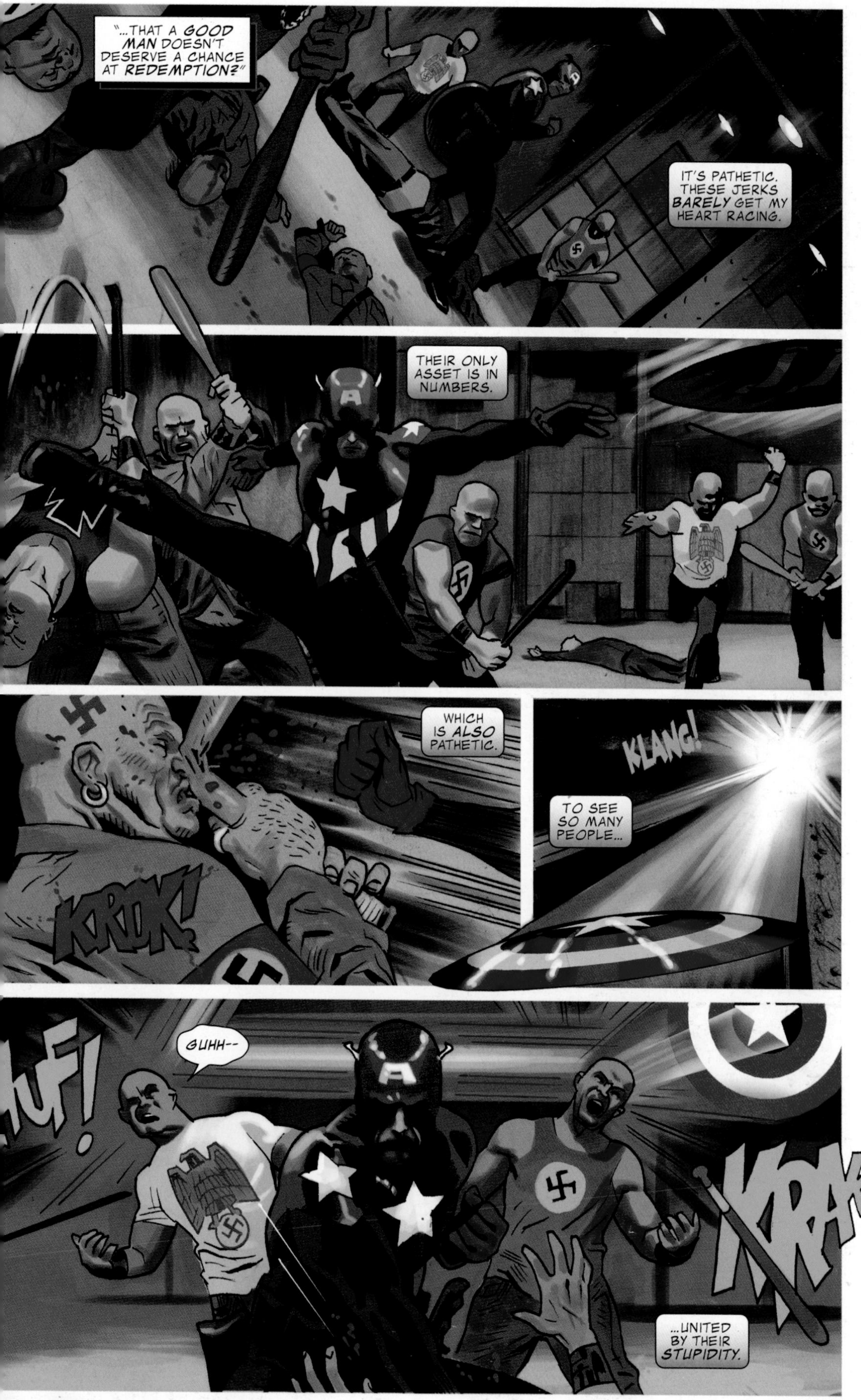
"...THAT A GOOD MAN DOESN'T DESERVE A CHANCE AT REDEMPTION?"
IT'S PATHETIC. THESE JERKS BARELY GET MY HEART RACING.
THEIR ONLY ASSET IS IN NUMBERS.
WHICH IS ALSO PATHETIC.
KROK!
KLANG!
TO SEE SO MANY PEOPLE...
GUHH--
KRAK
...UNITED BY THEIR STUPIDITY.

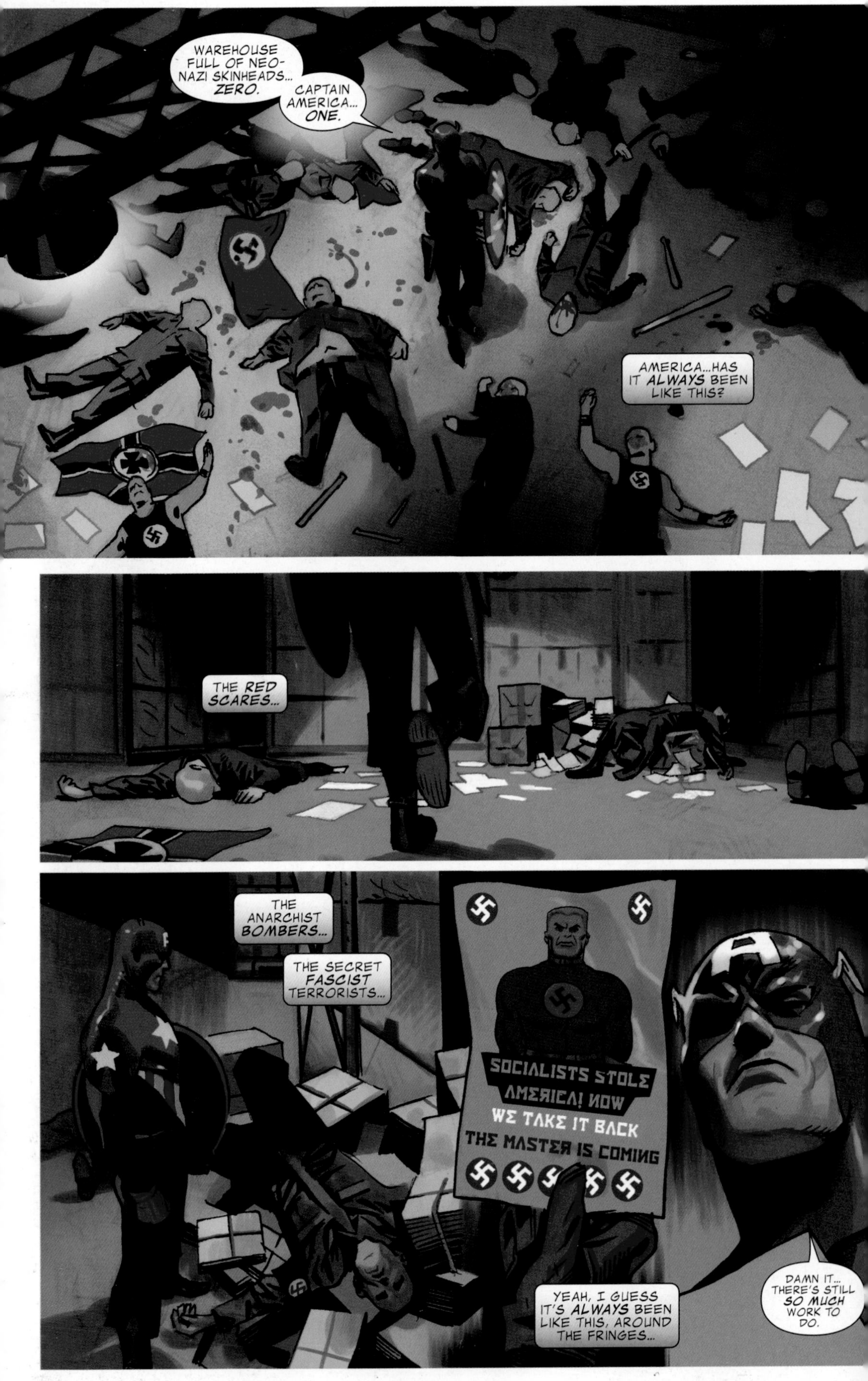
WAREHOUSE FULL OF NEO-NAZI SKINHEADS... ZERO.
CAPTAIN AMERICA... ONE.
AMERICA...HAS IT ALWAYS BEEN LIKE THIS?
THE RED SCARES...
THE ANARCHIST BOMBERS...
THE SECRET FASCIST TERRORISTS...
SOCIALISTS STOLE AMERICA! NOW WE TAKE IT BACK
THE MASTER IS COMING
YEAH, I GUESS IT'S ALWAYS BEEN LIKE THIS, AROUND THE FRINGES...
DAMN IT... THERE'S STILL SO MUCH WORK TO DO.

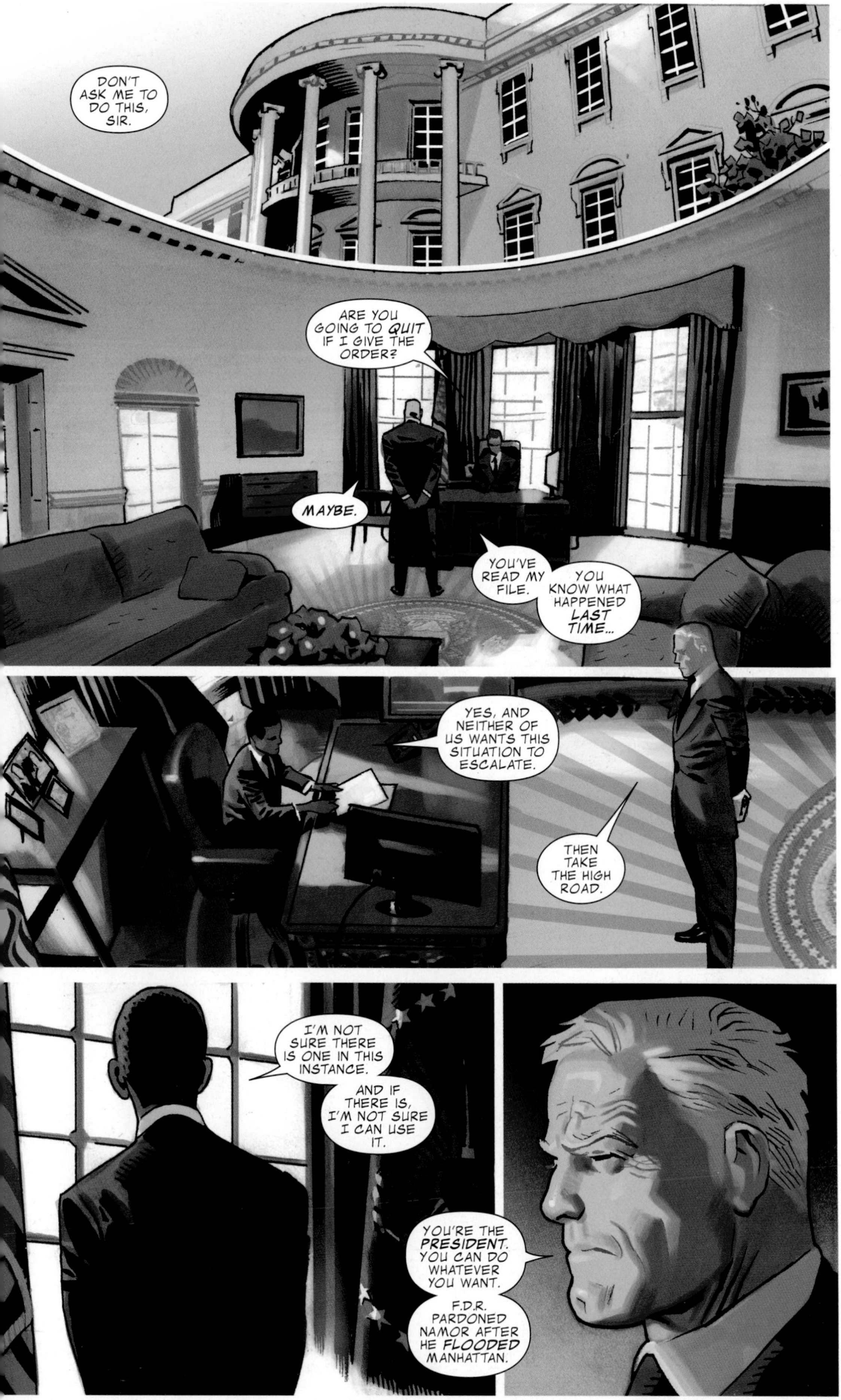
DON'T ASK ME TO DO THIS, SIR.
ARE YOU GOING TO QUIT IF I GIVE THE ORDER?
MAYBE.
YOU'VE READ MY FILE.
YOU KNOW WHAT HAPPENED LAST TIME...
YES, AND NEITHER OF US WANTS THIS SITUATION TO ESCALATE.
THEN TAKE THE HIGH ROAD.
I'M NOT SURE THERE IS ONE IN THIS INSTANCE.
AND IF THERE IS, I'M NOT SURE I CAN USE IT.
YOU'RE THE PRESIDENT. YOU CAN DO WHATEVER YOU WANT.
F.D.R. PARDONED NAMOR AFTER HE FLOODED MANHATTAN.

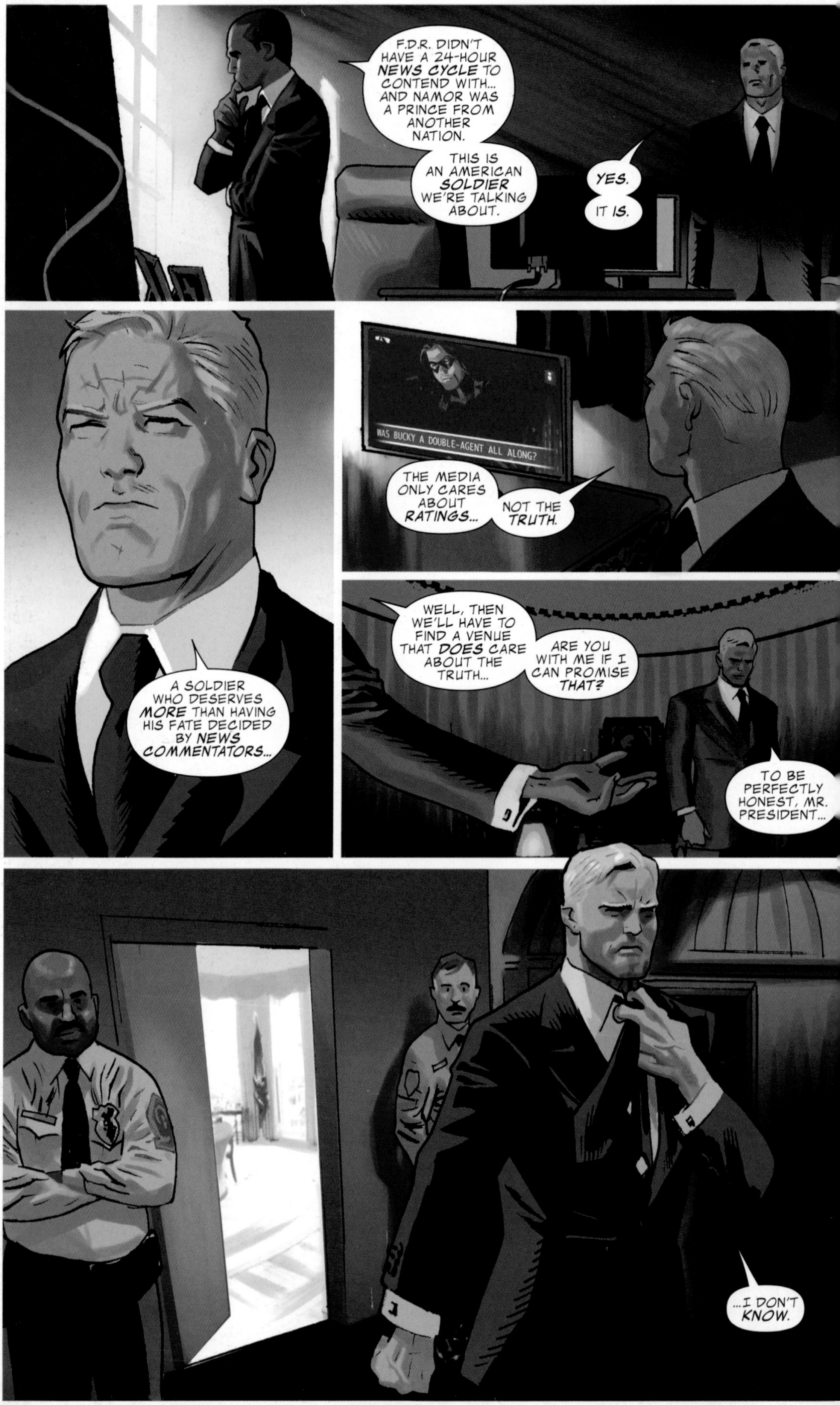

F.D.R. DIDN'T HAVE A 24-HOUR NEWS CYCLE TO CONTEND WITH... AND NAMOR WAS A PRINCE FROM ANOTHER NATION.
THIS IS AN AMERICAN SOLDIER WE'RE TALKING ABOUT.
YES.
IT IS.
A SOLDIER WHO DESERVES MORE THAN HAVING HIS FATE DECIDED BY NEWS COMMENTATORS...
WAS BUCKY A DOUBLE-AGENT ALL ALONG?
THE MEDIA ONLY CARES ABOUT RATINGS...
NOT THE TRUTH.
WELL, THEN WE'LL HAVE TO FIND A VENUE THAT DOES CARE ABOUT THE TRUTH...
ARE YOU WITH ME IF I CAN PROMISE THAT?
TO BE PERFECTLY HONEST, MR. PRESIDENT...
...I DON'T KNOW.

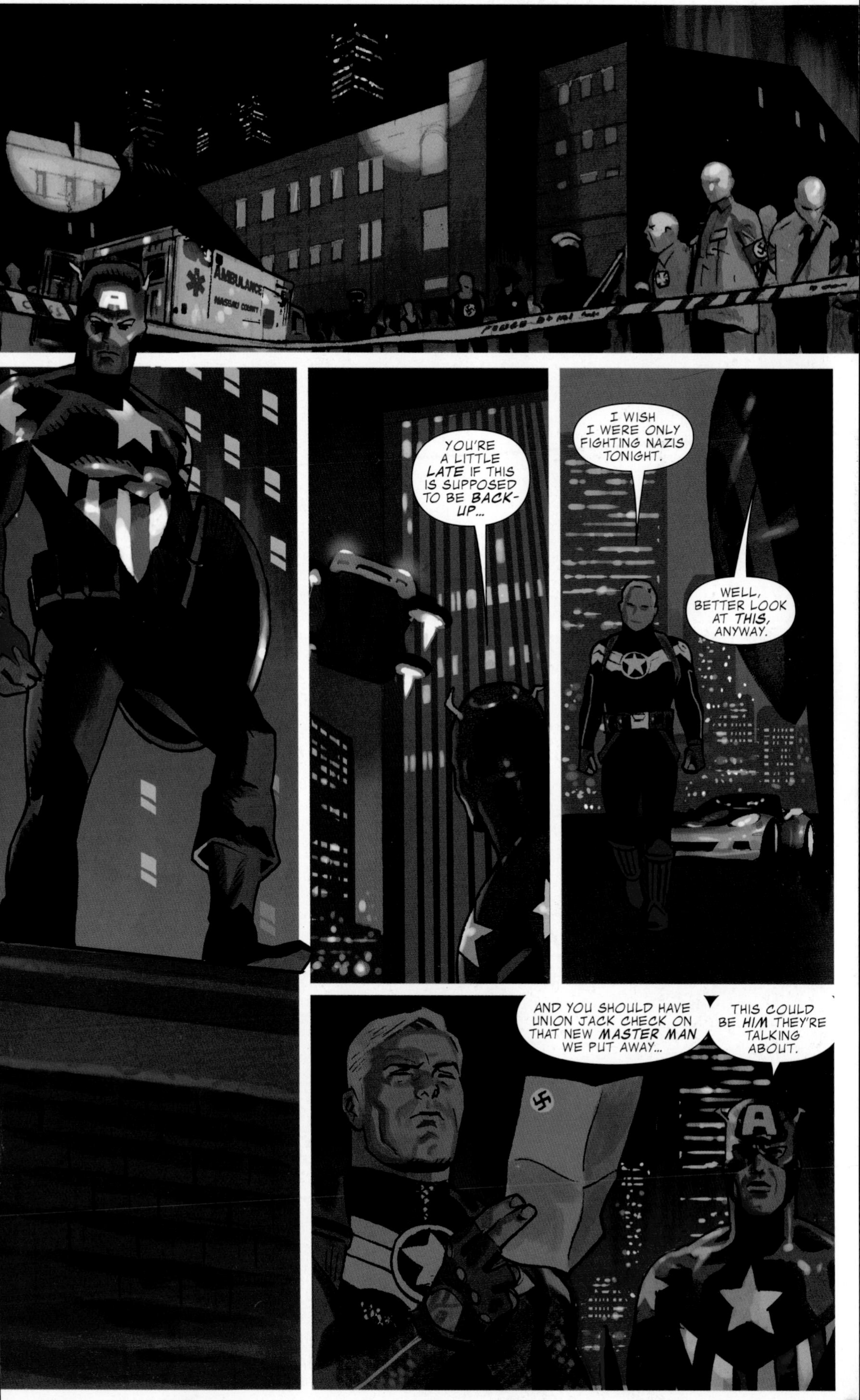

YOU'RE A LITTLE LATE IF THIS IS SUPPOSED TO BE BACK-UP...
I WISH I WERE ONLY FIGHTING NAZIS TONIGHT.
WELL, BETTER LOOK AT THIS, ANYWAY.
AND YOU SHOULD HAVE UNION JACK CHECK ON THAT NEW MASTER MAN WE PUT AWAY...
THIS COULD BE HIM THEY'RE TALKING ABOUT.

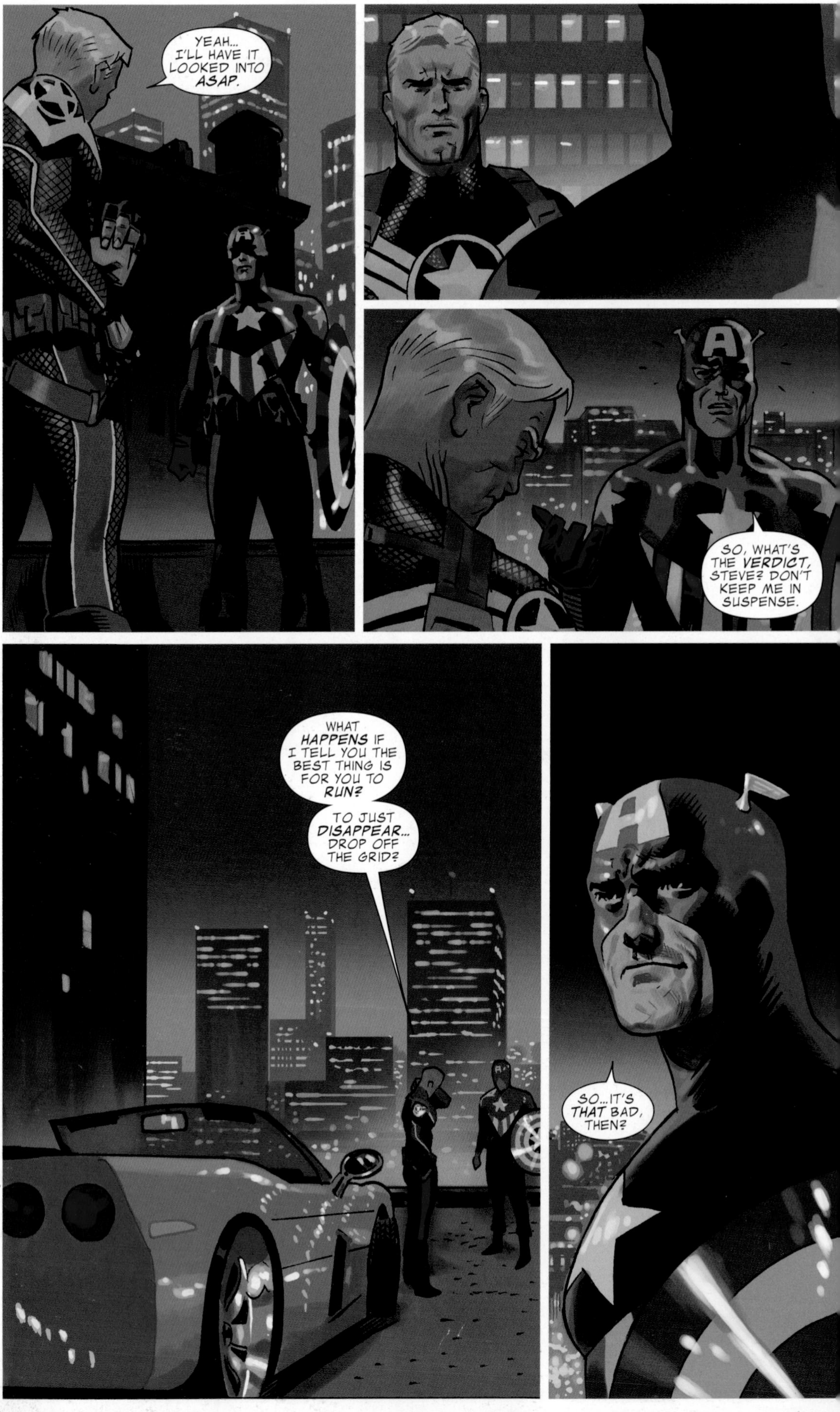
YEAH... I'LL HAVE IT LOOKED INTO ASAP.
SO, WHAT'S THE VERDICT, STEVE? DON'T KEEP ME IN SUSPENSE.
WHAT HAPPENS IF I TELL YOU THE BEST THING IS FOR YOU TO RUN?
TO JUST DISAPPEAR... DROP OFF THE GRID?
SO...IT'S THAT BAD, THEN?

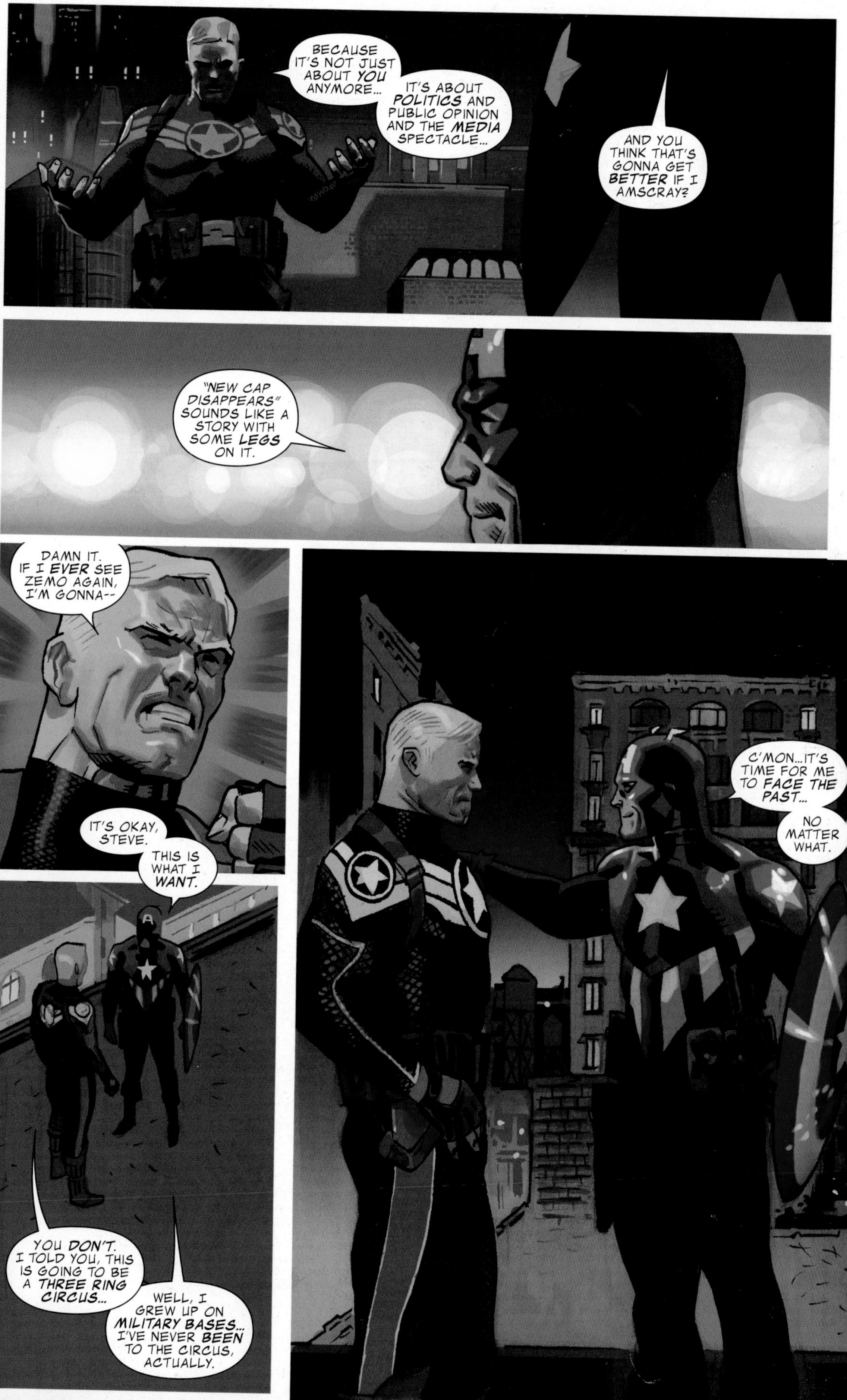
BECAUSE IT'S NOT JUST ABOUT YOU ANYMORE...
IT'S ABOUT POLITICS AND PUBLIC OPINION AND THE MEDIA SPECTACLE...
AND YOU THINK THAT'S GONNA GET BETTER IF I AMSCRAY?
"NEW CAP DISAPPEARS" SOUNDS LIKE A STORY WITH SOME LEGS ON IT.
DAMN IT. IF I EVER SEE ZEMO AGAIN, I'M GONNA--
IT'S OKAY, STEVE.
THIS IS WHAT I WANT.
YOU DON'T. I TOLD YOU, THIS IS GOING TO BE A THREE RING CIRCUS...
WELL, I GREW UP ON MILITARY BASES... I'VE NEVER BEEN TO THE CIRCUS, ACTUALLY.
C'MON...IT'S TIME FOR ME TO FACE THE PAST...
NO MATTER WHAT.

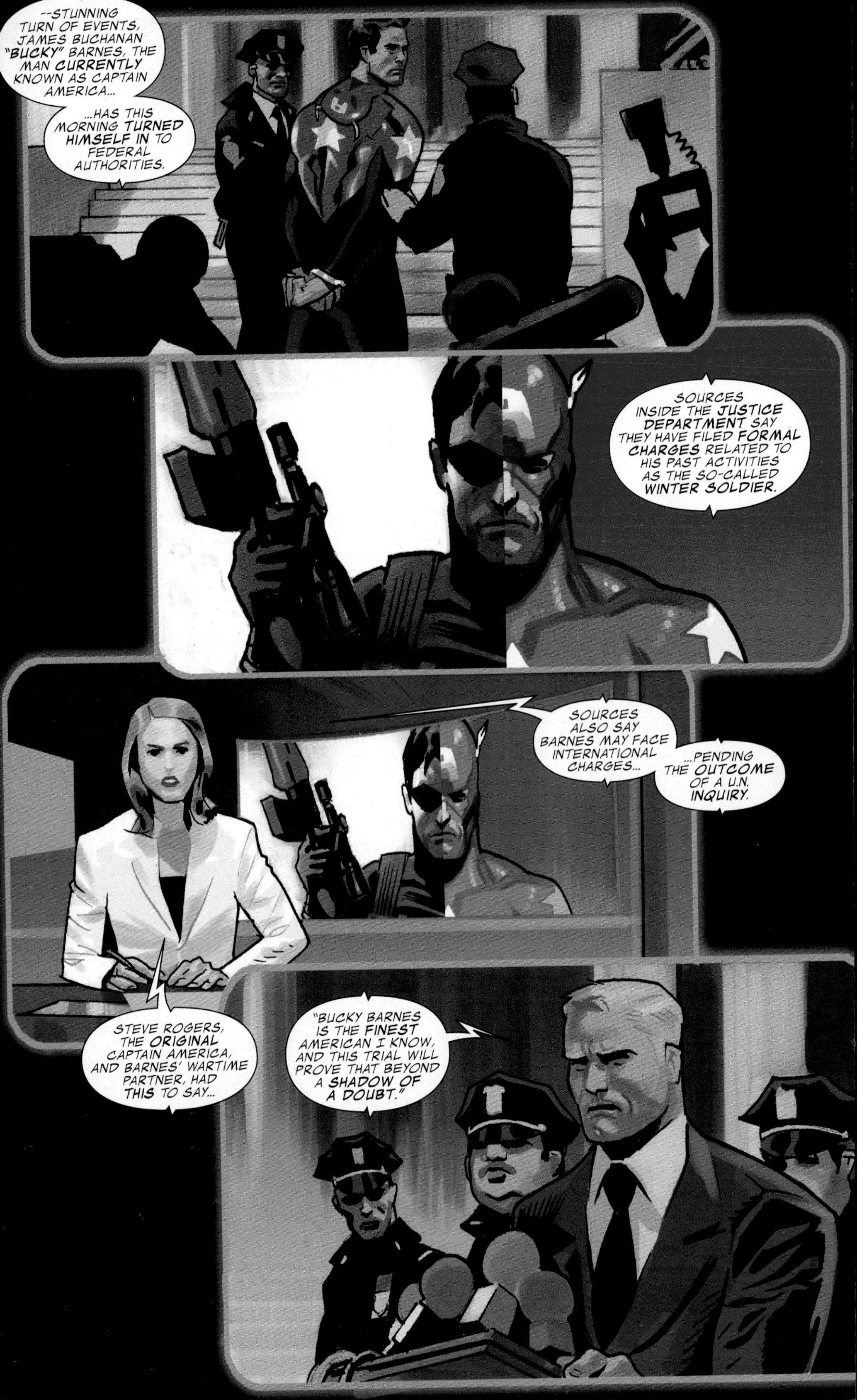
--STUNNING TURN OF EVENTS, JAMES BUCHANAN "BUCKY" BARNES, THE MAN CURRENTLY KNOWN AS CAPTAIN AMERICA...
...HAS THIS MORNING TURNED HIMSELF IN TO FEDERAL AUTHORITIES.
SOURCES INSIDE THE JUSTICE DEPARTMENT SAY THEY HAVE FILED FORMAL CHARGES RELATED TO HIS PAST ACTIVITIES AS THE SO-CALLED WINTER SOLDIER.
SOURCES ALSO SAY BARNES MAY FACE INTERNATIONAL CHARGES...
...PENDING THE OUTCOME OF A U.N. INQUIRY.
STEVE ROGERS, THE ORIGINAL CAPTAIN AMERICA, AND BARNES' WARTIME PARTNER, HAD THIS TO SAY...
"BUCKY BARNES IS THE FINEST AMERICAN I KNOW, AND THIS TRIAL WILL PROVE THAT BEYOND A SHADOW OF A DOUBT."

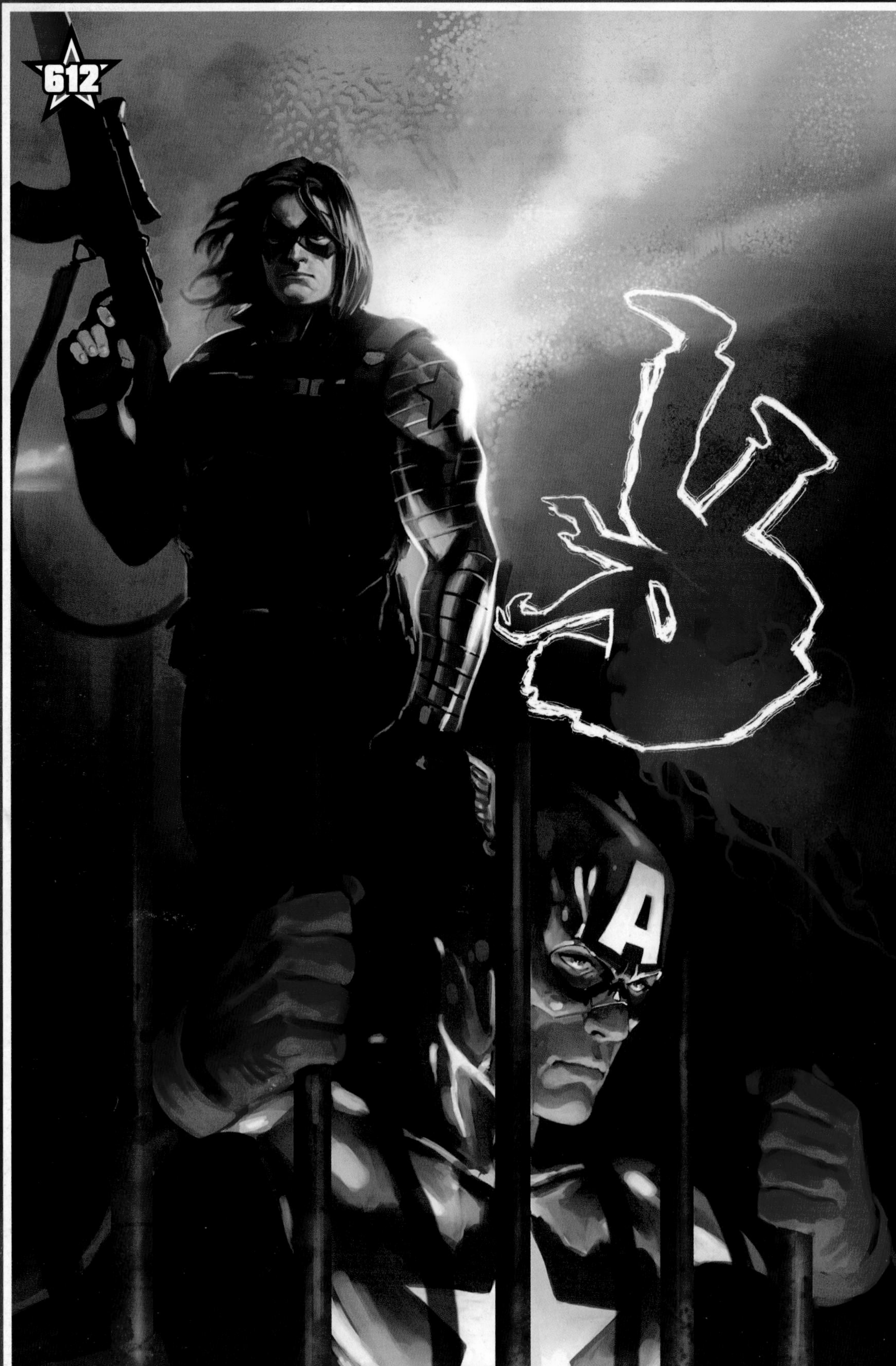
612

THE TRIAL OF CAPTAIN AMERICA PART 2

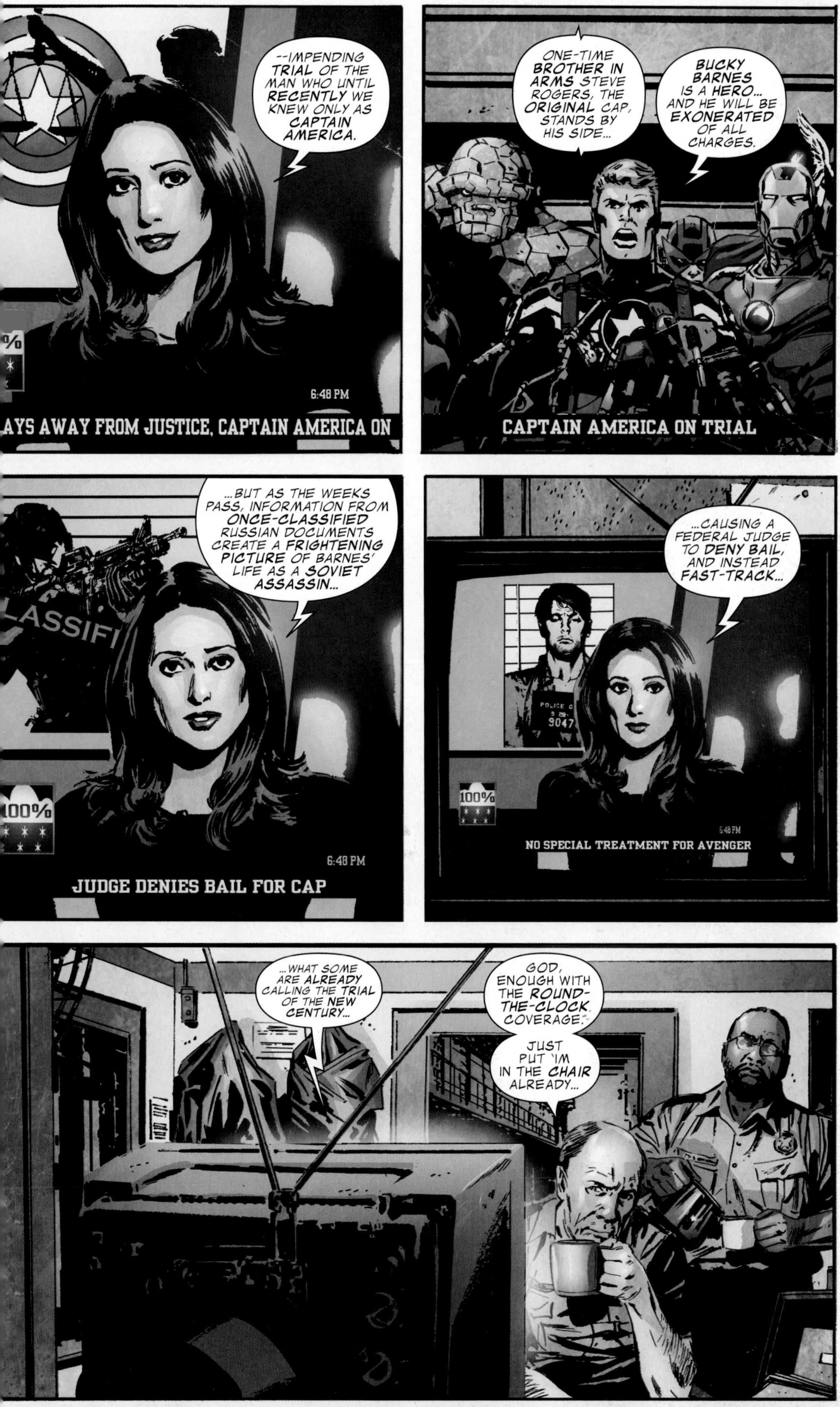
--IMPENDING TRIAL OF THE MAN WHO UNTIL RECENTLY WE KNEW ONLY AS CAPTAIN AMERICA.
6:48 PM
AYS AWAY FROM JUSTICE, CAPTAIN AMERICA ON
ONE-TIME BROTHER IN ARMS STEVE ROGERS, THE ORIGINAL CAP, STANDS BY HIS SIDE...
BUCKY BARNES IS A HERO... AND HE WILL BE EXONERATED OF ALL CHARGES.
CAPTAIN AMERICA ON TRIAL
...BUT AS THE WEEKS PASS, INFORMATION FROM ONCE-CLASSIFIED RUSSIAN DOCUMENTS CREATE A FRIGHTENING PICTURE OF BARNES' LIFE AS A SOVIET ASSASSIN...
LASSIFI
100%
6:48 PM
JUDGE DENIES BAIL FOR CAP
...CAUSING A FEDERAL JUDGE TO DENY BAIL, AND INSTEAD FAST-TRACK...
9047
100%
6:48 PM
NO SPECIAL TREATMENT FOR AVENGER
...WHAT SOME ARE ALREADY CALLING THE TRIAL OF THE NEW CENTURY...
GOD, ENOUGH WITH THE ROUND-THE-CLOCK COVERAGE.
JUST PUT 'IM IN THE CHAIR ALREADY...

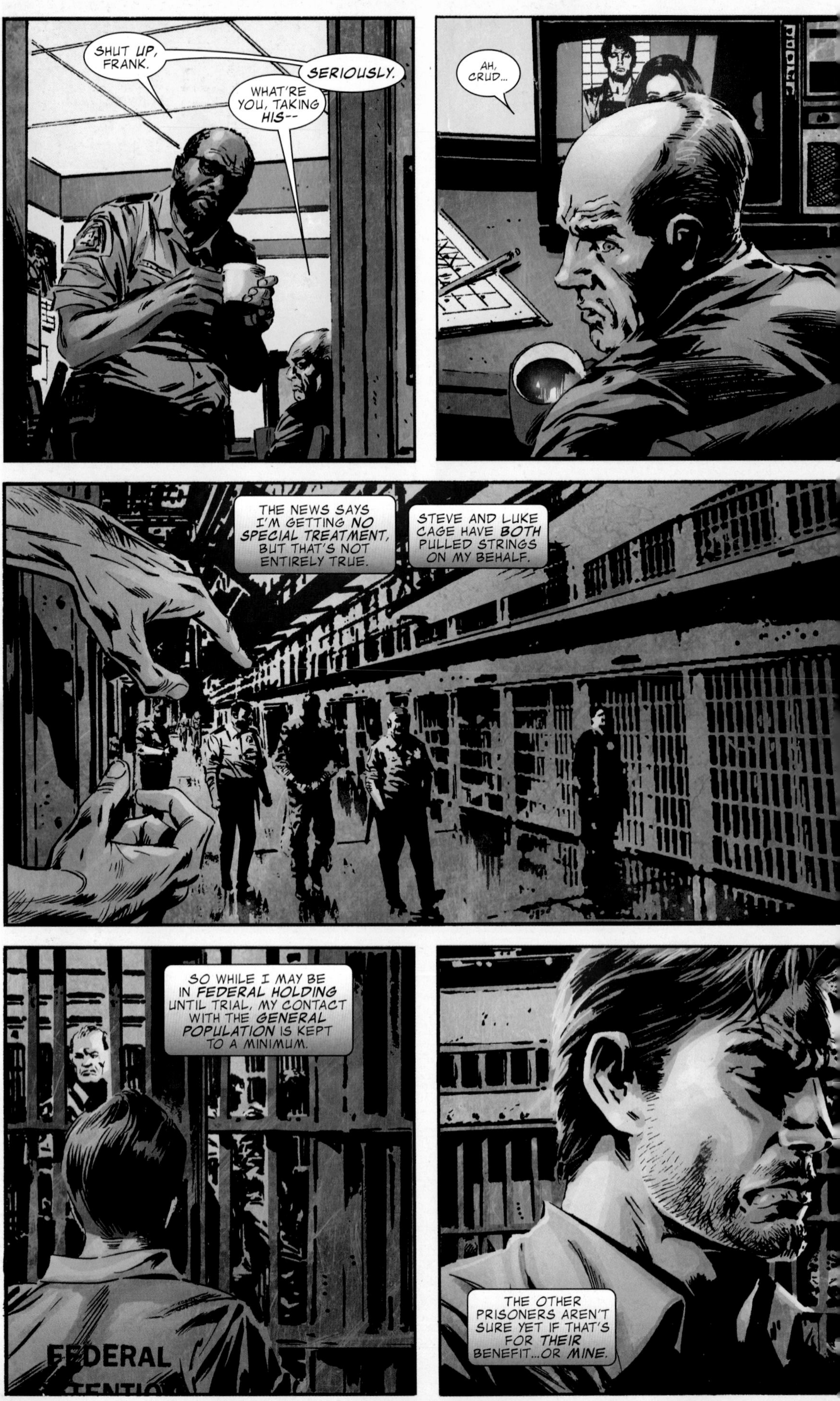
SHUT UP, FRANK.
SERIOUSLY.
WHAT'RE YOU, TAKING HIS--
AH, CRUD...
THE NEWS SAYS I'M GETTING NO SPECIAL TREATMENT, BUT THAT'S NOT ENTIRELY TRUE.
STEVE AND LUKE CAGE HAVE BOTH PULLED STRINGS ON MY BEHALF.
SO WHILE I MAY BE IN FEDERAL HOLDING UNTIL TRIAL, MY CONTACT WITH THE GENERAL POPULATION IS KEPT TO A MINIMUM.
FEDERAL
THE OTHER PRISONERS AREN'T SURE YET IF THAT'S FOR THEIR BENEFIT...OR MINE.

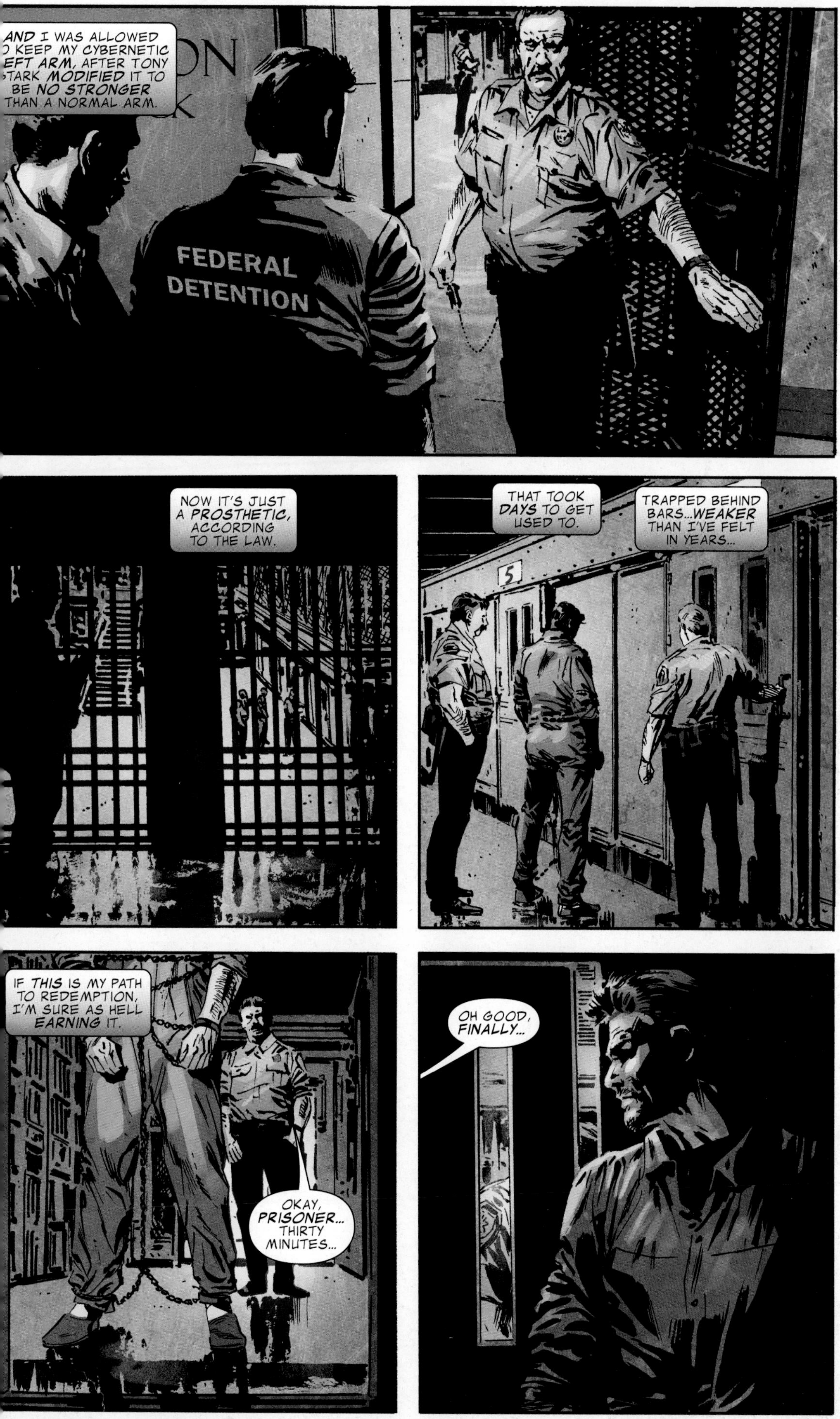
AND I WAS ALLOWED TO KEEP MY CYBERNETIC LEFT ARM, AFTER TONY STARK MODIFIED IT TO BE NO STRONGER THAN A NORMAL ARM.
FEDERAL DETENTION
NOW IT'S JUST A PROSTHETIC, ACCORDING TO THE LAW.
THAT TOOK DAYS TO GET USED TO.
TRAPPED BEHIND BARS...WEAKER THAN I'VE FELT IN YEARS...
5
IF THIS IS MY PATH TO REDEMPTION, I'M SURE AS HELL EARNING IT.
OKAY, PRISONER... THIRTY MINUTES...
OH GOOD, FINALLY...

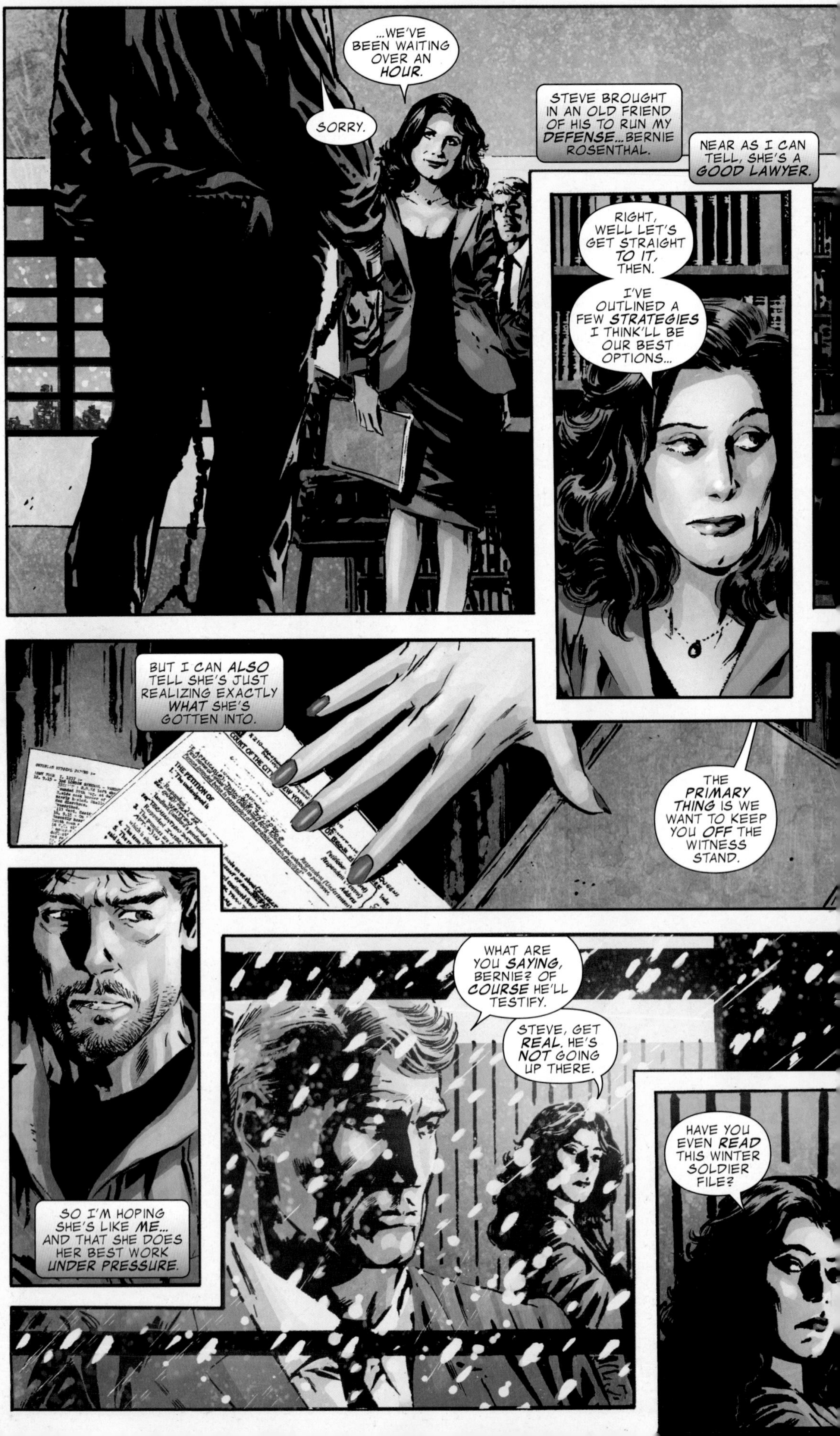
...WE'VE BEEN WAITING OVER AN HOUR.
SORRY.
STEVE BROUGHT IN AN OLD FRIEND OF HIS TO RUN MY DEFENSE...BERNIE ROSENTHAL.
NEAR AS I CAN TELL, SHE'S A GOOD LAWYER.
RIGHT, WELL LET'S GET STRAIGHT TO IT, THEN.
I'VE OUTLINED A FEW STRATEGIES I THINK'LL BE OUR BEST OPTIONS...
BUT I CAN ALSO TELL SHE'S JUST REALIZING EXACTLY WHAT SHE'S GOTTEN INTO.
THE PRIMARY THING IS WE WANT TO KEEP YOU OFF THE WITNESS STAND.
WHAT ARE YOU SAYING, BERNIE? OF COURSE HE'LL TESTIFY.
STEVE, GET REAL. HE'S NOT GOING UP THERE.
HAVE YOU EVEN READ THIS WINTER SOLDIER FILE?
SO I'M HOPING SHE'S LIKE ME... AND THAT SHE DOES HER BEST WORK UNDER PRESSURE.

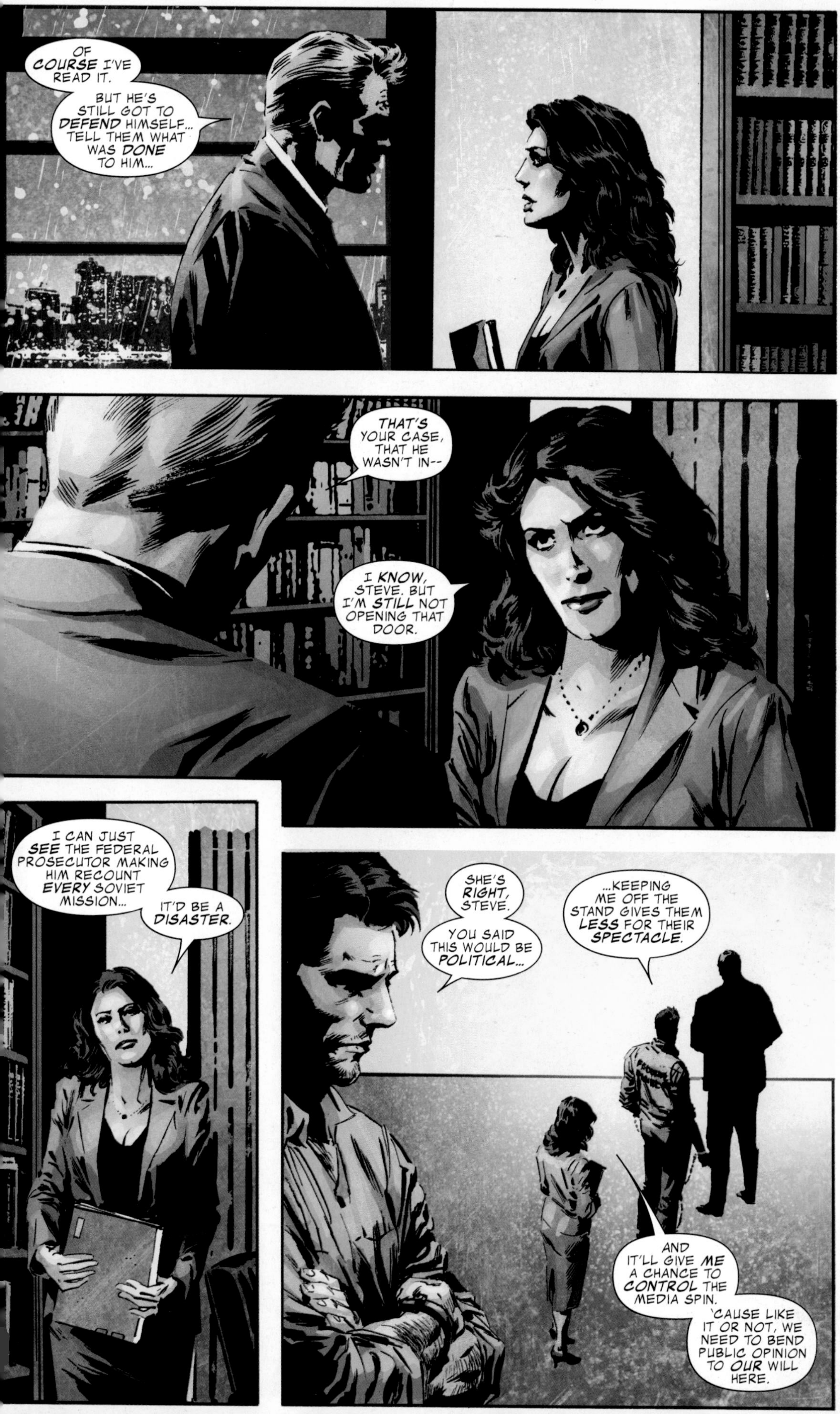
OF COURSE I'VE READ IT.
BUT HE'S STILL GOT TO DEFEND HIMSELF... TELL THEM WHAT WAS DONE TO HIM...
THAT'S YOUR CASE, THAT HE WASN'T IN--
I KNOW, STEVE. BUT I'M STILL NOT OPENING THAT DOOR.
I CAN JUST SEE THE FEDERAL PROSECUTOR MAKING HIM RECOUNT EVERY SOVIET MISSION...
IT'D BE A DISASTER.
SHE'S RIGHT, STEVE.
YOU SAID THIS WOULD BE POLITICAL...
...KEEPING ME OFF THE STAND GIVES THEM LESS FOR THEIR SPECTACLE.
AND IT'LL GIVE ME A CHANCE TO CONTROL THE MEDIA SPIN.
'CAUSE LIKE IT OR NOT, WE NEED TO BEND PUBLIC OPINION TO OUR WILL HERE.

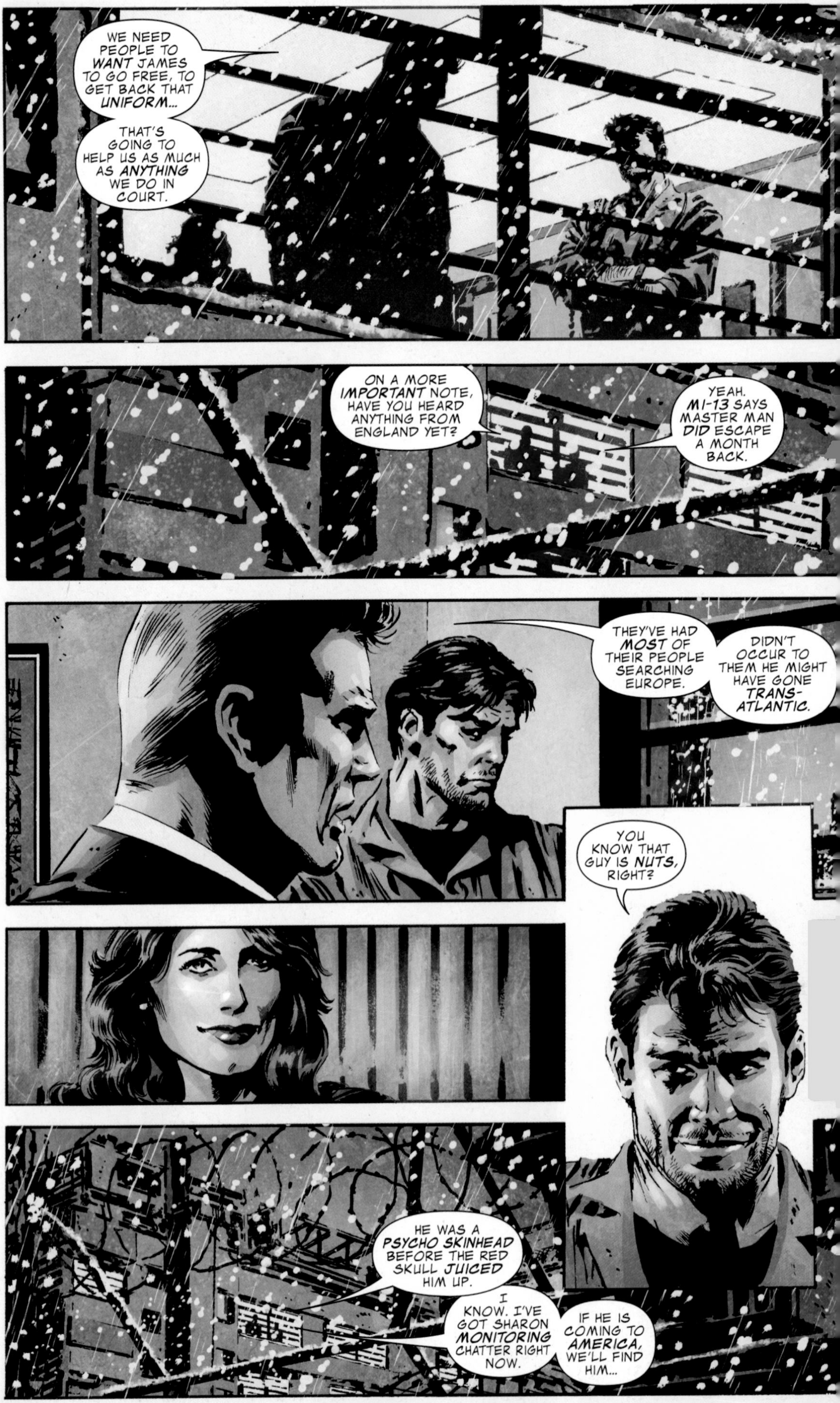

WE NEED PEOPLE TO WANT JAMES TO GO FREE, TO GET BACK THAT UNIFORM...
THAT'S GOING TO HELP US AS MUCH AS ANYTHING WE DO IN COURT.
ON A MORE IMPORTANT NOTE, HAVE YOU HEARD ANYTHING FROM ENGLAND YET?
YEAH. MI-13 SAYS MASTER MAN DID ESCAPE A MONTH BACK.
THEY'VE HAD MOST OF THEIR PEOPLE SEARCHING EUROPE.
DIDN'T OCCUR TO THEM HE MIGHT HAVE GONE TRANS-ATLANTIC.
YOU KNOW THAT GUY IS NUTS, RIGHT?
HE WAS A PSYCHO SKINHEAD BEFORE THE RED SKULL JUICED HIM UP.
I KNOW. I'VE GOT SHARON MONITORING CHATTER RIGHT NOW.
IF HE IS COMING TO AMERICA, WE'LL FIND HIM...

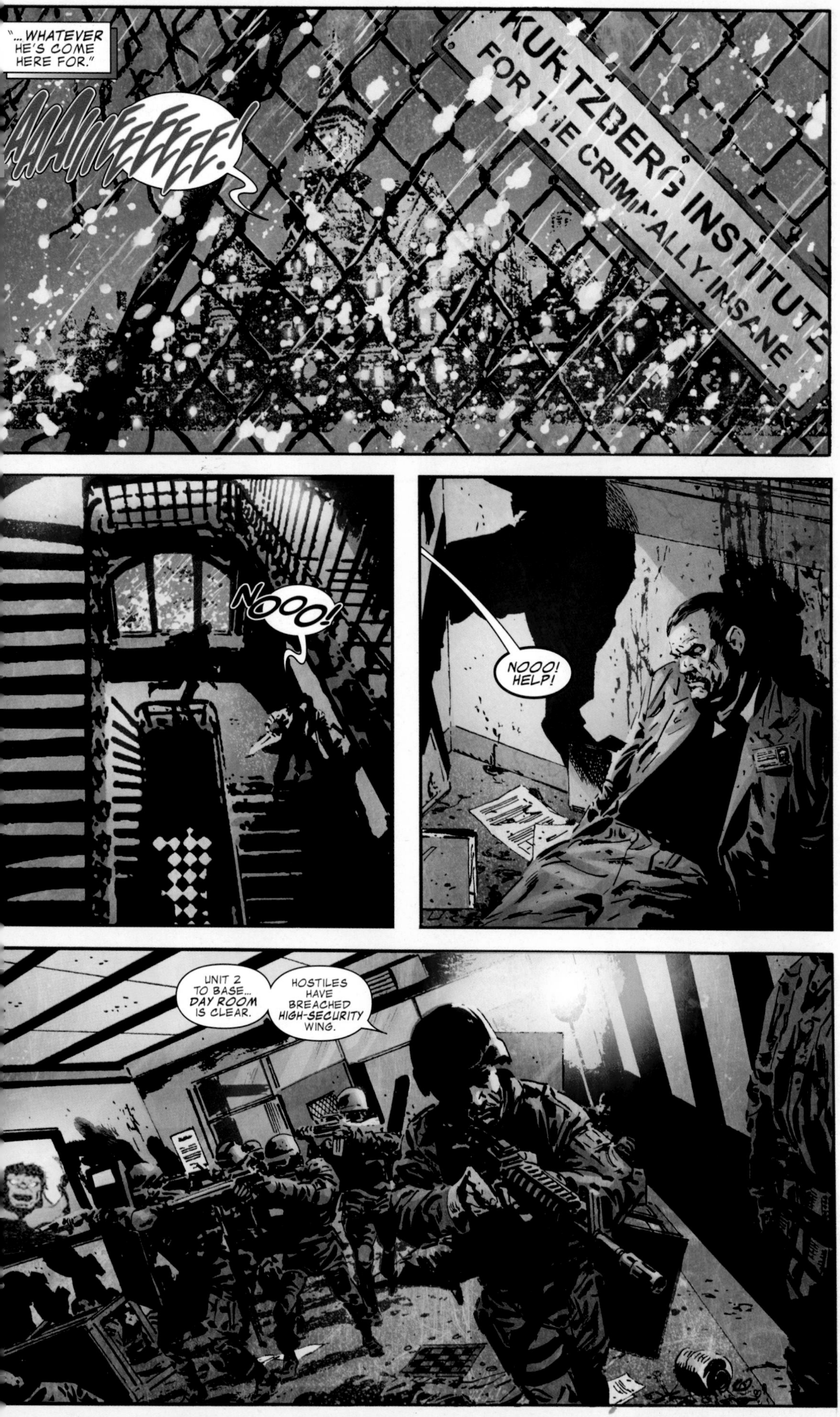
"...WHATEVER HE'S COME HERE FOR."
AAAAIIEEEEE!
KURTZBERG INSTITUTE FOR THE CRIMINALLY INSANE
NOOO!
NOOO! HELP!
UNIT 2 TO BASE... DAY ROOM IS CLEAR.
HOSTILES HAVE BREACHED HIGH-SECURITY WING.

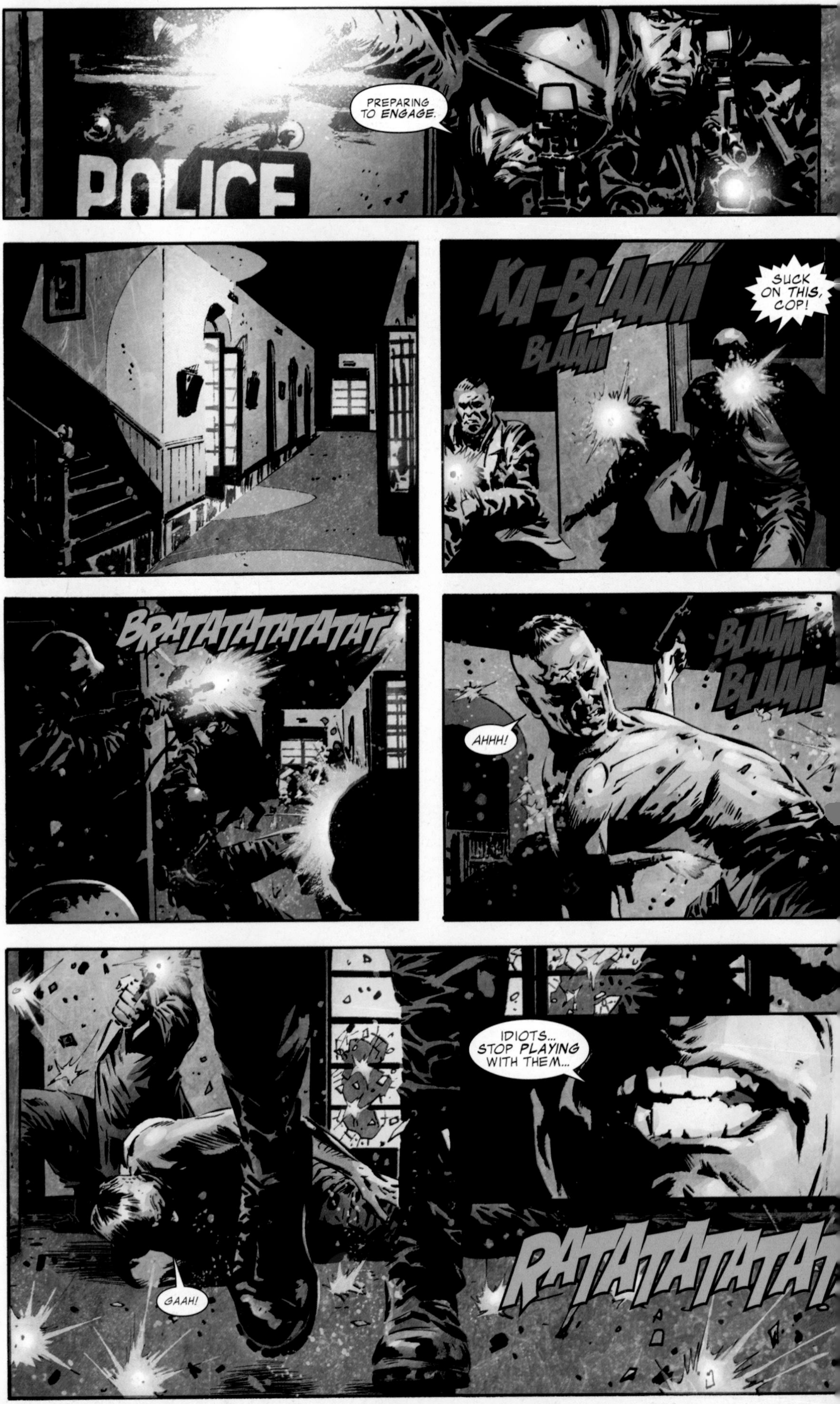
POLICE
PREPARING TO ENGAGE.
KA-BLAAM
BLAAM
SUCK ON THIS, COP!
BRATATATATATAT
BLAAM BLAAM
AHHH!
IDIOTS... STOP PLAYING WITH THEM...
RATATATATAT
GAAH!

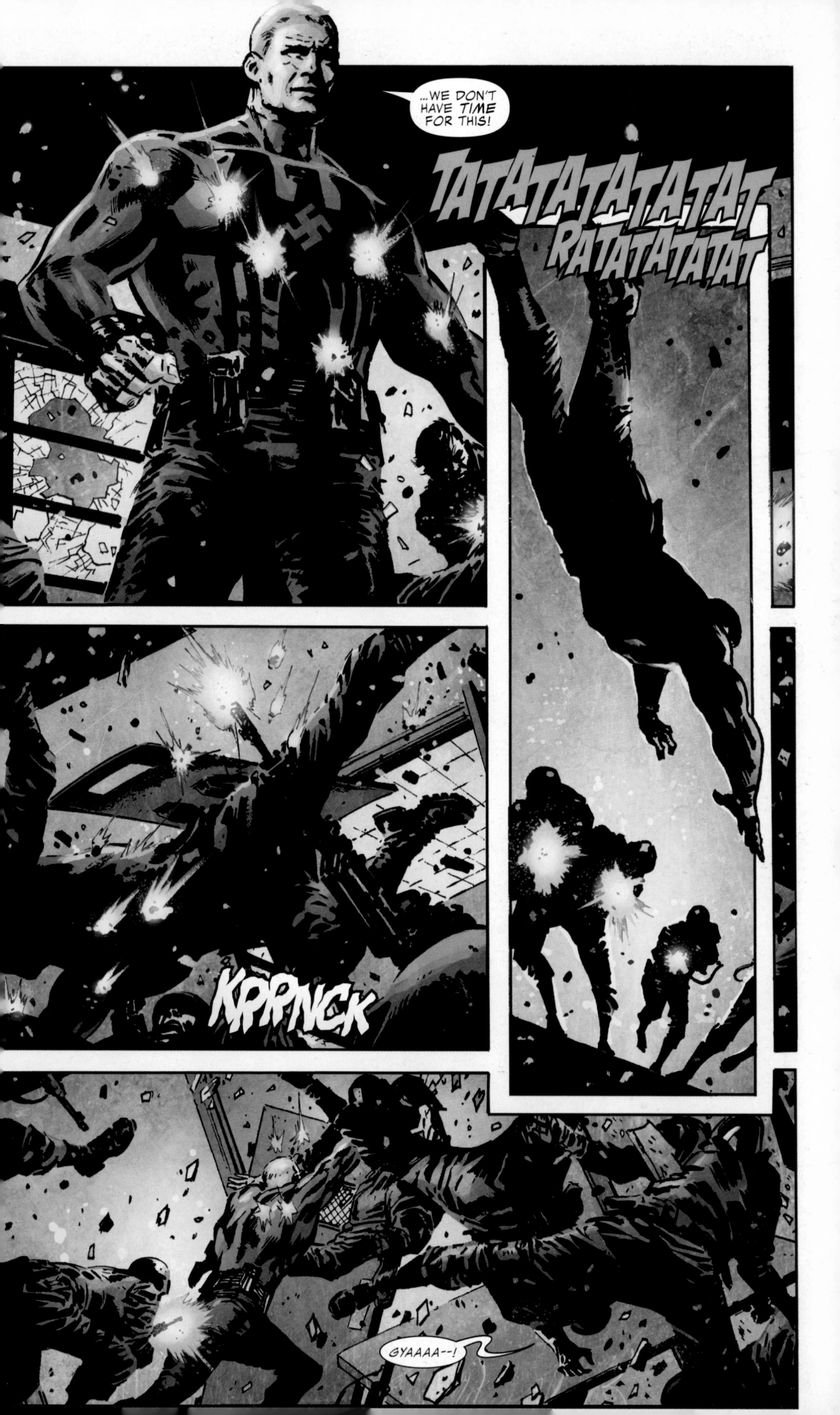
...WE DON'T HAVE TIME FOR THIS!
TATATATATATATAT
RATATATATAT
KRRNCK
GYAAAA--!

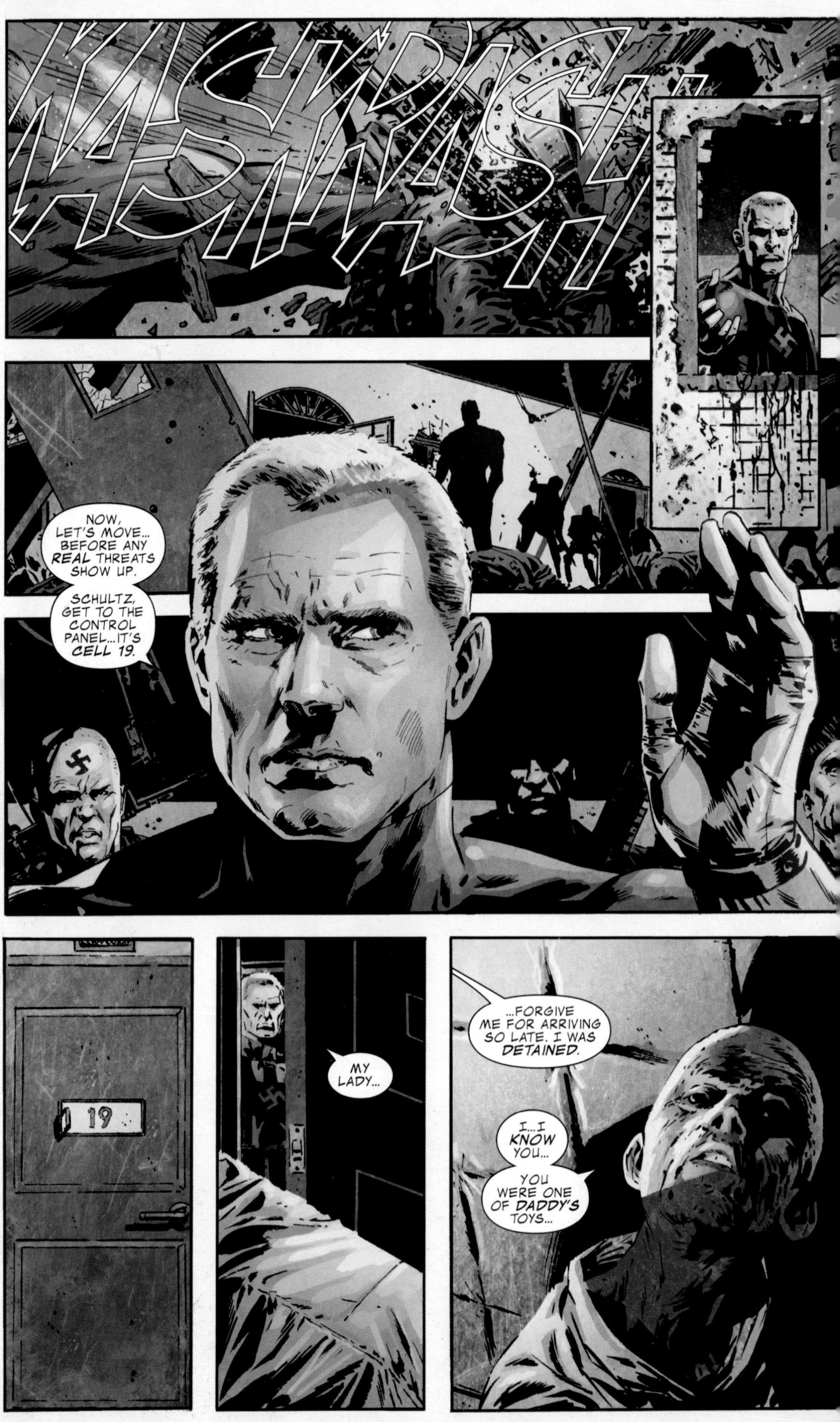

KA-CHUNK-KA-SHANG!! ...
NOW, LET'S MOVE... BEFORE ANY REAL THREATS SHOW UP.
SCHULTZ, GET TO THE CONTROL PANEL...IT'S CELL 19.
19
MY LADY...
...FORGIVE ME FOR ARRIVING SO LATE. I WAS DETAINED.
I...I KNOW YOU...
YOU WERE ONE OF DADDY'S TOYS...

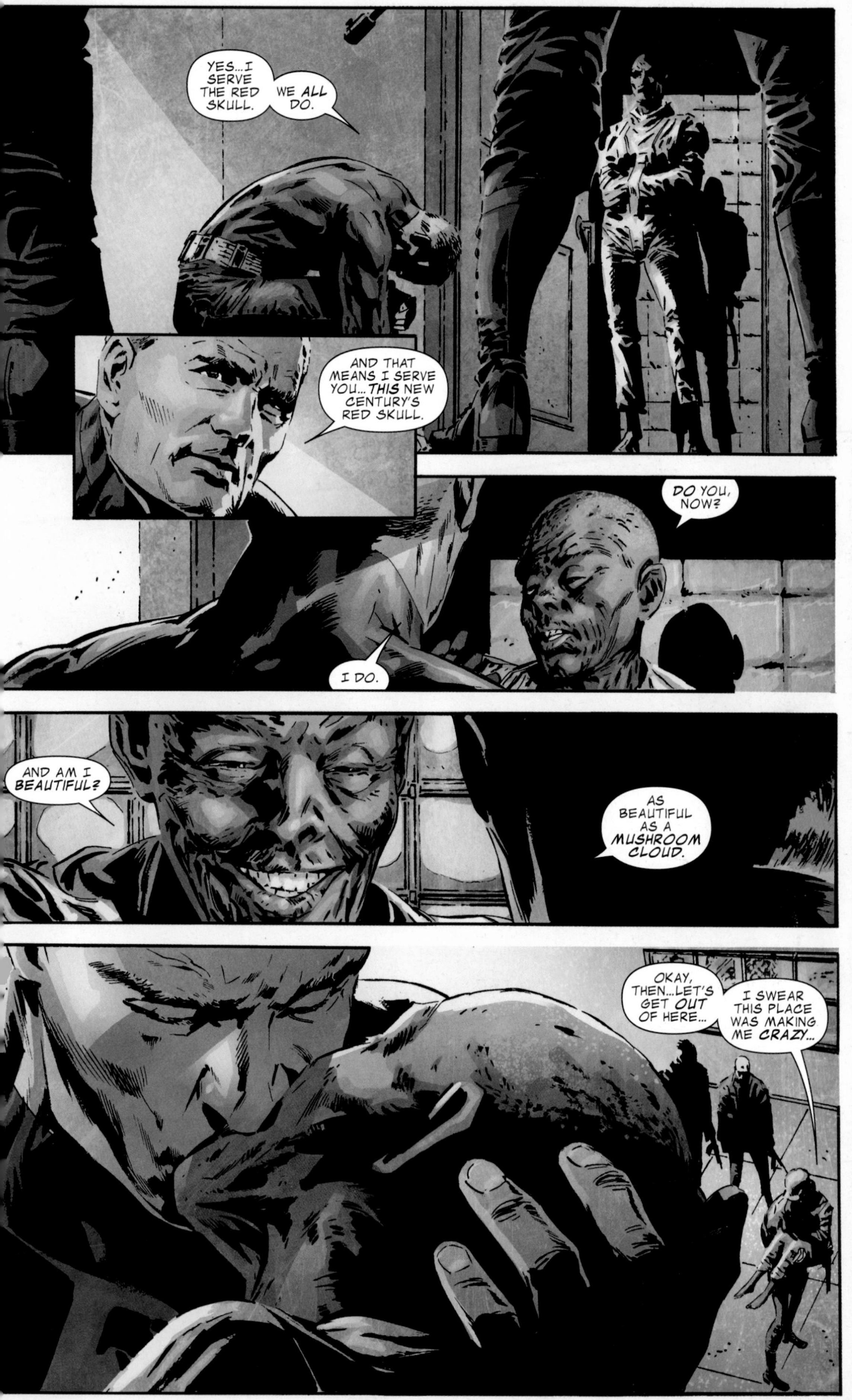

YES...I SERVE THE RED SKULL.
WE ALL DO.
AND THAT MEANS I SERVE YOU...THIS NEW CENTURY'S RED SKULL.
DO YOU, NOW?
I DO.
AND AM I BEAUTIFUL?
AS BEAUTIFUL AS A MUSHROOM CLOUD.
OKAY, THEN...LET'S GET OUT OF HERE...
I SWEAR THIS PLACE WAS MAKING ME CRAZY...

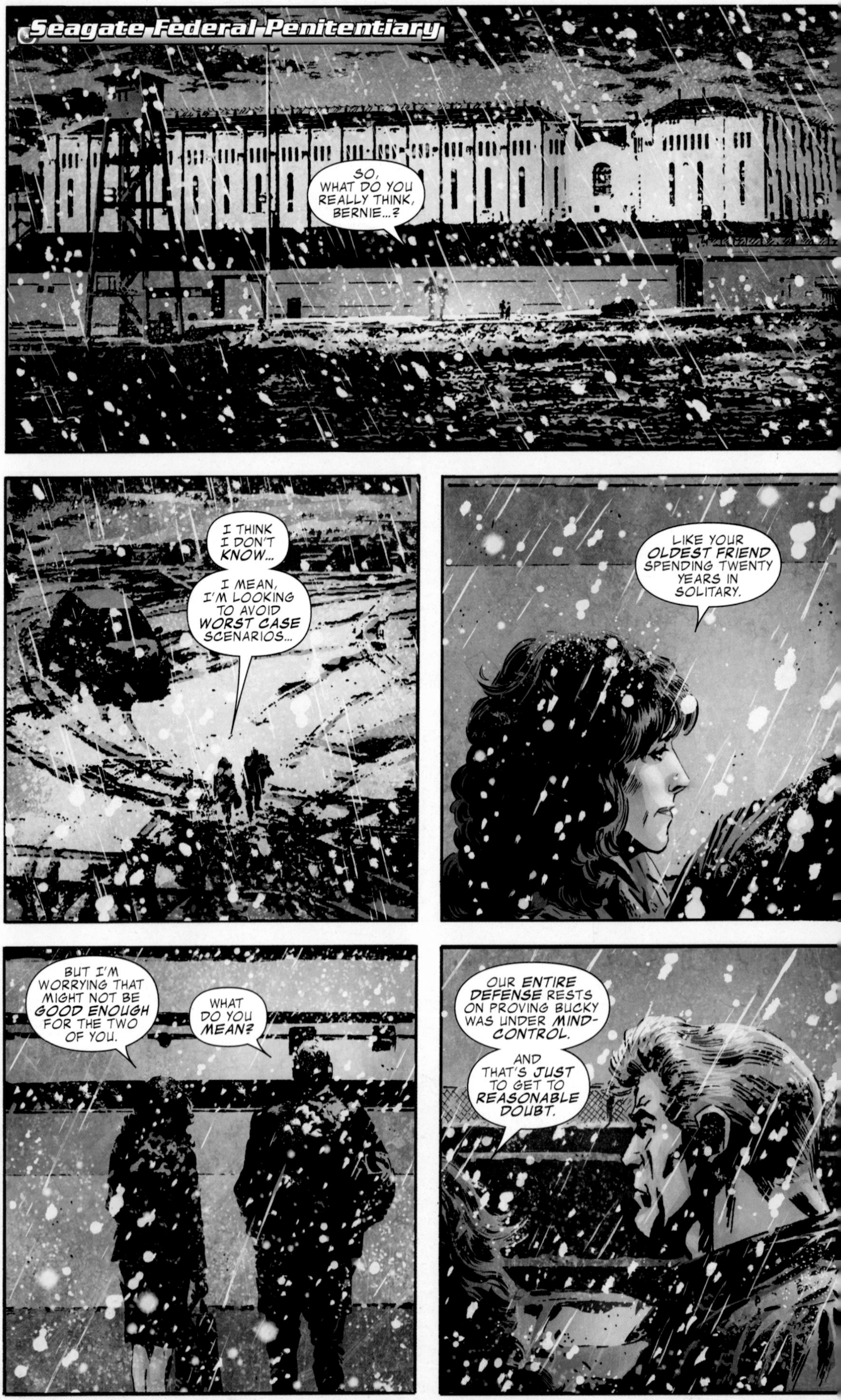
Seagate Federal Penitentiary
SO, WHAT DO YOU REALLY THINK, BERNIE...?
I THINK I DON'T KNOW...
I MEAN, I'M LOOKING TO AVOID WORST CASE SCENARIOS...
LIKE YOUR OLDEST FRIEND SPENDING TWENTY YEARS IN SOLITARY.
BUT I'M WORRYING THAT MIGHT NOT BE GOOD ENOUGH FOR THE TWO OF YOU.
WHAT DO YOU MEAN?
OUR ENTIRE DEFENSE RESTS ON PROVING BUCKY WAS UNDER MIND-CONTROL.
AND THAT'S JUST TO GET TO REASONABLE DOUBT.

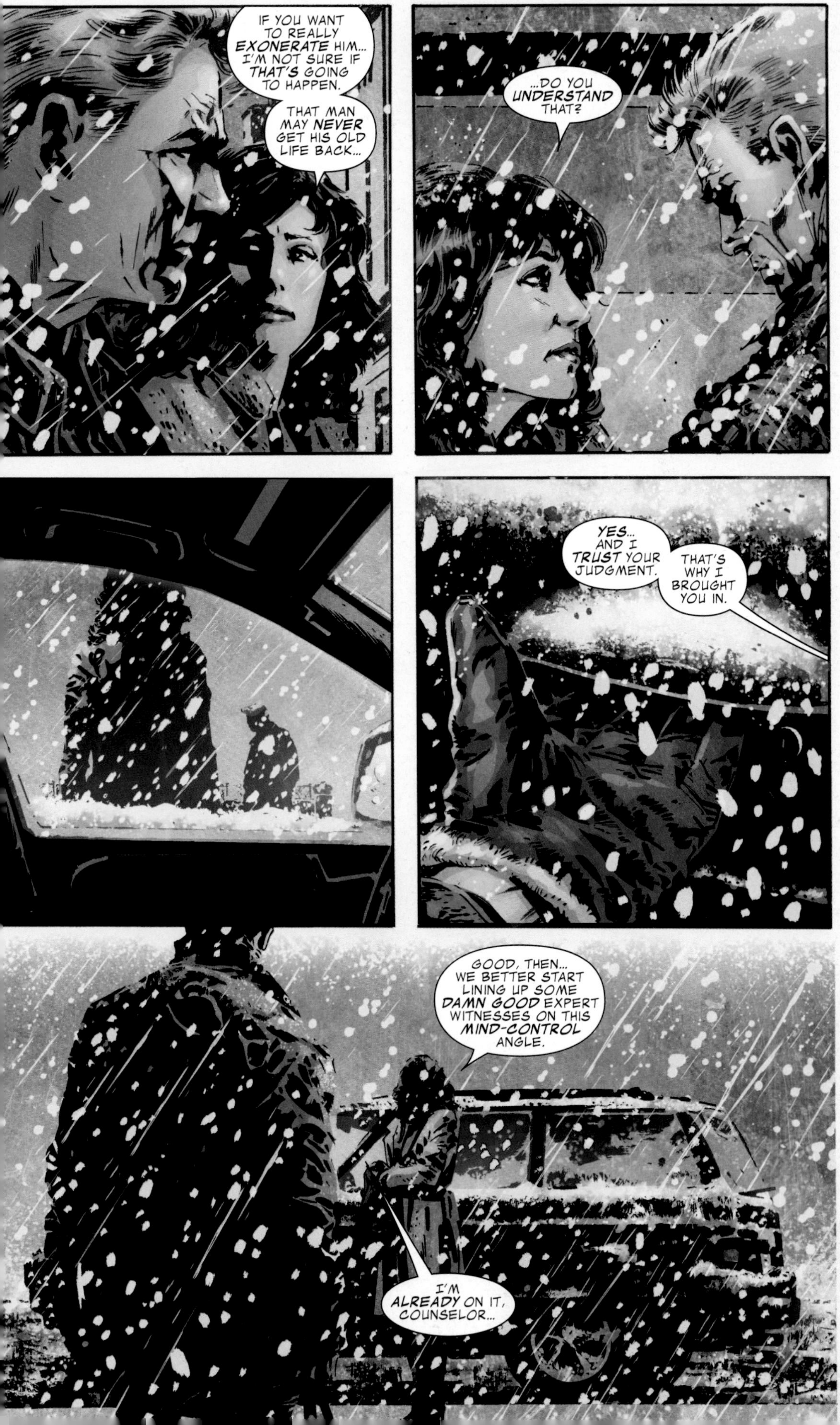
IF YOU WANT TO REALLY EXONERATE HIM... I'M NOT SURE IF THAT'S GOING TO HAPPEN.
THAT MAN MAY NEVER GET HIS OLD LIFE BACK...
...DO YOU UNDERSTAND THAT?
YES... AND I TRUST YOUR JUDGMENT.
THAT'S WHY I BROUGHT YOU IN.
GOOD, THEN... WE BETTER START LINING UP SOME DAMN GOOD EXPERT WITNESSES ON THIS MIND-CONTROL ANGLE.
I'M ALREADY ON IT, COUNSELOR...

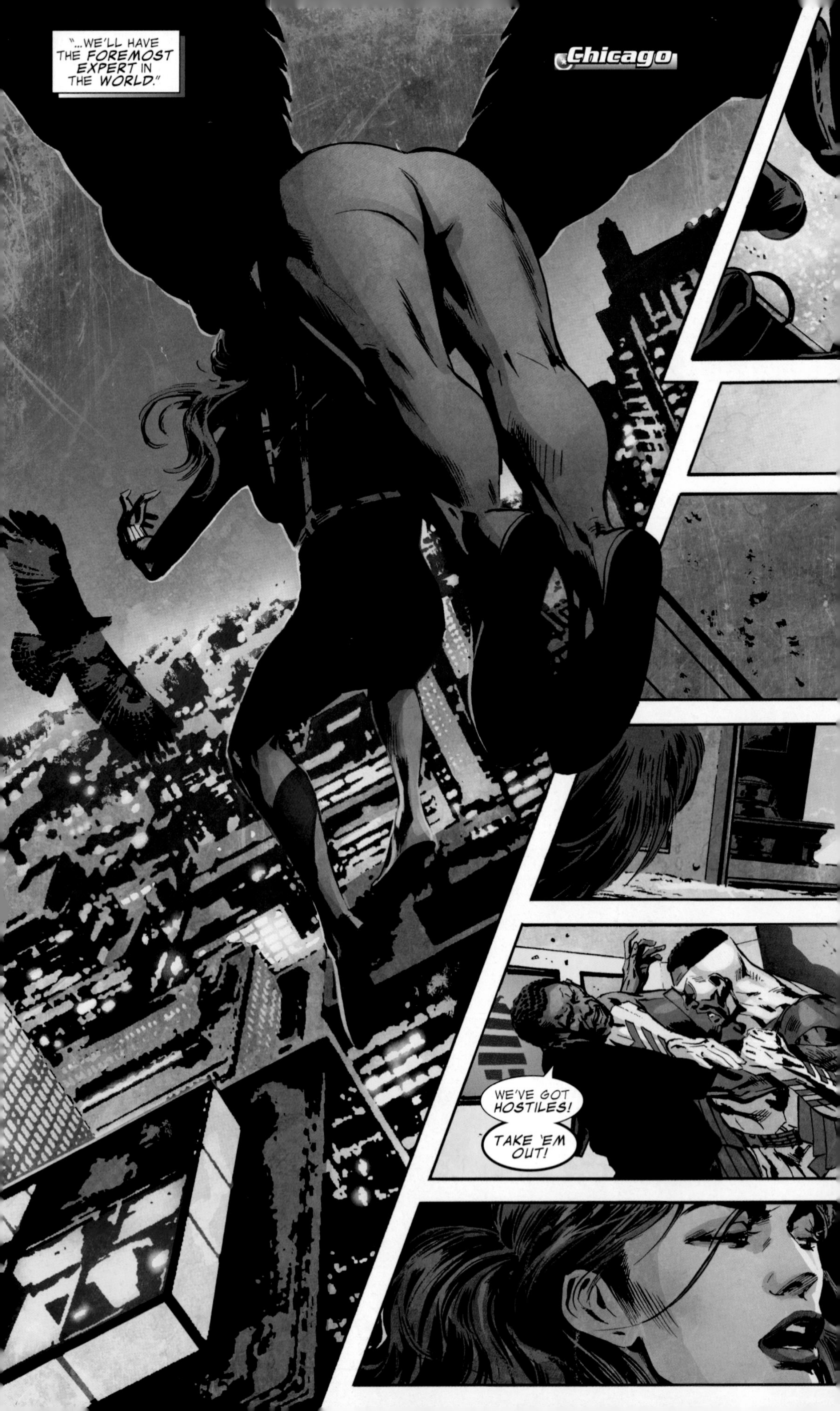
"...WE'LL HAVE THE FOREMOST EXPERT IN THE WORLD."
Chicago
WE'VE GOT HOSTILES!
TAKE 'EM OUT!

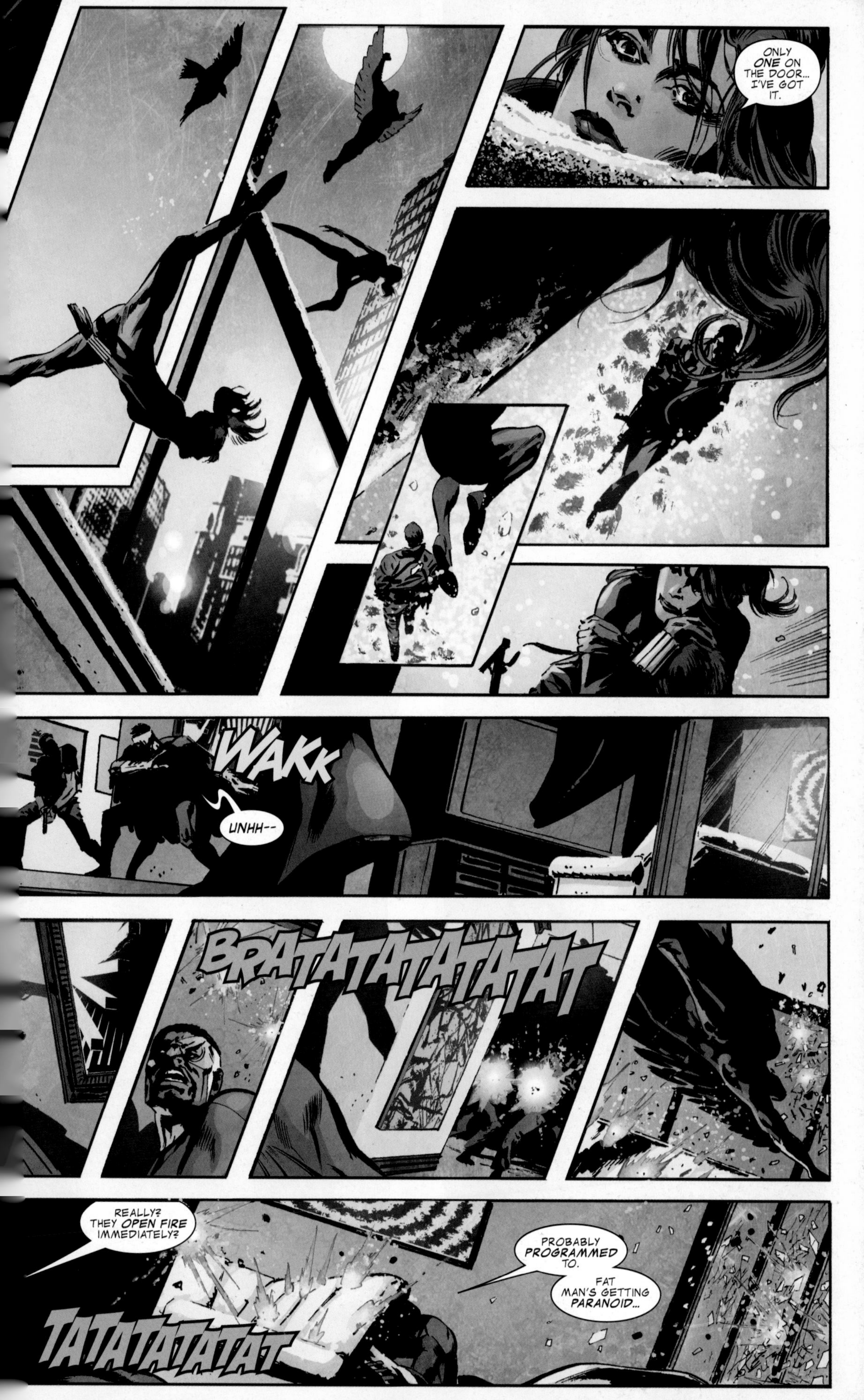
ONLY ONE ON THE DOOR... I'VE GOT IT.
WAKK
UNHH--
BRATATATATATATAT
REALLY? THEY OPEN FIRE IMMEDIATELY?
PROBABLY PROGRAMMED TO.
FAT MAN'S GETTING PARANOID...
TATATATATAT

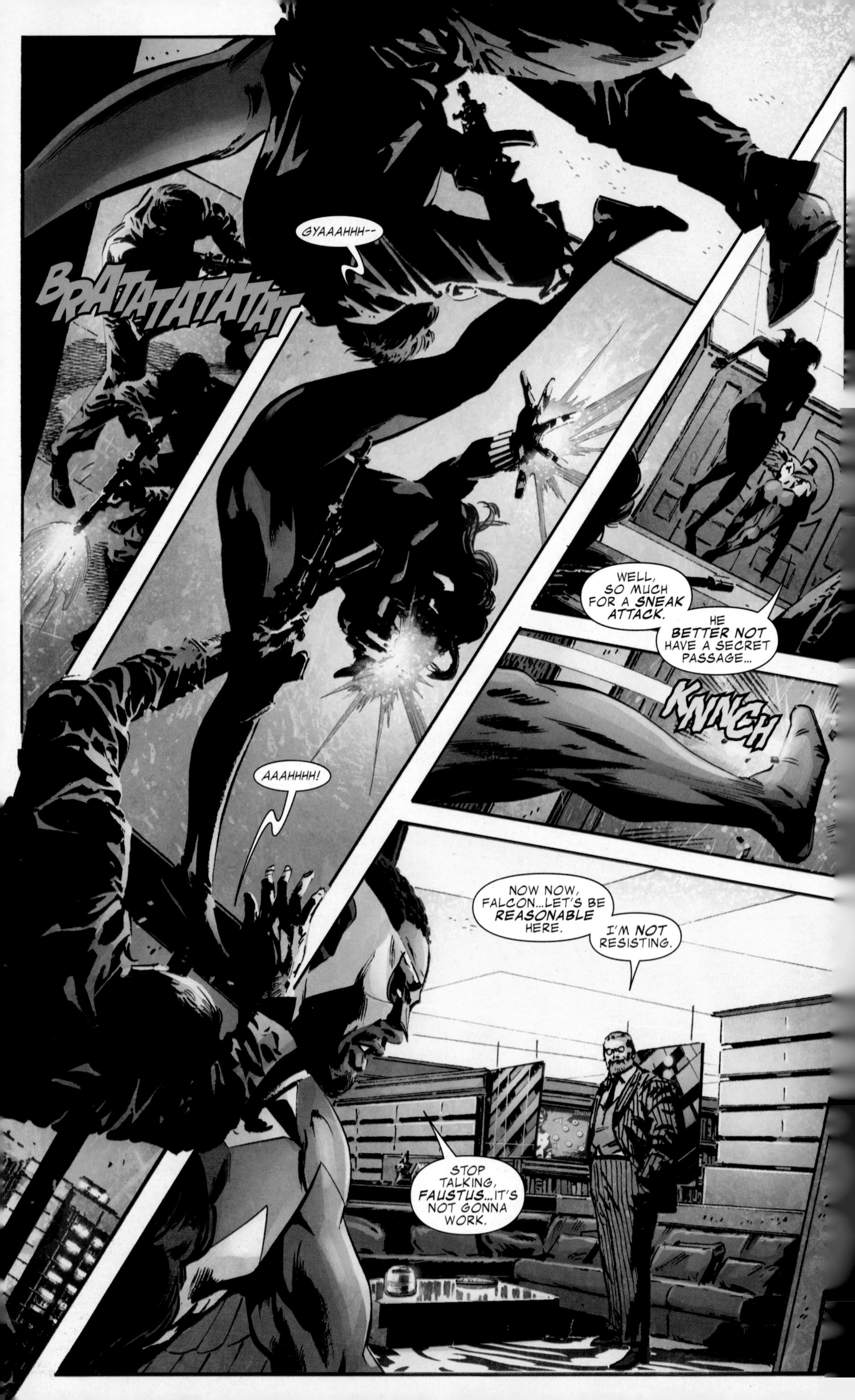
GYAAAHHH--
BRATATATATATAT
AAAHHHH!
WELL, SO MUCH FOR A SNEAK ATTACK.
HE BETTER NOT HAVE A SECRET PASSAGE...
KNNCH
NOW NOW, FALCON...LET'S BE REASONABLE HERE.
I'M NOT RESISTING.
STOP TALKING, FAUSTUS...IT'S NOT GONNA WORK.

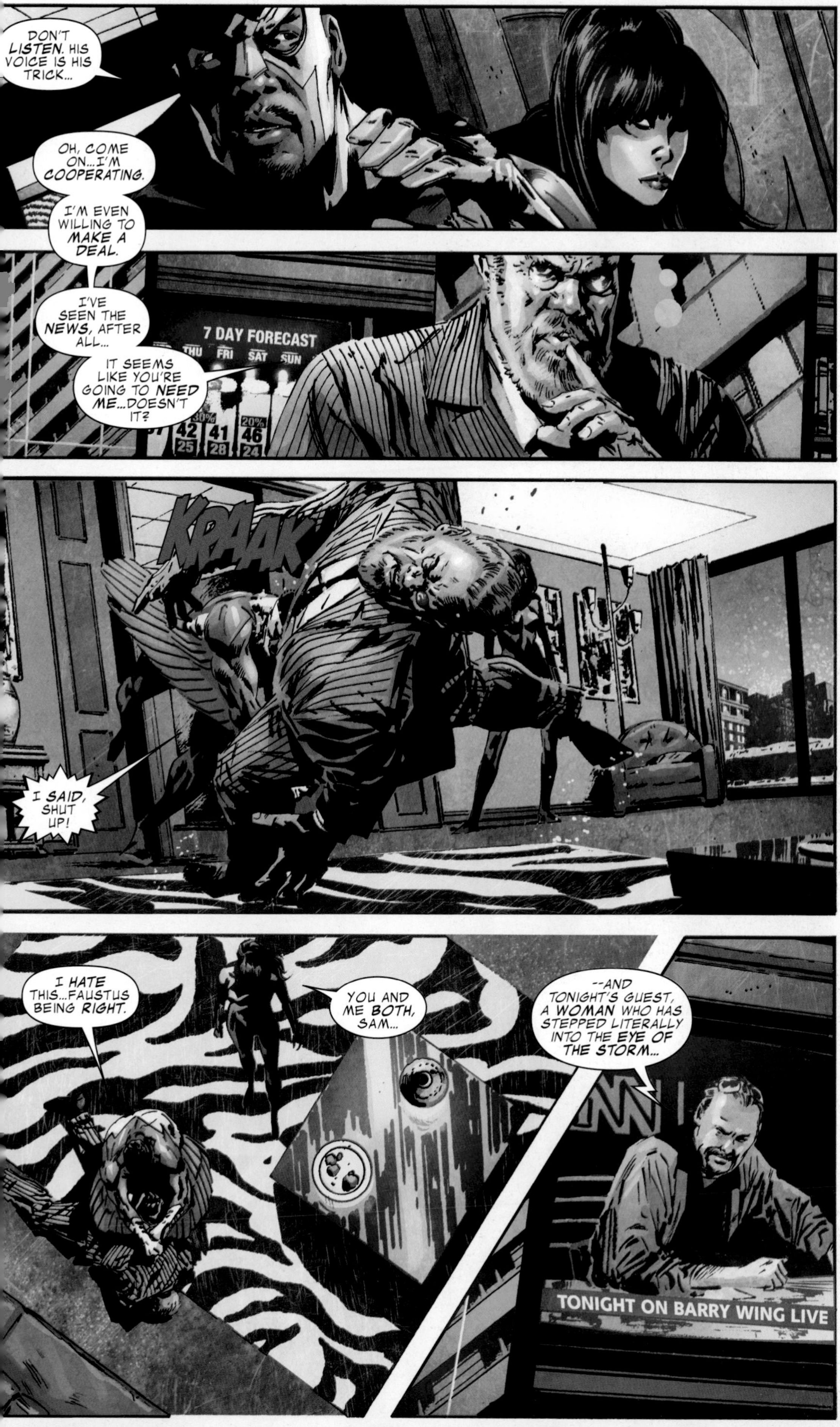
DON'T LISTEN. HIS VOICE IS HIS TRICK...
OH, COME ON...I'M COOPERATING.
I'M EVEN WILLING TO MAKE A DEAL.
I'VE SEEN THE NEWS, AFTER ALL...
IT SEEMS LIKE YOU'RE GOING TO NEED ME...DOESN'T IT?
7 DAY FORECAST
THU FRI SAT SUN
KRAAK
I SAID, SHUT UP!
I HATE THIS...FAUSTUS BEING RIGHT.
YOU AND ME BOTH, SAM...
--AND TONIGHT'S GUEST, A WOMAN WHO HAS STEPPED LITERALLY INTO THE EYE OF THE STORM...
TONIGHT ON BARRY WING LIVE

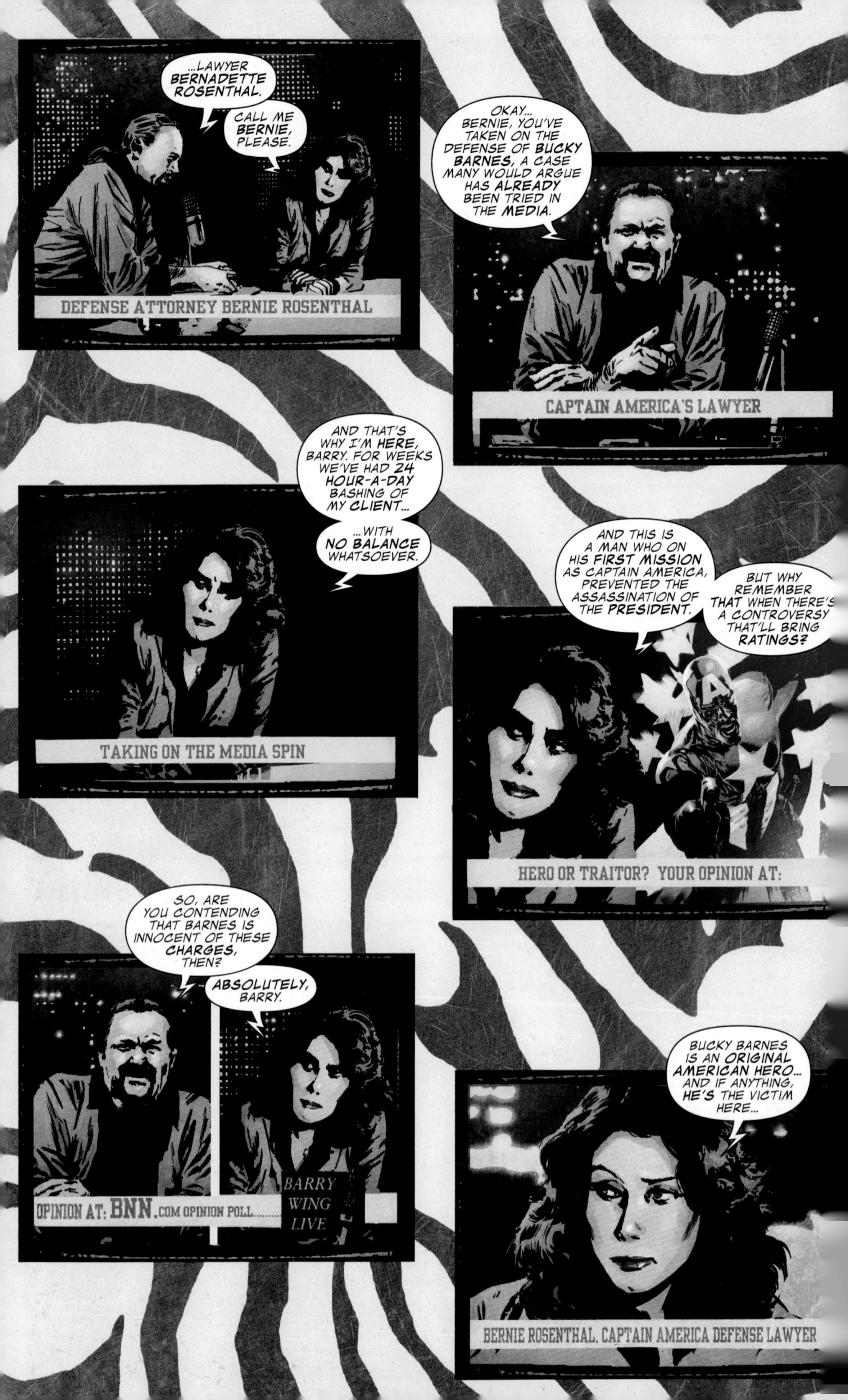
...LAWYER BERNADETTE ROSENTHAL.
CALL ME BERNIE, PLEASE.
DEFENSE ATTORNEY BERNIE ROSENTHAL
OKAY... BERNIE, YOU'VE TAKEN ON THE DEFENSE OF BUCKY BARNES, A CASE MANY WOULD ARGUE HAS ALREADY BEEN TRIED IN THE MEDIA.
CAPTAIN AMERICA'S LAWYER
AND THAT'S WHY I'M HERE, BARRY. FOR WEEKS WE'VE HAD 24 HOUR-A-DAY BASHING OF MY CLIENT...
...WITH NO BALANCE WHATSOEVER.
TAKING ON THE MEDIA SPIN
AND THIS IS A MAN WHO ON HIS FIRST MISSION AS CAPTAIN AMERICA, PREVENTED THE ASSASSINATION OF THE PRESIDENT.
BUT WHY REMEMBER THAT WHEN THERE'S A CONTROVERSY THAT'LL BRING RATINGS?
HERO OR TRAITOR? YOUR OPINION AT:
SO, ARE YOU CONTENDING THAT BARNES IS INNOCENT OF THESE CHARGES, THEN?
ABSOLUTELY, BARRY.
OPINION AT: BNN.COM OPINION POLL.........
BARRY WING LIVE
BUCKY BARNES IS AN ORIGINAL AMERICAN HERO... AND IF ANYTHING, HE'S THE VICTIM HERE...
BERNIE ROSENTHAL, CAPTAIN AMERICA DEFENSE LAWYER

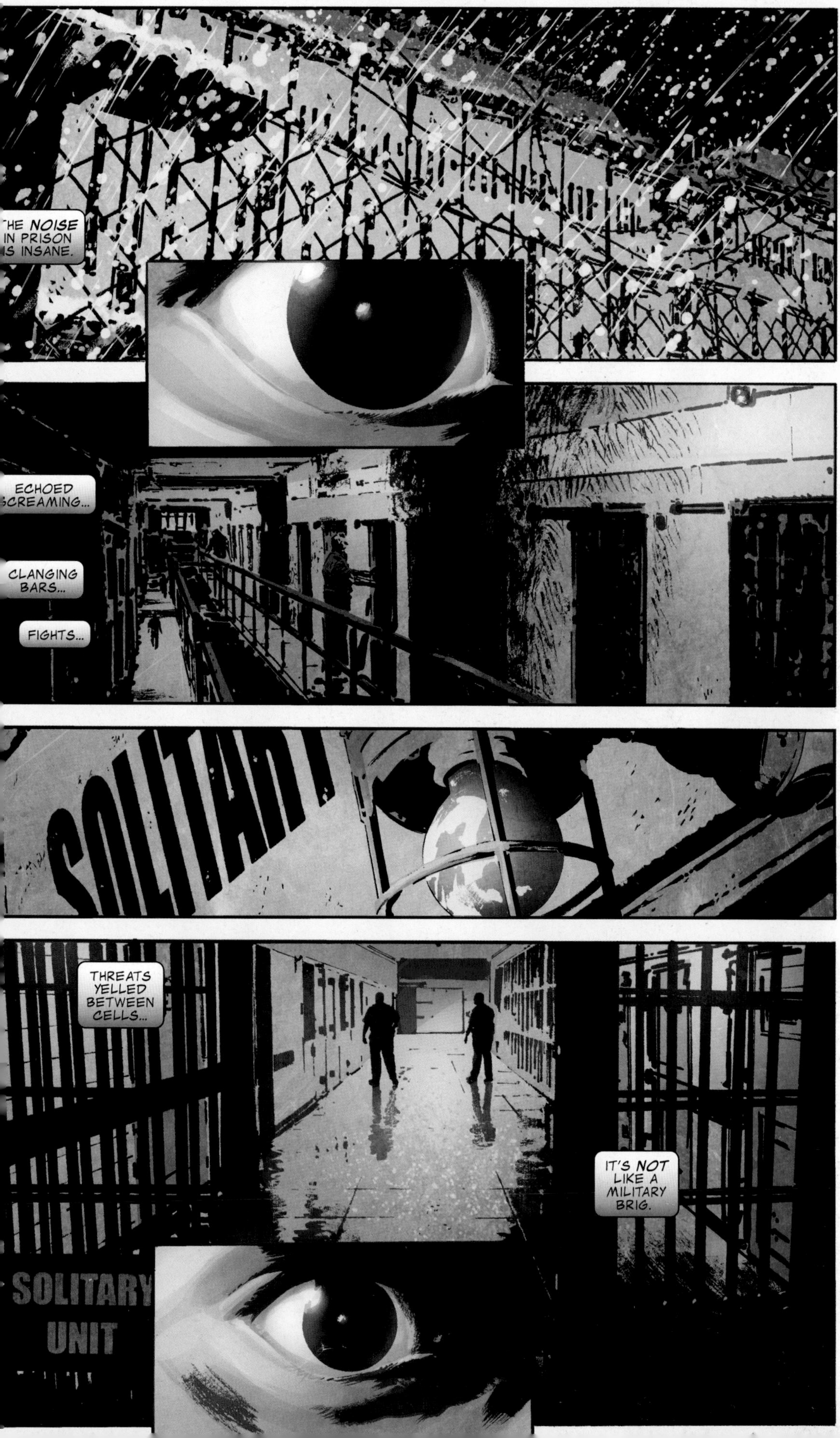
THE NOISE IN PRISON IS INSANE.
ECHOED SCREAMING...
CLANGING BARS...
FIGHTS...
SOLITARY
THREATS YELLED BETWEEN CELLS...
IT'S NOT LIKE A MILITARY BRIG.
SOLITARY UNIT

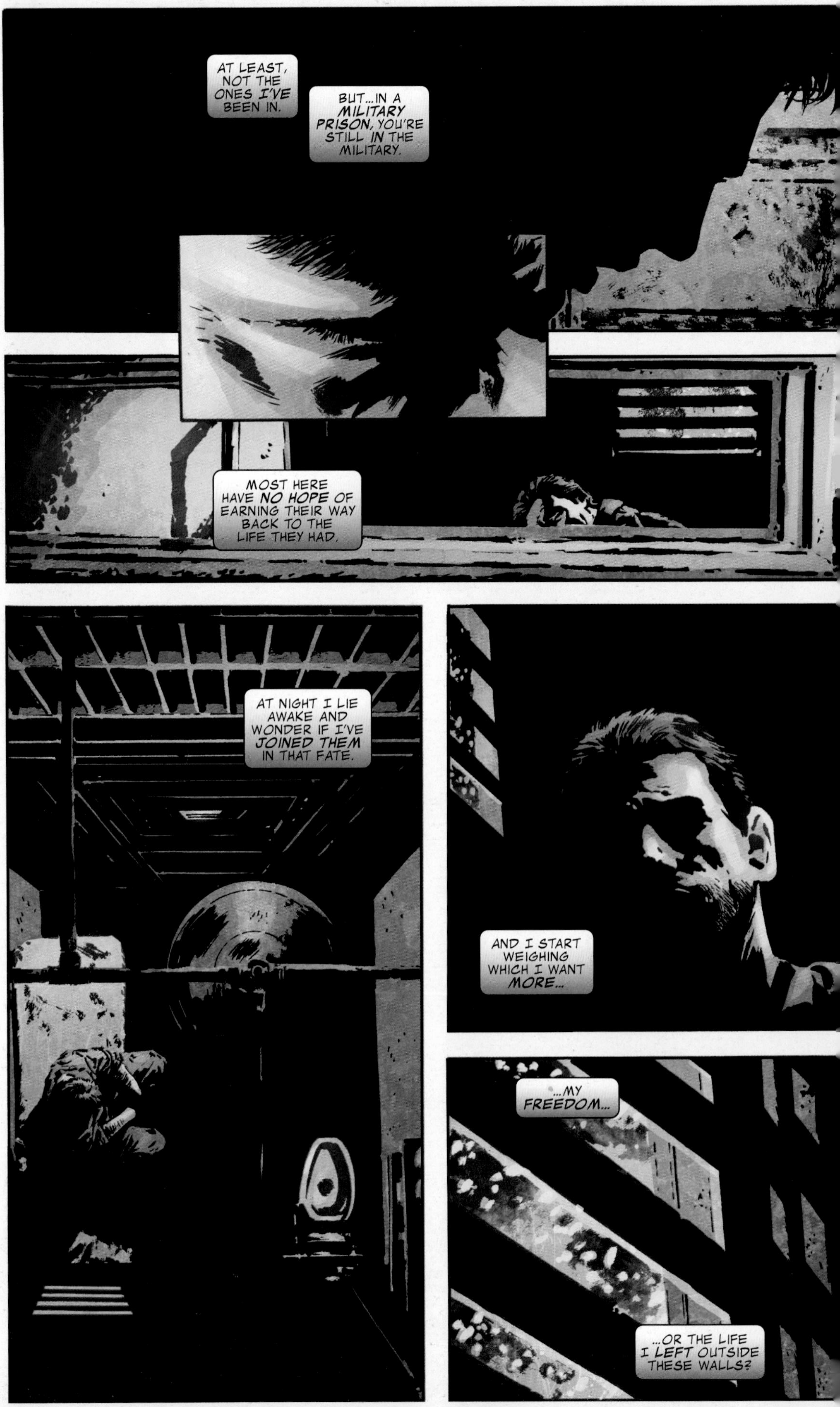
AT LEAST, NOT THE ONES I'VE BEEN IN.
BUT...IN A MILITARY PRISON, YOU'RE STILL IN THE MILITARY.
MOST HERE HAVE NO HOPE OF EARNING THEIR WAY BACK TO THE LIFE THEY HAD.
AT NIGHT I LIE AWAKE AND WONDER IF I'VE JOINED THEM IN THAT FATE.
AND I START WEIGHING WHICH I WANT MORE...
...MY FREEDOM...
...OR THE LIFE I LEFT OUTSIDE THESE WALLS?

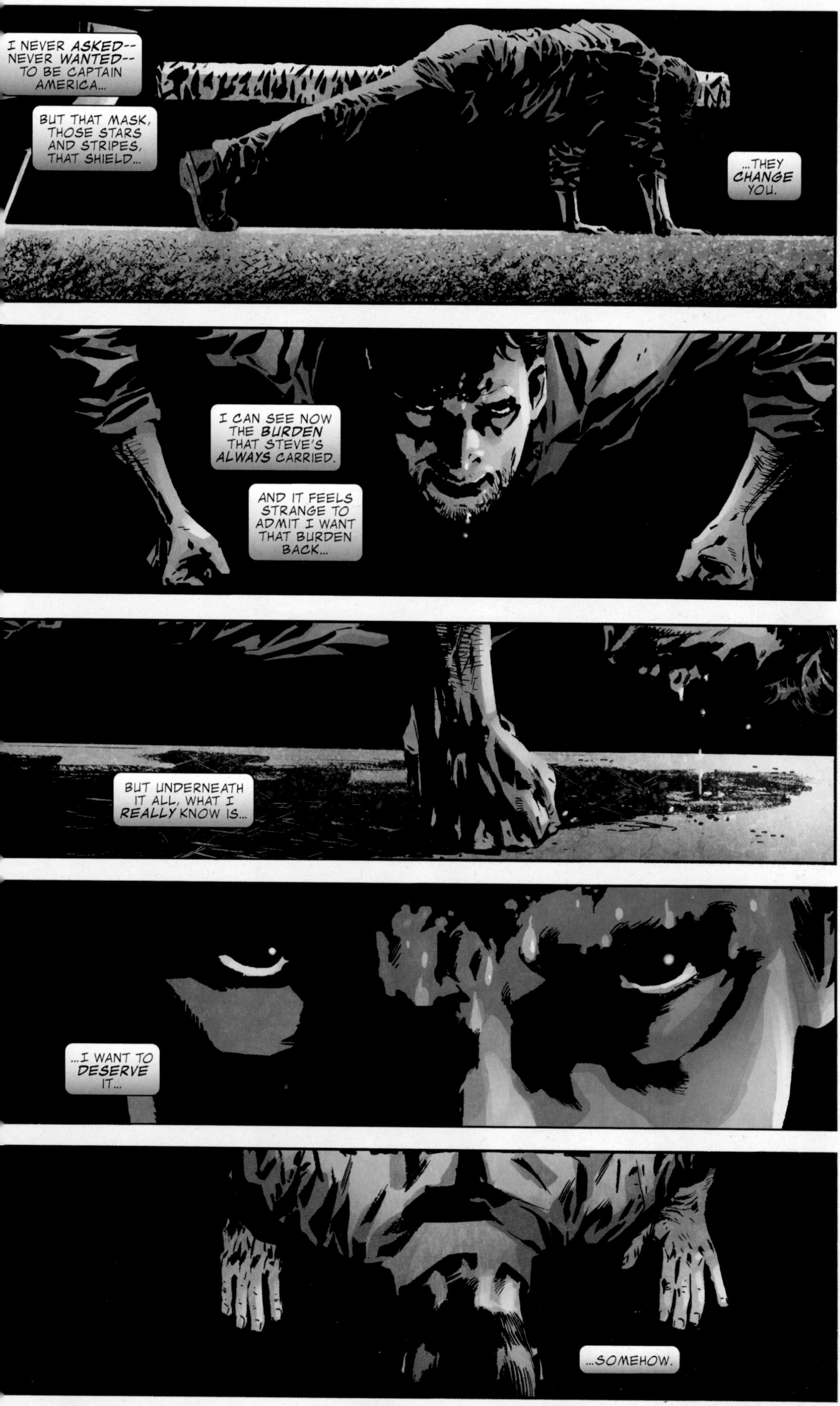

I NEVER ASKED-- NEVER WANTED-- TO BE CAPTAIN AMERICA...
BUT THAT MASK, THOSE STARS AND STRIPES, THAT SHIELD...
...THEY CHANGE YOU.
I CAN SEE NOW THE BURDEN THAT STEVE'S ALWAYS CARRIED.
AND IT FEELS STRANGE TO ADMIT I WANT THAT BURDEN BACK...
BUT UNDERNEATH IT ALL, WHAT I REALLY KNOW IS...
...I WANT TO DESERVE IT...
...SOMEHOW.

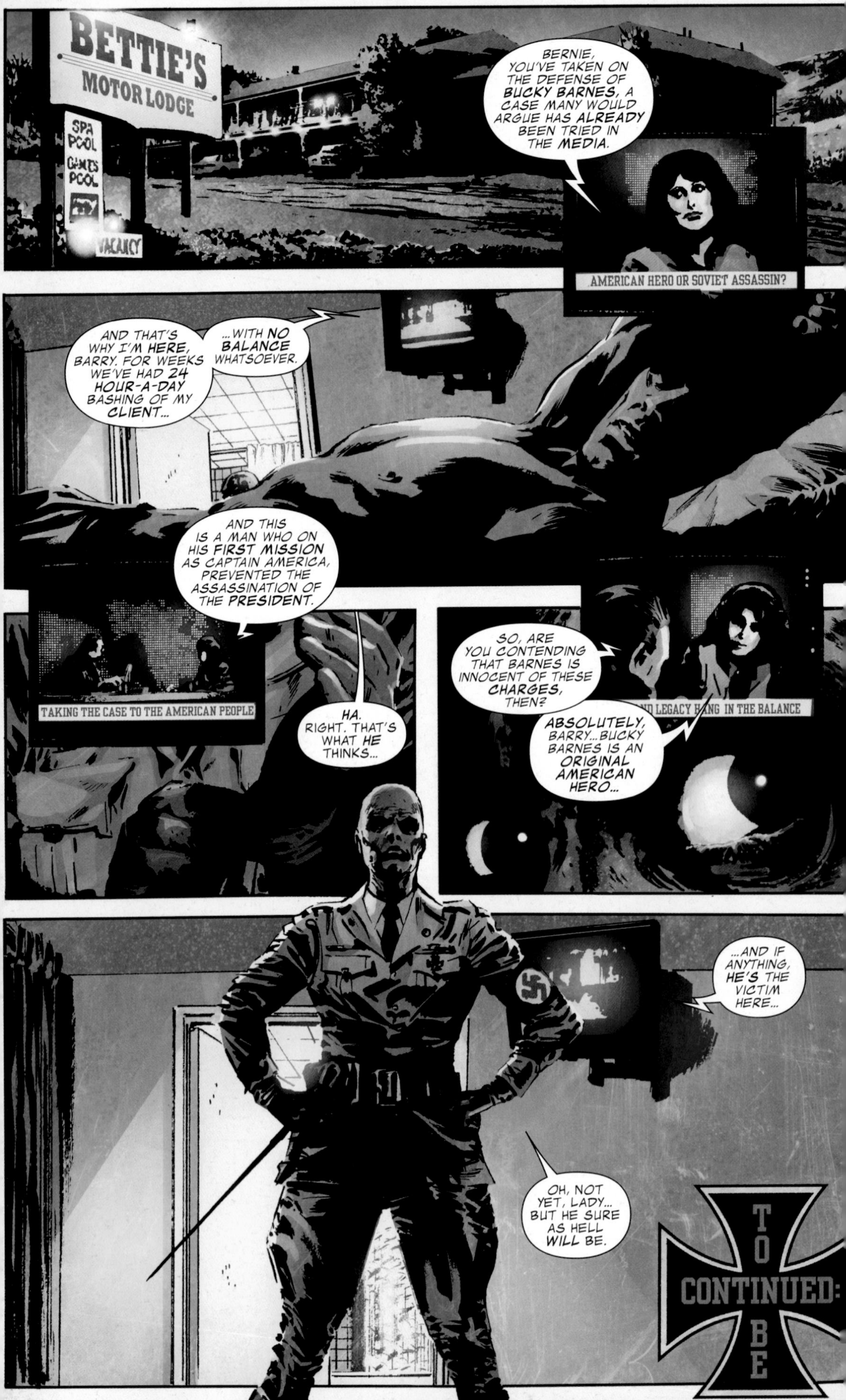
BETTIE'S MOTOR LODGE
SPA POOL
GAMES POOL
VACANCY
BERNIE, YOU'VE TAKEN ON THE DEFENSE OF BUCKY BARNES, A CASE MANY WOULD ARGUE HAS ALREADY BEEN TRIED IN THE MEDIA.
AMERICAN HERO OR SOVIET ASSASSIN?
AND THAT'S WHY I'M HERE, BARRY. FOR WEEKS WE'VE HAD 24 HOUR-A-DAY BASHING OF MY CLIENT...
...WITH NO BALANCE WHATSOEVER.
AND THIS IS A MAN WHO ON HIS FIRST MISSION AS CAPTAIN AMERICA, PREVENTED THE ASSASSINATION OF THE PRESIDENT.
TAKING THE CASE TO THE AMERICAN PEOPLE
HA. RIGHT. THAT'S WHAT HE THINKS...
SO, ARE YOU CONTENDING THAT BARNES IS INNOCENT OF THESE CHARGES, THEN?
LEGACY HANG IN THE BALANCE
ABSOLUTELY, BARRY...BUCKY BARNES IS AN ORIGINAL AMERICAN HERO...
...AND IF ANYTHING, HE'S THE VICTIM HERE...
OH, NOT YET, LADY... BUT HE SURE AS HELL WILL BE.
TO BE CONTINUED:

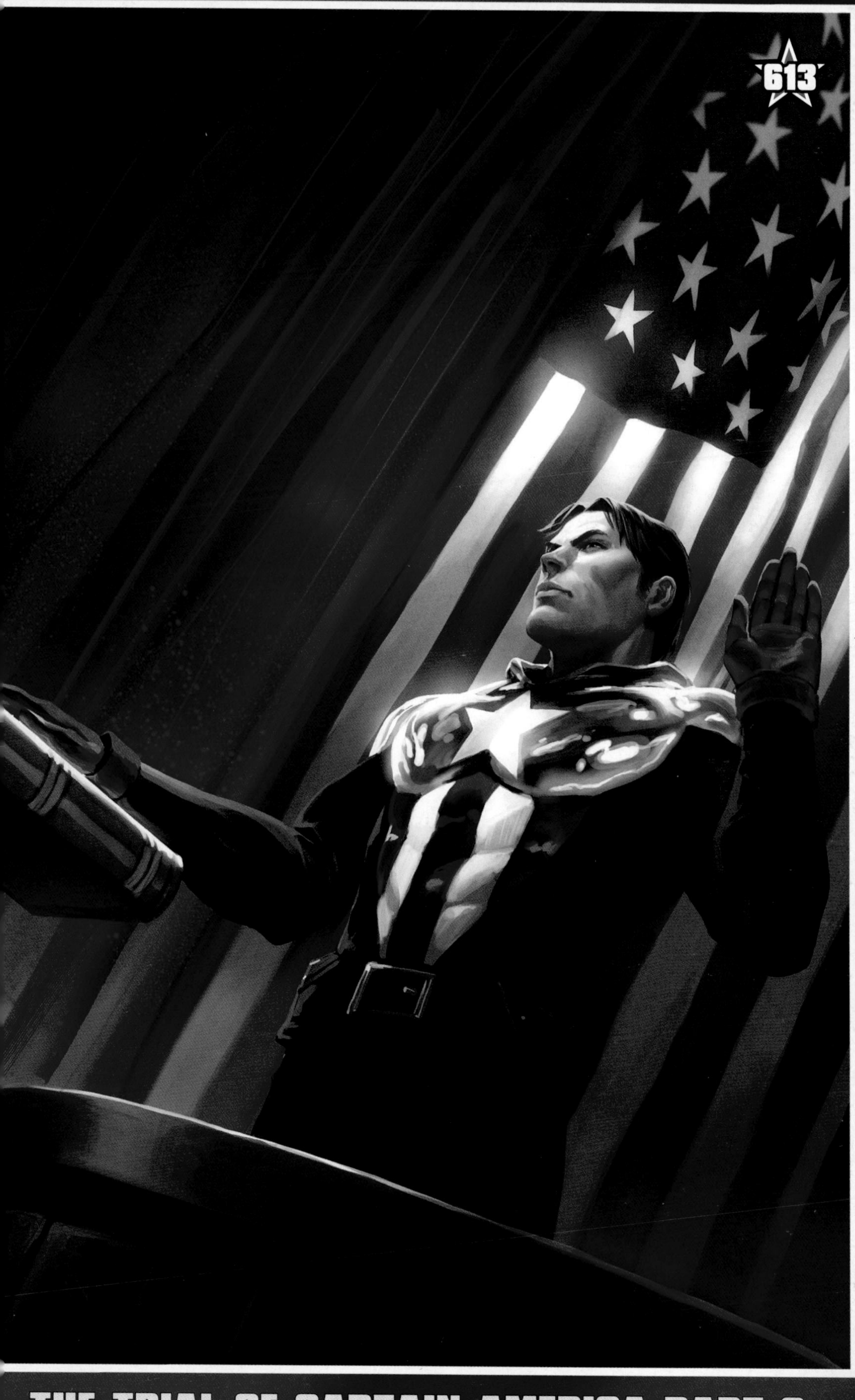
613

THE TRIAL OF CAPTAIN AMERICA PART 3

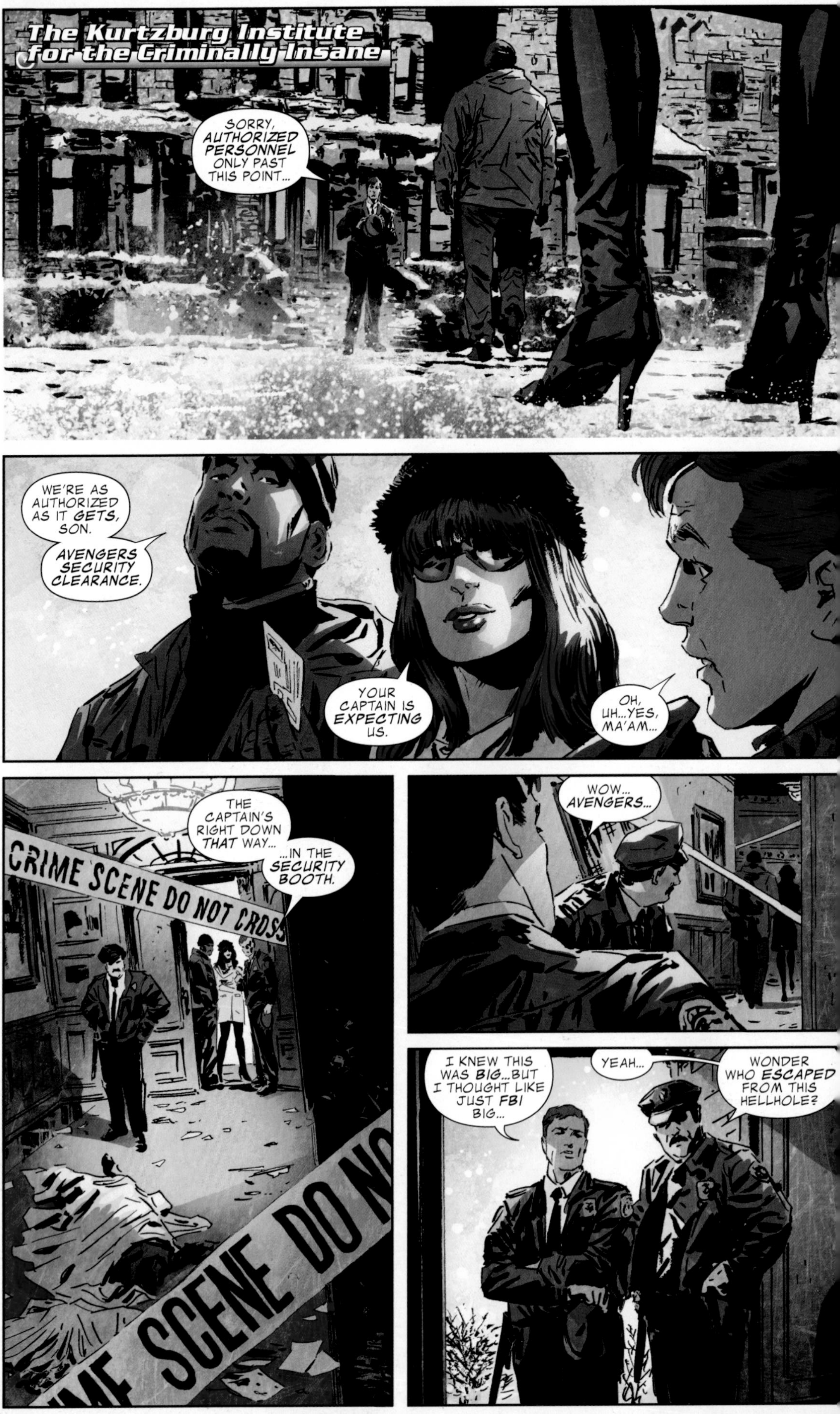
The Kurtzburg Institute for the Criminally Insane
SORRY, AUTHORIZED PERSONNEL ONLY PAST THIS POINT...
WE'RE AS AUTHORIZED AS IT GETS, SON.
AVENGERS SECURITY CLEARANCE.
YOUR CAPTAIN IS EXPECTING US.
OH, UH...YES, MA'AM...
THE CAPTAIN'S RIGHT DOWN THAT WAY...
...IN THE SECURITY BOOTH.
CRIME SCENE DO NOT CROSS
WOW... AVENGERS...
I KNEW THIS WAS BIG...BUT I THOUGHT LIKE JUST FBI BIG...
YEAH...
WONDER WHO ESCAPED FROM THIS HELLHOLE?

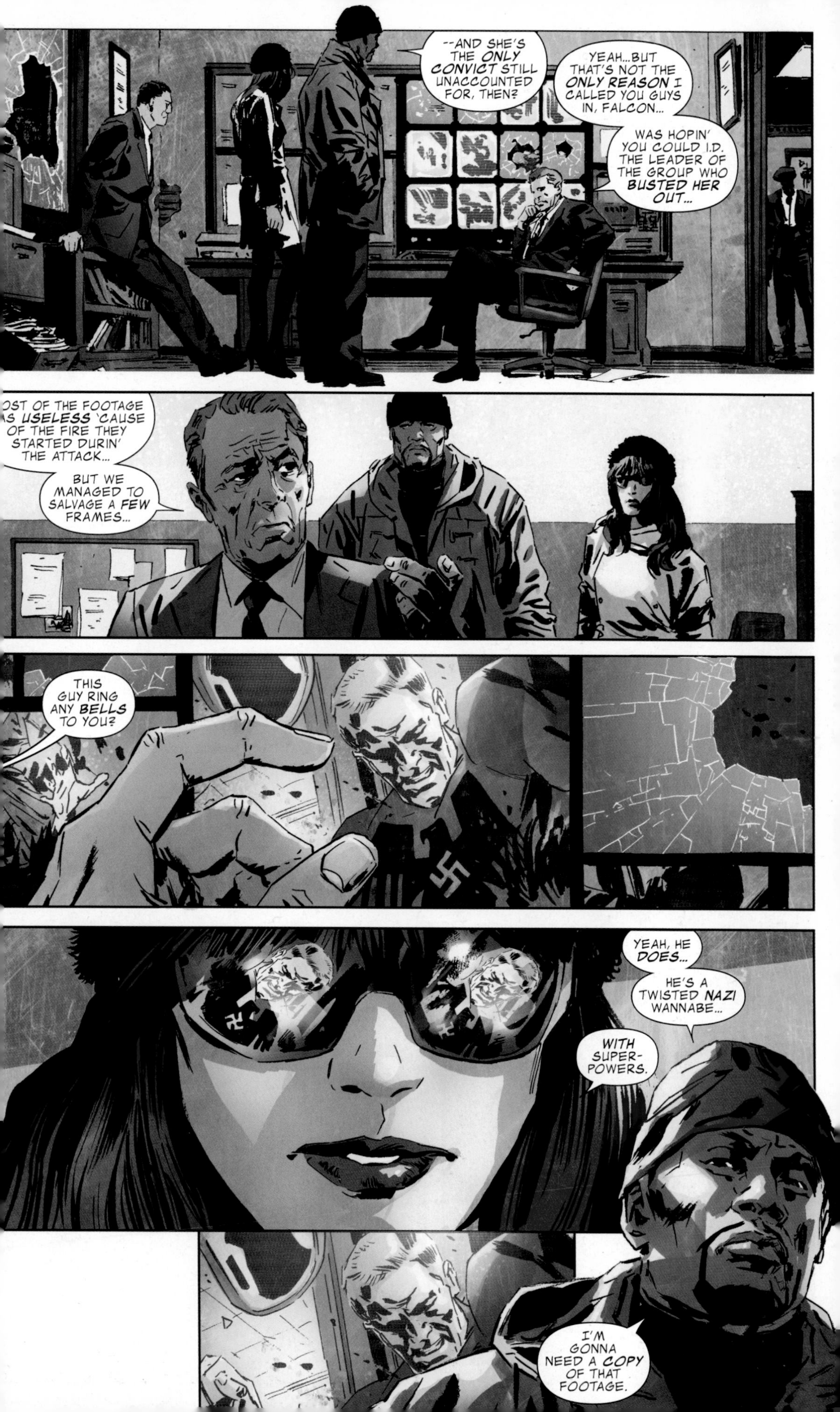
--AND SHE'S THE ONLY CONVICT STILL UNACCOUNTED FOR, THEN?
YEAH...BUT THAT'S NOT THE ONLY REASON I CALLED YOU GUYS IN, FALCON...
WAS HOPIN' YOU COULD I.D. THE LEADER OF THE GROUP WHO BUSTED HER OUT...
OST OF THE FOOTAGE AS USELESS 'CAUSE OF THE FIRE THEY STARTED DURIN' THE ATTACK...
BUT WE MANAGED TO SALVAGE A FEW FRAMES...
THIS GUY RING ANY BELLS TO YOU?
YEAH, HE DOES...
HE'S A TWISTED NAZI WANNABE...
WITH SUPER-POWERS.
I'M GONNA NEED A COPY OF THAT FOOTAGE.

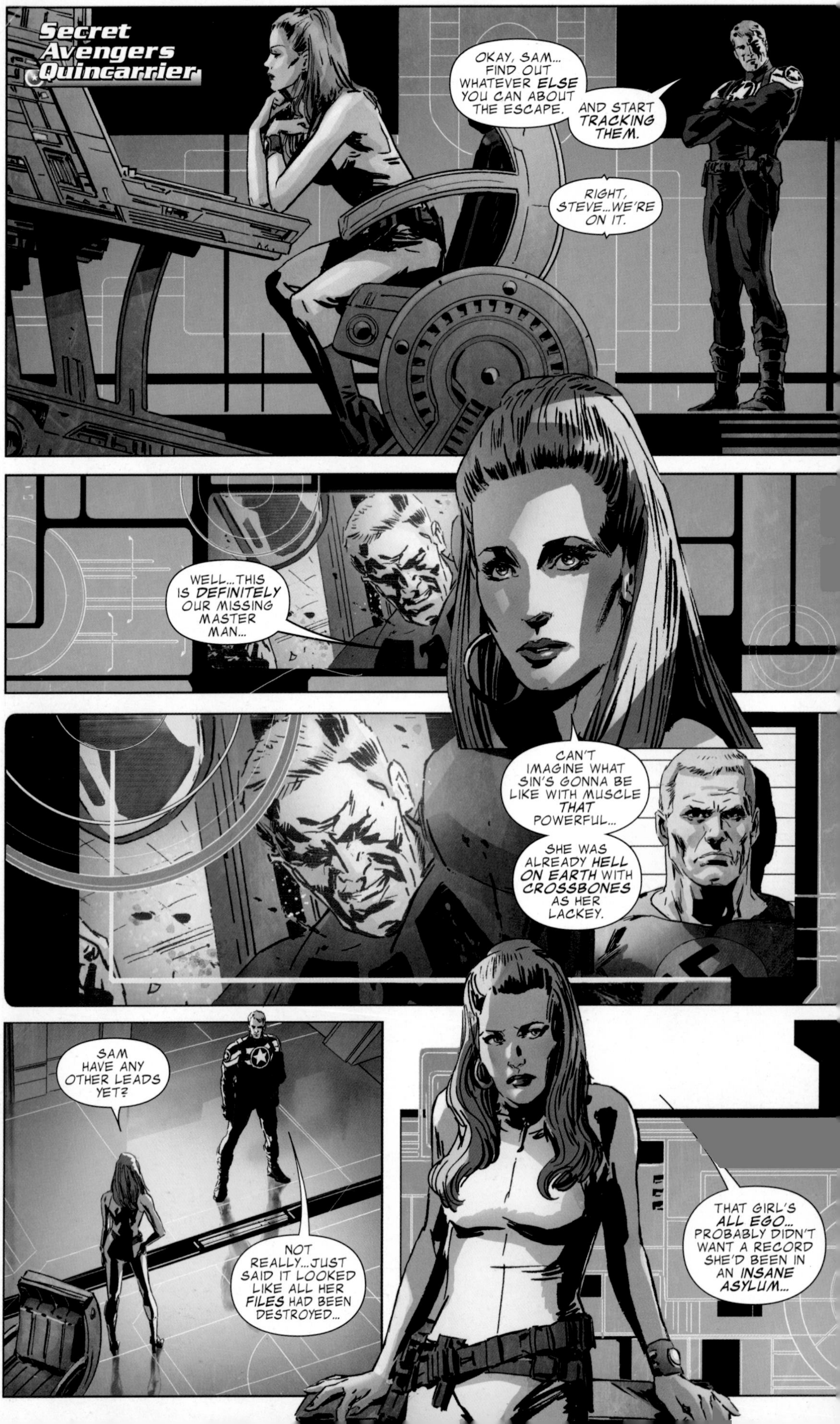
Secret Avengers Quincarrier
OKAY, SAM... FIND OUT WHATEVER ELSE YOU CAN ABOUT THE ESCAPE.
AND START TRACKING THEM.
RIGHT, STEVE...WE'RE ON IT.
WELL...THIS IS DEFINITELY OUR MISSING MASTER MAN...
CAN'T IMAGINE WHAT SIN'S GONNA BE LIKE WITH MUSCLE THAT POWERFUL...
SHE WAS ALREADY HELL ON EARTH WITH CROSSBONES AS HER LACKEY.
SAM HAVE ANY OTHER LEADS YET?
NOT REALLY...JUST SAID IT LOOKED LIKE ALL HER FILES HAD BEEN DESTROYED...
THAT GIRL'S ALL EGO... PROBABLY DIDN'T WANT A RECORD SHE'D BEEN IN AN INSANE ASYLUM...

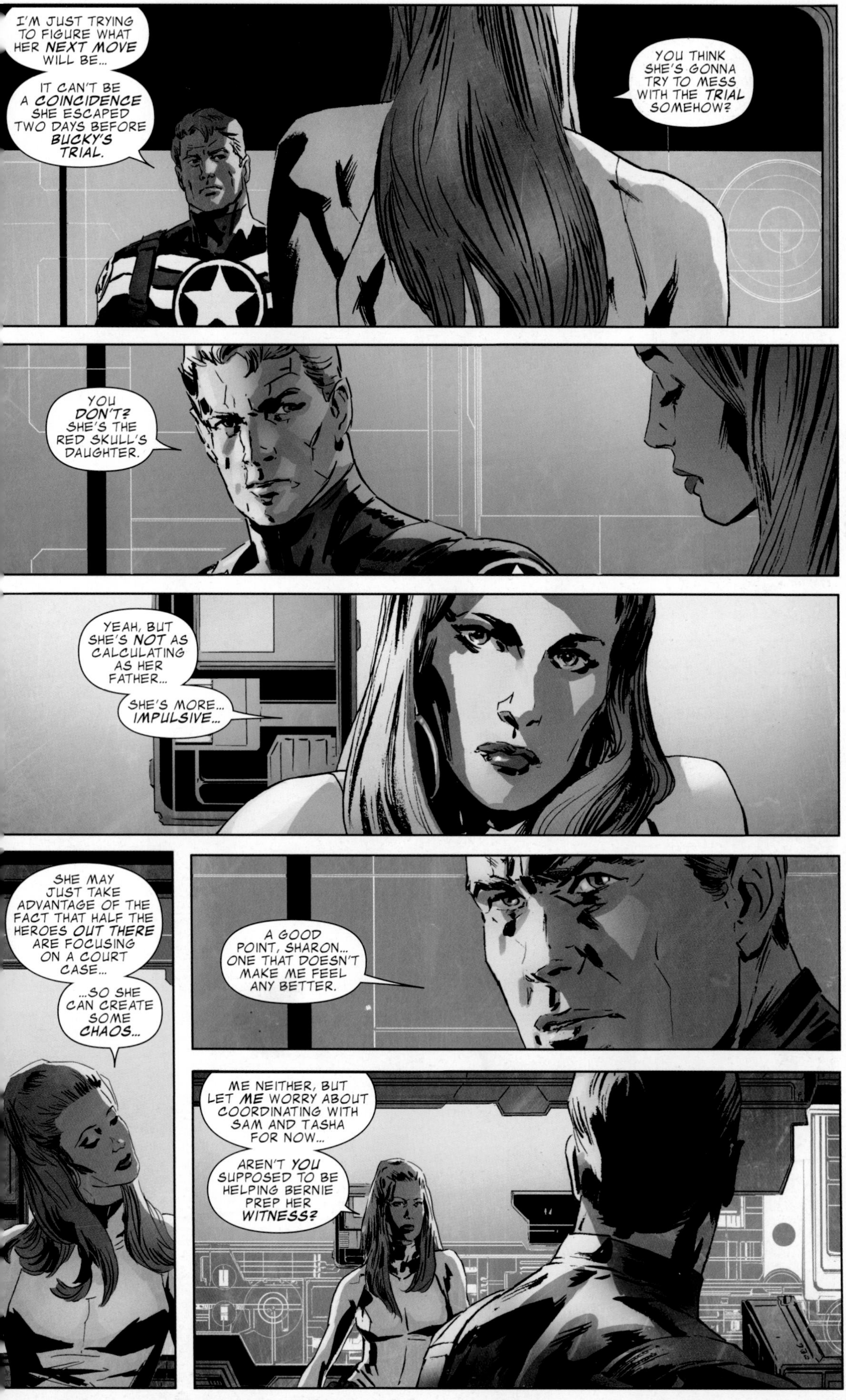

I'M JUST TRYING TO FIGURE WHAT HER NEXT MOVE WILL BE...
IT CAN'T BE A COINCIDENCE SHE ESCAPED TWO DAYS BEFORE BUCKY'S TRIAL.
YOU THINK SHE'S GONNA TRY TO MESS WITH THE TRIAL SOMEHOW?
YOU DON'T? SHE'S THE RED SKULL'S DAUGHTER.
YEAH, BUT SHE'S NOT AS CALCULATING AS HER FATHER...
SHE'S MORE... IMPULSIVE...
SHE MAY JUST TAKE ADVANTAGE OF THE FACT THAT HALF THE HEROES OUT THERE ARE FOCUSING ON A COURT CASE...
...SO SHE CAN CREATE SOME CHAOS...
A GOOD POINT, SHARON... ONE THAT DOESN'T MAKE ME FEEL ANY BETTER.
ME NEITHER, BUT LET ME WORRY ABOUT COORDINATING WITH SAM AND TASHA FOR NOW...
AREN'T YOU SUPPOSED TO BE HELPING BERNIE PREP HER WITNESS?

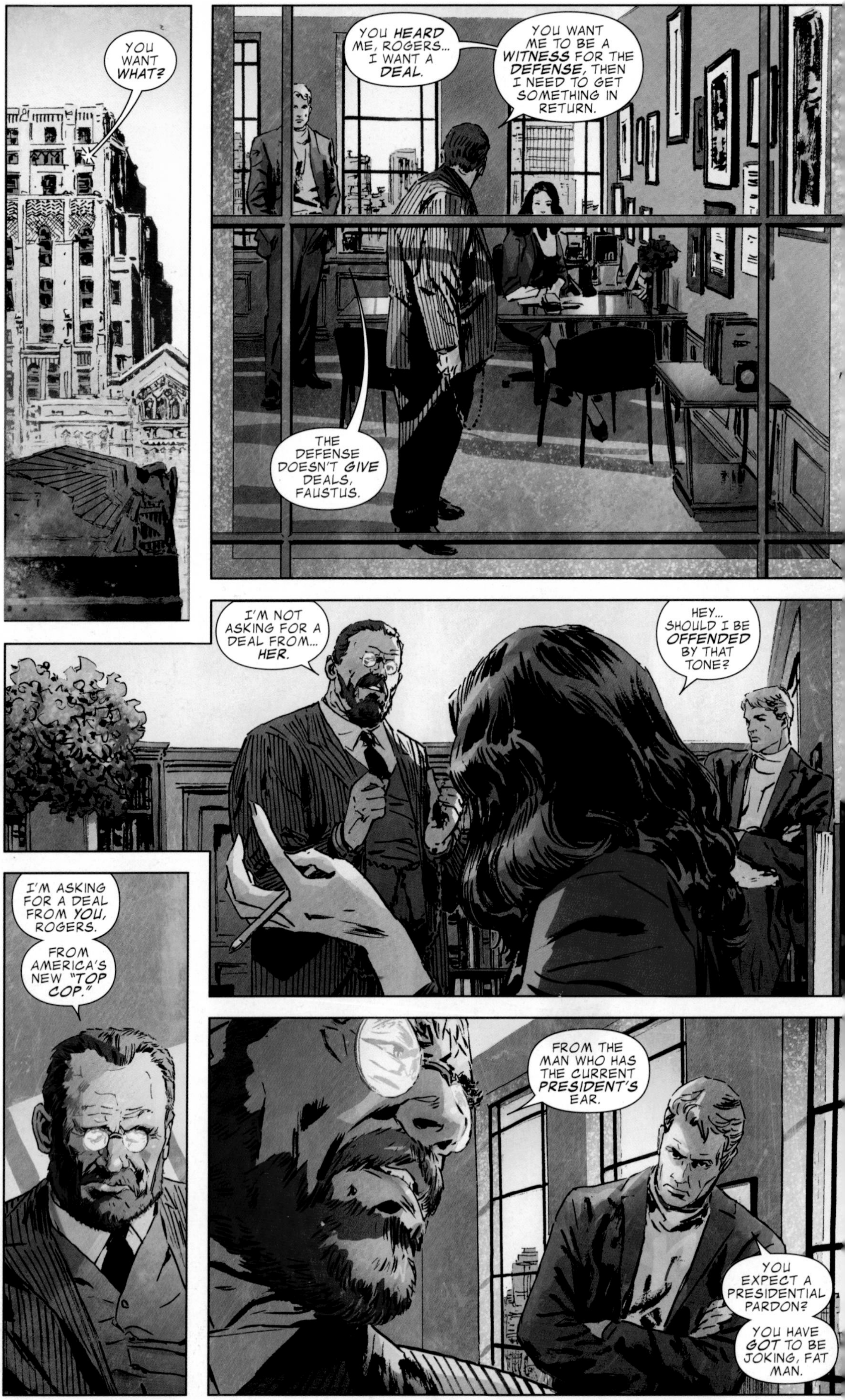
YOU WANT WHAT?
YOU HEARD ME, ROGERS... I WANT A DEAL.
YOU WANT ME TO BE A WITNESS FOR THE DEFENSE, THEN I NEED TO GET SOMETHING IN RETURN.
THE DEFENSE DOESN'T GIVE DEALS, FAUSTUS.
I'M NOT ASKING FOR A DEAL FROM... HER.
HEY... SHOULD I BE OFFENDED BY THAT TONE?
I'M ASKING FOR A DEAL FROM YOU, ROGERS.
FROM AMERICA'S NEW "TOP COP."
FROM THE MAN WHO HAS THE CURRENT PRESIDENT'S EAR.
YOU EXPECT A PRESIDENTIAL PARDON?
YOU HAVE GOT TO BE JOKING, FAT MAN.

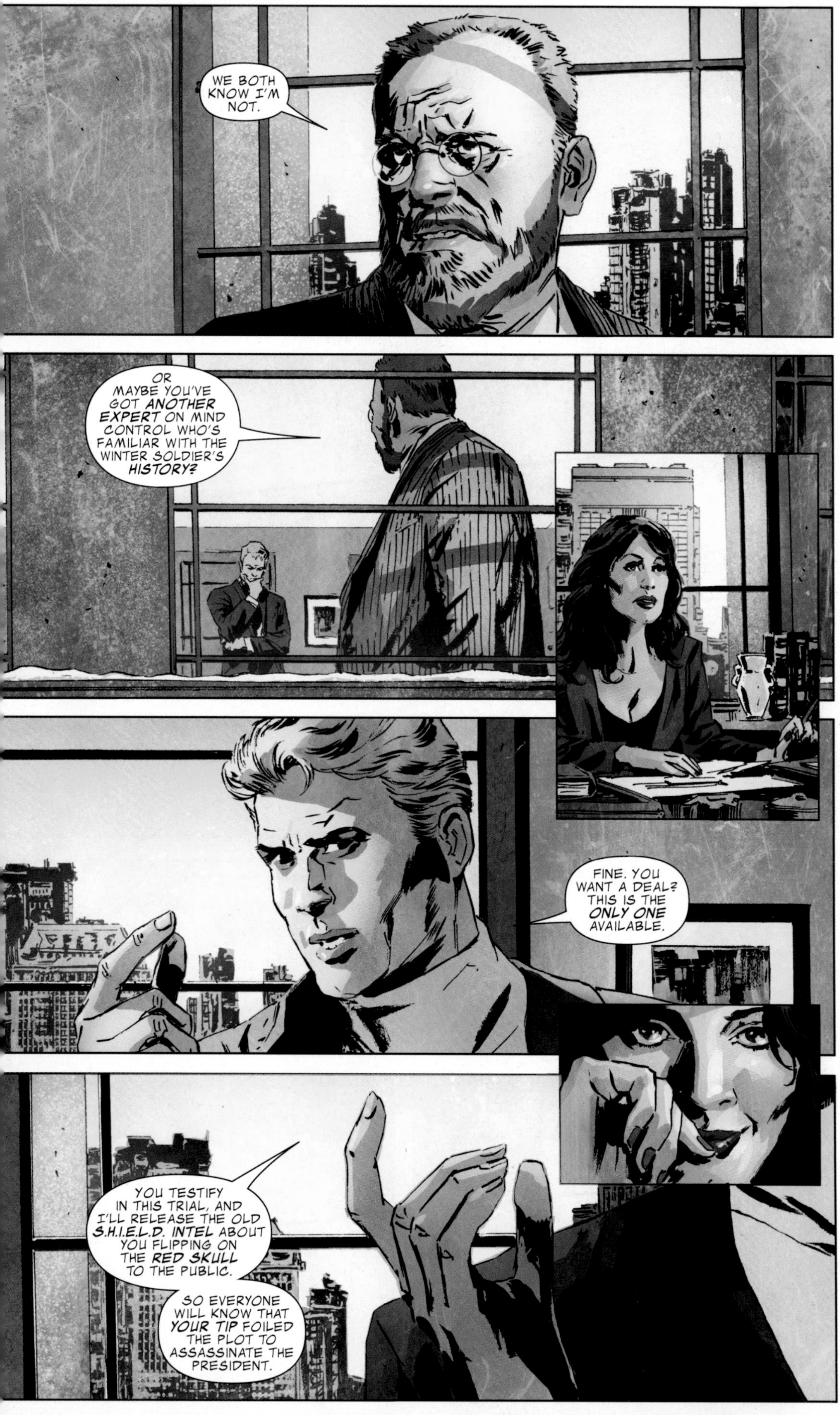
WE BOTH KNOW I'M NOT.
OR MAYBE YOU'VE GOT ANOTHER EXPERT ON MIND CONTROL WHO'S FAMILIAR WITH THE WINTER SOLDIER'S HISTORY?
FINE. YOU WANT A DEAL? THIS IS THE ONLY ONE AVAILABLE.
YOU TESTIFY IN THIS TRIAL, AND I'LL RELEASE THE OLD S.H.I.E.L.D. INTEL ABOUT YOU FLIPPING ON THE RED SKULL TO THE PUBLIC.
SO EVERYONE WILL KNOW THAT YOUR TIP FOILED THE PLOT TO ASSASSINATE THE PRESIDENT.

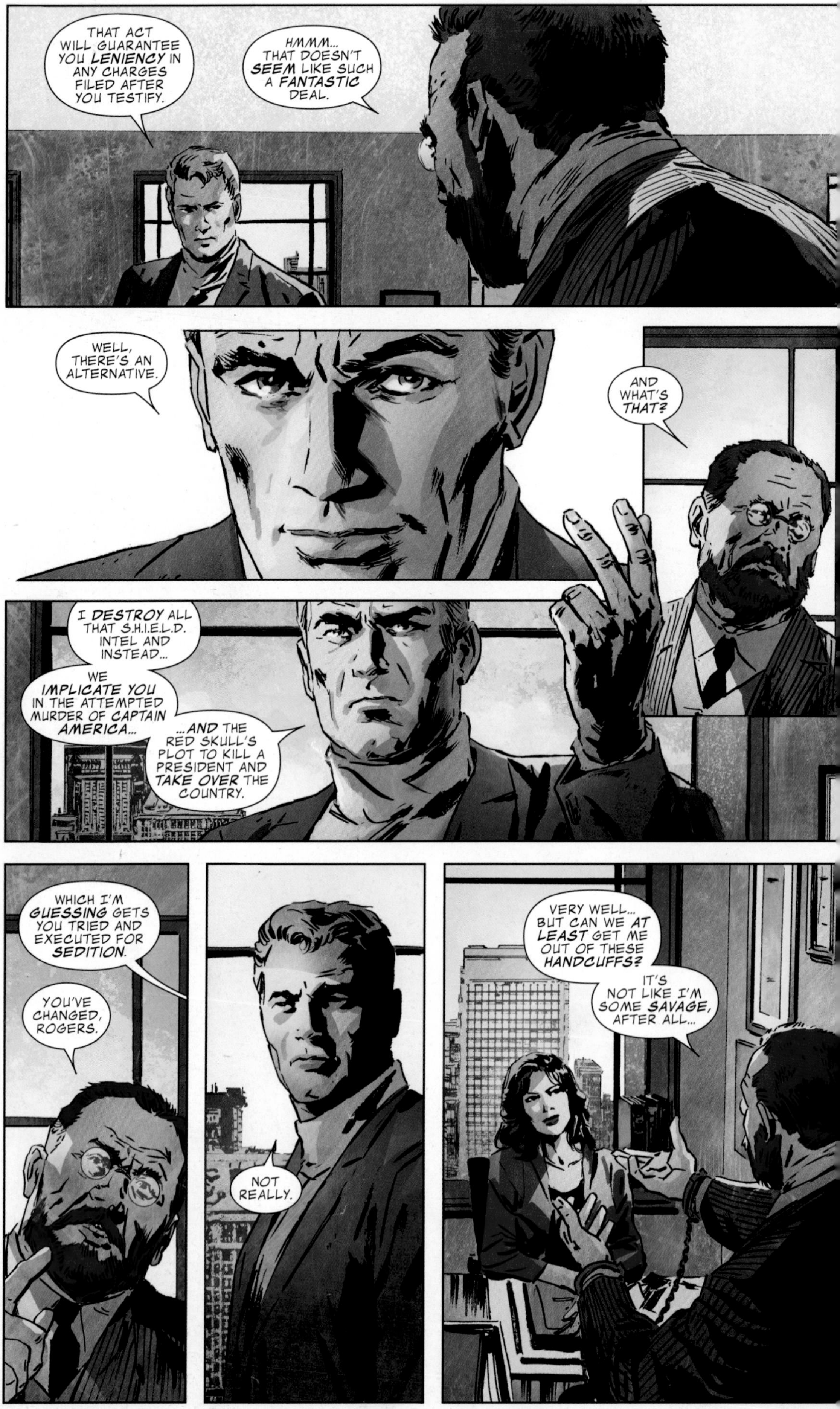
THAT ACT WILL GUARANTEE YOU LENIENCY IN ANY CHARGES FILED AFTER YOU TESTIFY.
HMMM... THAT DOESN'T SEEM LIKE SUCH A FANTASTIC DEAL.
WELL, THERE'S AN ALTERNATIVE.
AND WHAT'S THAT?
I DESTROY ALL THAT S.H.I.E.L.D. INTEL AND INSTEAD...
WE IMPLICATE YOU IN THE ATTEMPTED MURDER OF CAPTAIN AMERICA...
...AND THE RED SKULL'S PLOT TO KILL A PRESIDENT AND TAKE OVER THE COUNTRY.
WHICH I'M GUESSING GETS YOU TRIED AND EXECUTED FOR SEDITION.
YOU'VE CHANGED, ROGERS.
NOT REALLY.
VERY WELL... BUT CAN WE AT LEAST GET ME OUT OF THESE HANDCUFFS?
IT'S NOT LIKE I'M SOME SAVAGE, AFTER ALL...

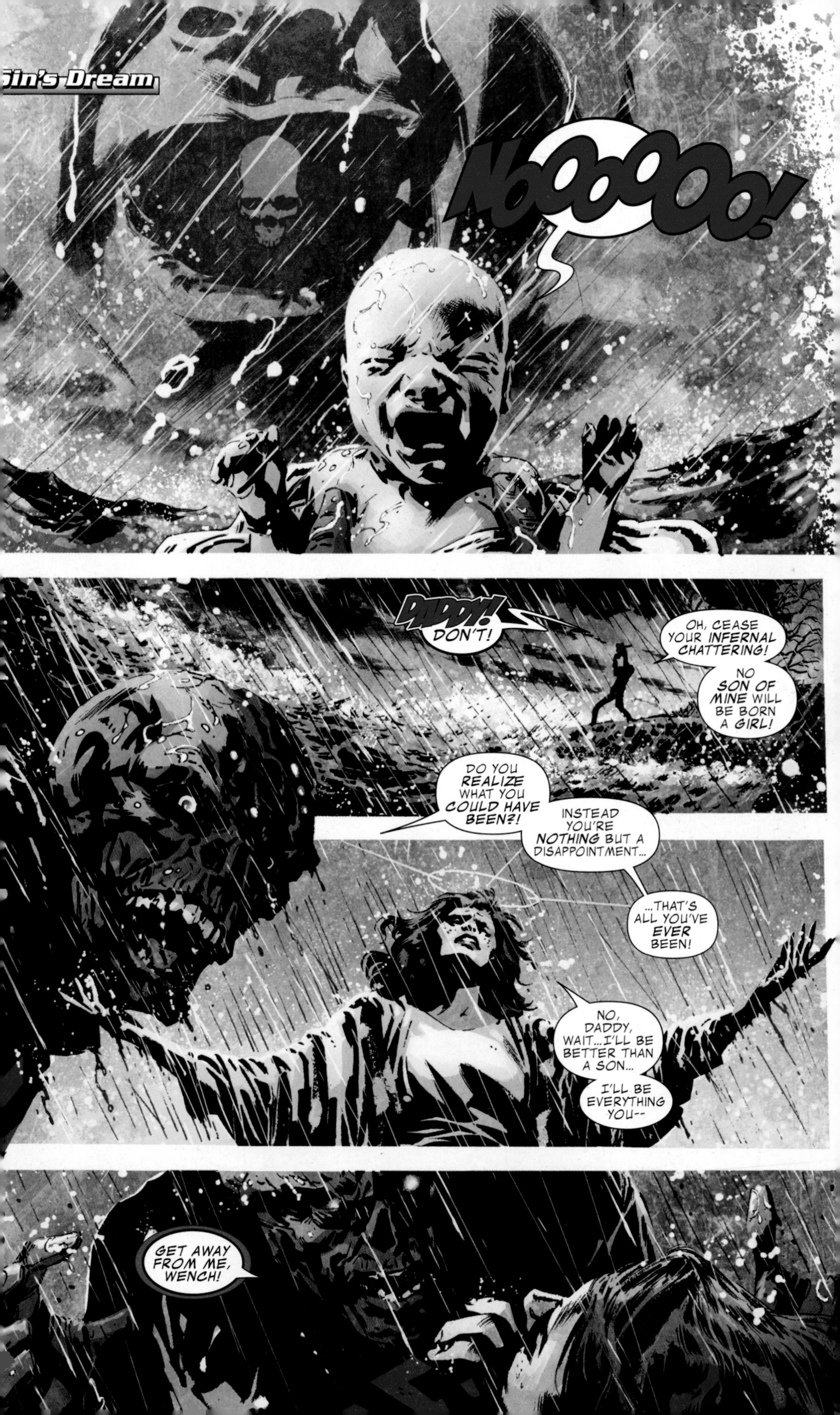
Sin's Dream
NOOOOOO!
DADDY! DON'T!
OH, CEASE YOUR INFERNAL CHATTERING!
NO SON OF MINE WILL BE BORN A GIRL!
DO YOU REALIZE WHAT YOU COULD HAVE BEEN?!
INSTEAD YOU'RE NOTHING BUT A DISAPPOINTMENT...
...THAT'S ALL YOU'VE EVER BEEN!
NO, DADDY, WAIT...I'LL BE BETTER THAN A SON...
I'LL BE EVERYTHING YOU--
GET AWAY FROM ME, WENCH!

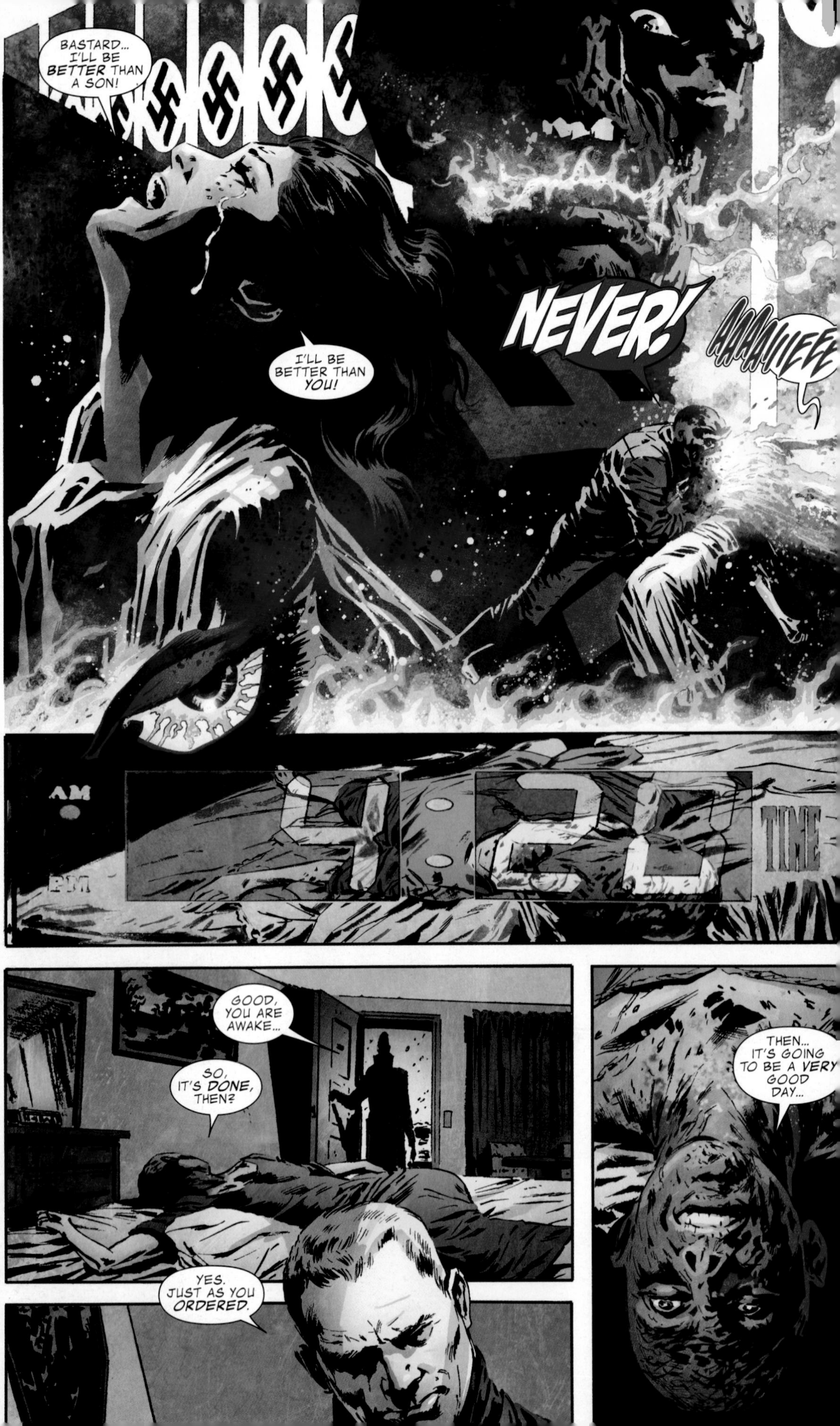
BASTARD... I'LL BE BETTER THAN A SON!
I'LL BE BETTER THAN YOU!
NEVER!
AAAAIIEEE
AM
PM
TIME
GOOD, YOU ARE AWAKE...
SO, IT'S DONE, THEN?
YES. JUST AS YOU ORDERED.
THEN... IT'S GOING TO BE A VERY GOOD DAY...

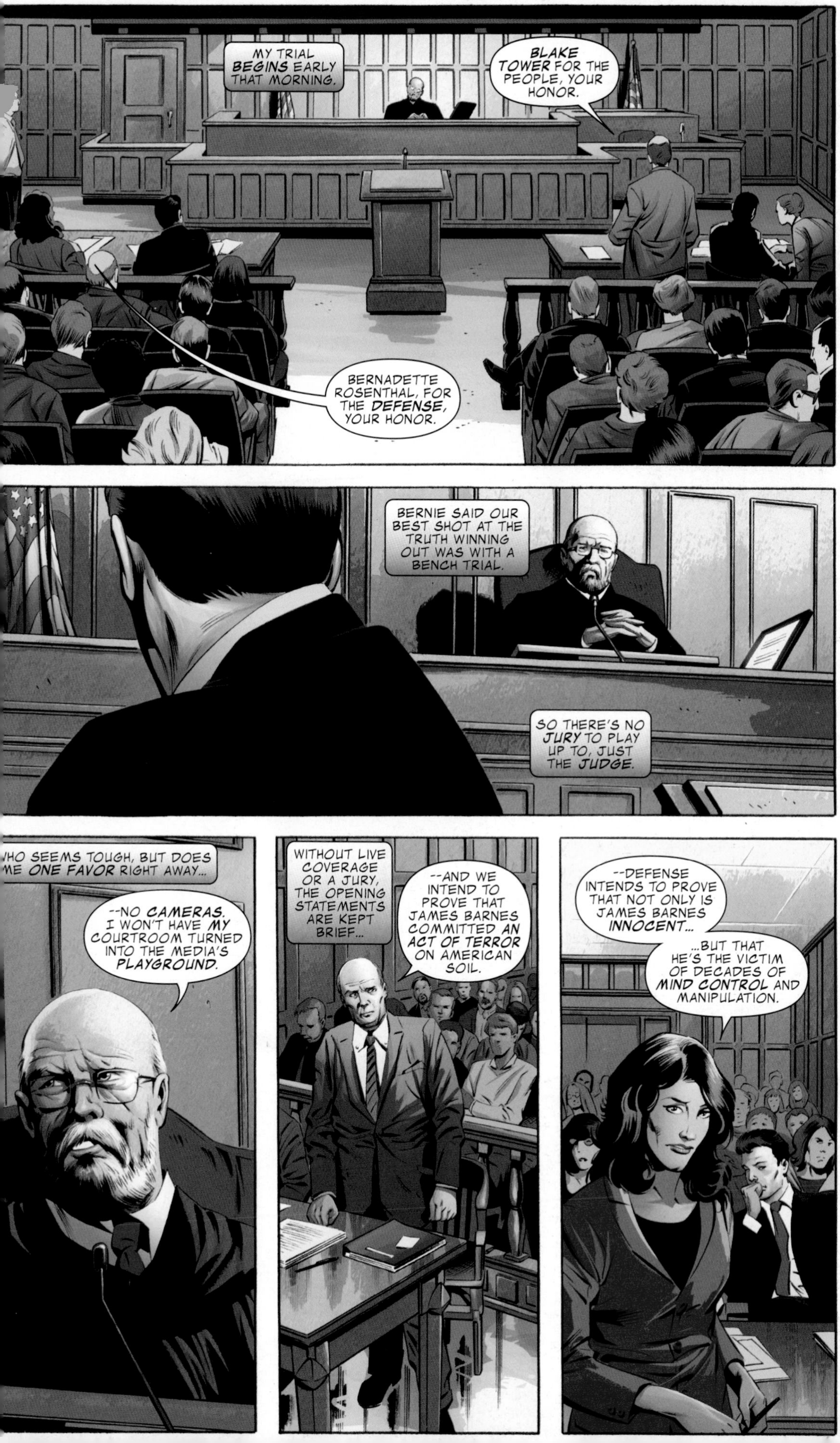

MY TRIAL BEGINS EARLY THAT MORNING.
BLAKE TOWER FOR THE PEOPLE, YOUR HONOR.
BERNADETTE ROSENTHAL, FOR THE DEFENSE, YOUR HONOR.
BERNIE SAID OUR BEST SHOT AT THE TRUTH WINNING OUT WAS WITH A BENCH TRIAL.
SO THERE'S NO JURY TO PLAY UP TO, JUST THE JUDGE.
WHO SEEMS TOUGH, BUT DOES ME ONE FAVOR RIGHT AWAY...
--NO CAMERAS. I WON'T HAVE MY COURTROOM TURNED INTO THE MEDIA'S PLAYGROUND.
WITHOUT LIVE COVERAGE OR A JURY, THE OPENING STATEMENTS ARE KEPT BRIEF...
--AND WE INTEND TO PROVE THAT JAMES BARNES COMMITTED AN ACT OF TERROR ON AMERICAN SOIL.
--DEFENSE INTENDS TO PROVE THAT NOT ONLY IS JAMES BARNES INNOCENT...
...BUT THAT HE'S THE VICTIM OF DECADES OF MIND CONTROL AND MANIPULATION.

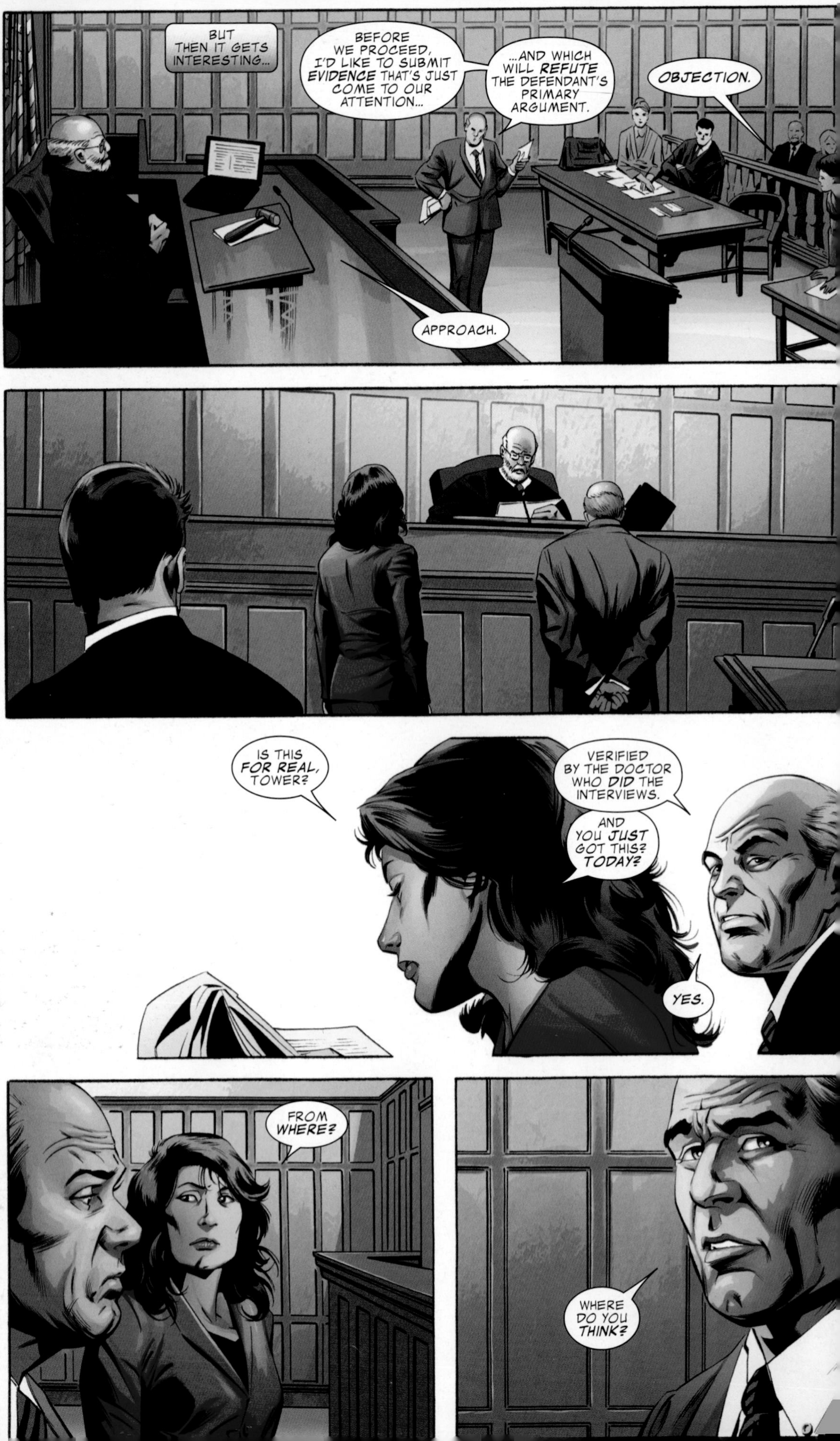
BUT THEN IT GETS INTERESTING...
BEFORE WE PROCEED, I'D LIKE TO SUBMIT EVIDENCE THAT'S JUST COME TO OUR ATTENTION...
...AND WHICH WILL REFUTE THE DEFENDANT'S PRIMARY ARGUMENT.
OBJECTION.
APPROACH.
IS THIS FOR REAL, TOWER?
VERIFIED BY THE DOCTOR WHO DID THE INTERVIEWS.
AND YOU JUST GOT THIS? TODAY?
YES.
FROM WHERE?
WHERE DO YOU THINK?

WS
ED:

KULL'S DAUGHTER REVEALS COURTROOM BOMBSHELL...

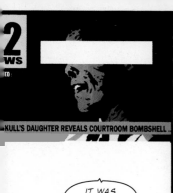

--SHOCKING REVELATIONS IN THE TAPED **CONFESSIONS** OF THE RED SKULL'S EVIL DAUGHTER...

IT WAS ALL A TRICK... A SET-UP...

BREAKING NEWS

NO, IDIOT, BARNES WAS MY FATHER'S **OPERATIVE** FOR YEARS...THEY **CLAIM** HE WAS BRAINWASHED, BUT IT'S A LIE...

LIVE

--INTERVIEWS CONDUCTED **WELL** **BEFORE** THE NEW CAPTAIN AMERICA'S IDENTITY...AND HIS **DARK** HISTORY...BECAME PUBLIC...

THE RUSSIANS JUST **TURNED** HIM.

BREAKING NEWS

...SHOCKING NEW REVELATIONS...HAS IT ALL BEEN A LIE? **BNN**

CHANNEL
7 BREAKING NEWS

HIM **SAVING** THE PRESIDENT, CLAIMING **REDEMPTION**... IT WAS A FAKE...

DADDY DIDN'T WANT HIS OWN PRESIDENT...

...HE WANTED HIS OWN **CAPTAIN AMERICA.**

12
NEWS

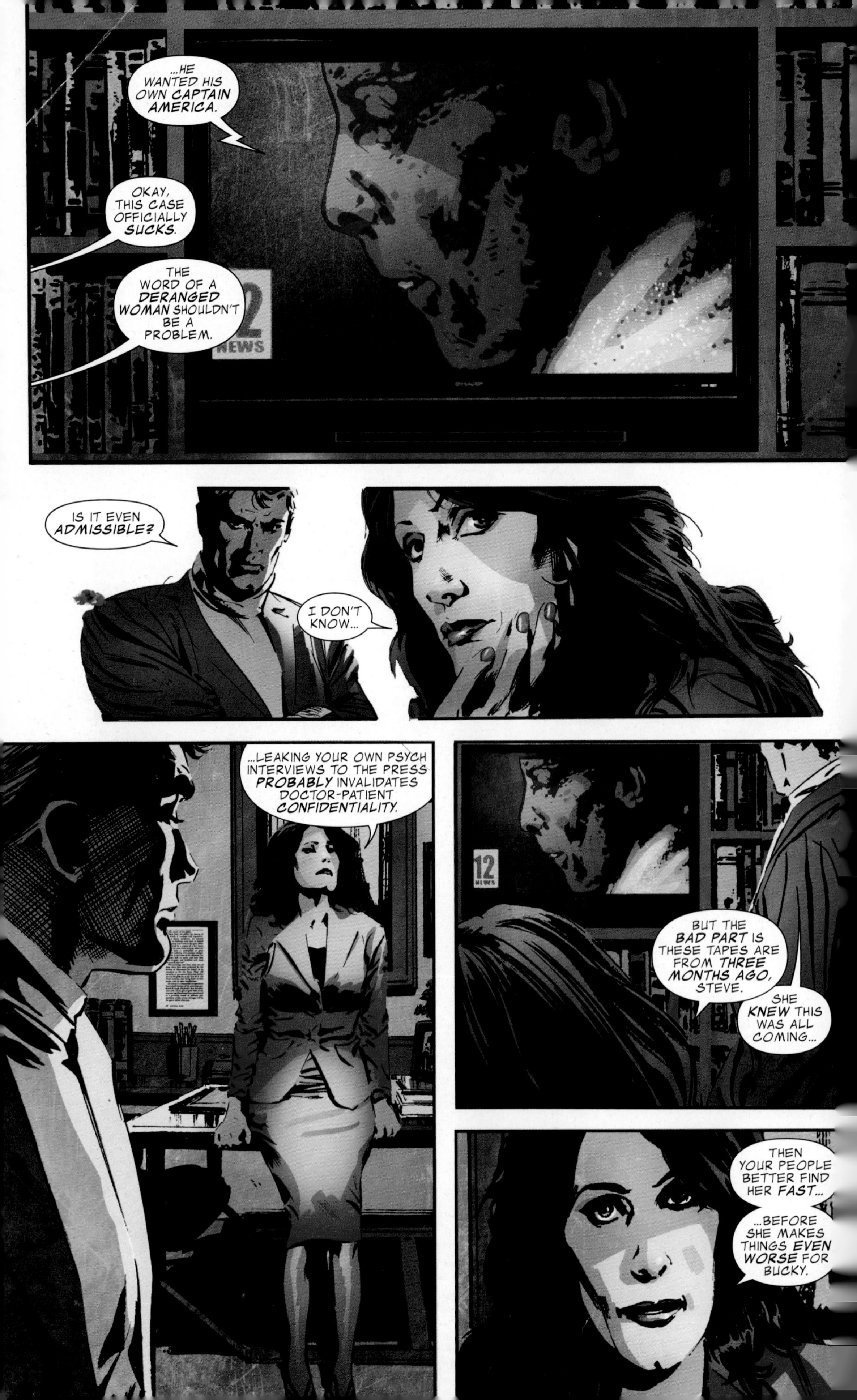
...HE WANTED HIS OWN CAPTAIN AMERICA.
OKAY, THIS CASE OFFICIALLY SUCKS.
THE WORD OF A DERANGED WOMAN SHOULDN'T BE A PROBLEM.
12 NEWS
IS IT EVEN ADMISSIBLE?
I DON'T KNOW...
...LEAKING YOUR OWN PSYCH INTERVIEWS TO THE PRESS PROBABLY INVALIDATES DOCTOR-PATIENT CONFIDENTIALITY.
12 NEWS
BUT THE BAD PART IS THESE TAPES ARE FROM THREE MONTHS AGO, STEVE.
SHE KNEW THIS WAS ALL COMING...
THEN YOUR PEOPLE BETTER FIND HER FAST...
...BEFORE SHE MAKES THINGS EVEN WORSE FOR BUCKY.

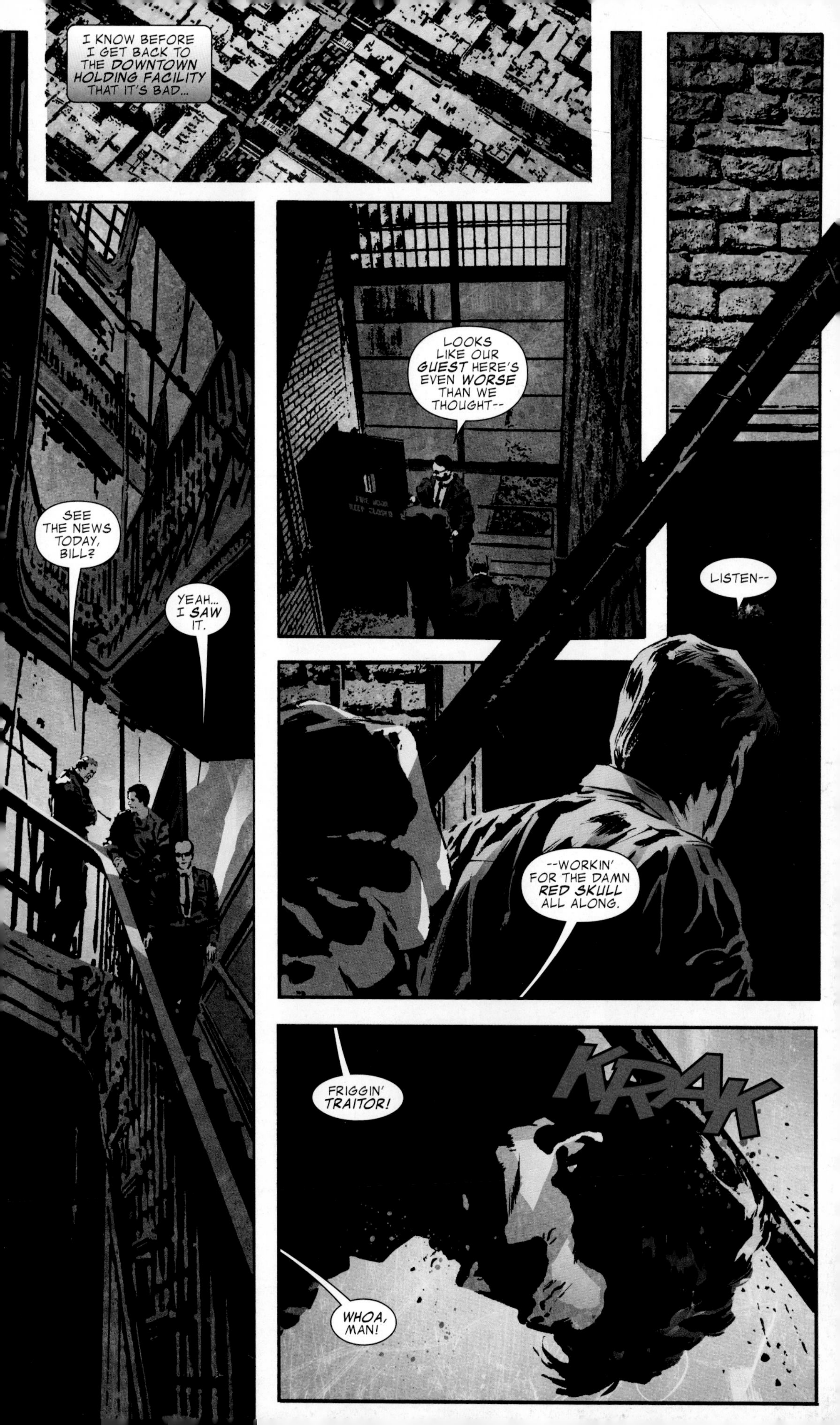
I KNOW BEFORE I GET BACK TO THE DOWNTOWN HOLDING FACILITY THAT IT'S BAD...
SEE THE NEWS TODAY, BILL?
YEAH... I SAW IT.
LOOKS LIKE OUR GUEST HERE'S EVEN WORSE THAN WE THOUGHT--
LISTEN--
--WORKIN' FOR THE DAMN RED SKULL ALL ALONG.
FRIGGIN' TRAITOR!
KRAK
WHOA, MAN!

I HEAR STEVE'S VOICE IN MY HEAD... TELLING ME TO JUST STAY CALM...
...TO RISE ABOVE.
BUT I DON'T WANT TO.
OH YEAH? WELL C'MON THEN, TOUGH GUY!
PAFF
DAILY BUGLE
EARLY MORNING EDITION
CAP ASSAULTS GUARD
AND STILL, MY "INNER STEVE" WINS THE ARGUMENT.

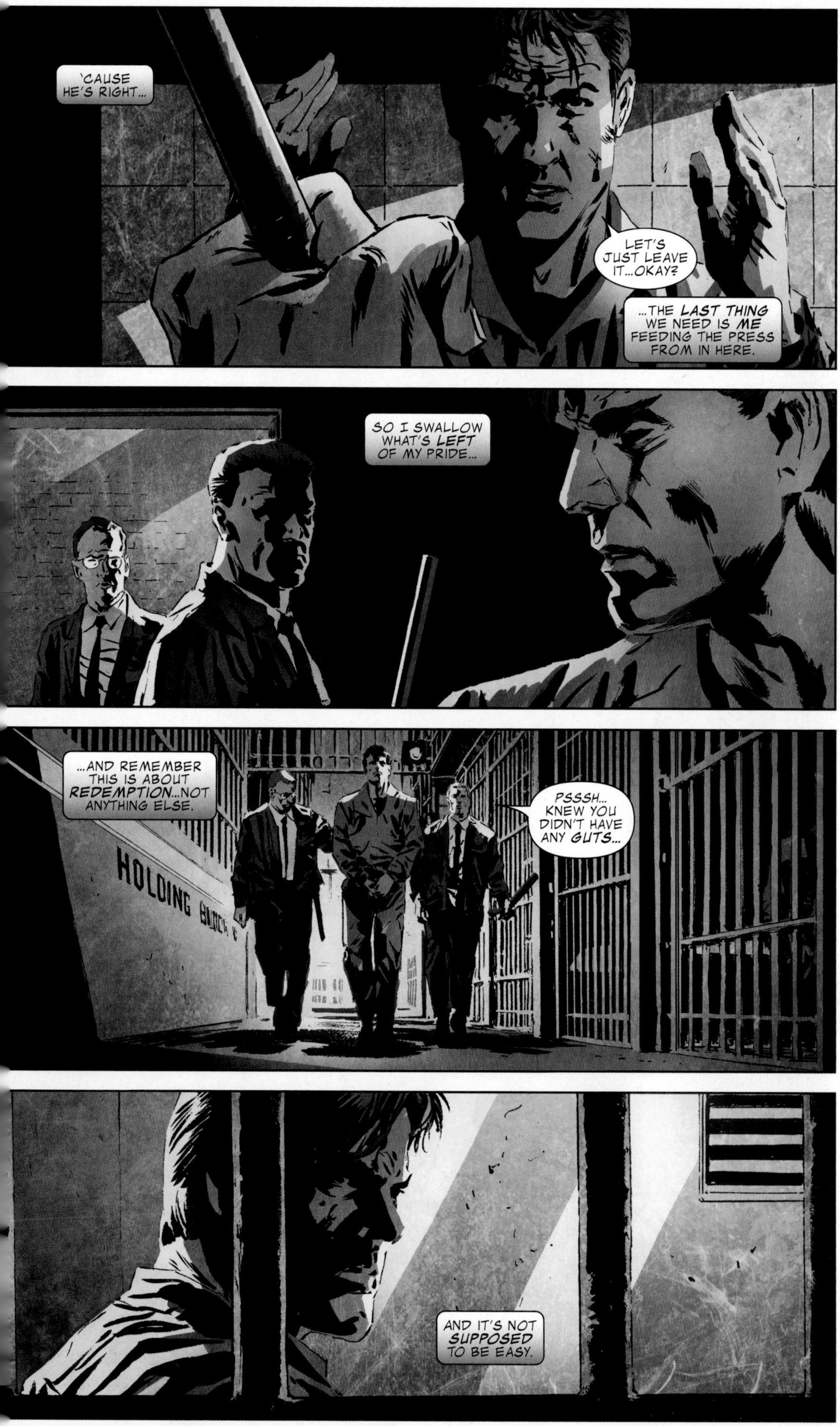
'CAUSE HE'S RIGHT...
LET'S JUST LEAVE IT...OKAY?
...THE LAST THING WE NEED IS ME FEEDING THE PRESS FROM IN HERE.
SO I SWALLOW WHAT'S LEFT OF MY PRIDE...
...AND REMEMBER THIS IS ABOUT REDEMPTION...NOT ANYTHING ELSE.
HOLDING BLOCK C
PSSSH... KNEW YOU DIDN'T HAVE ANY GUTS...
AND IT'S NOT SUPPOSED TO BE EASY.

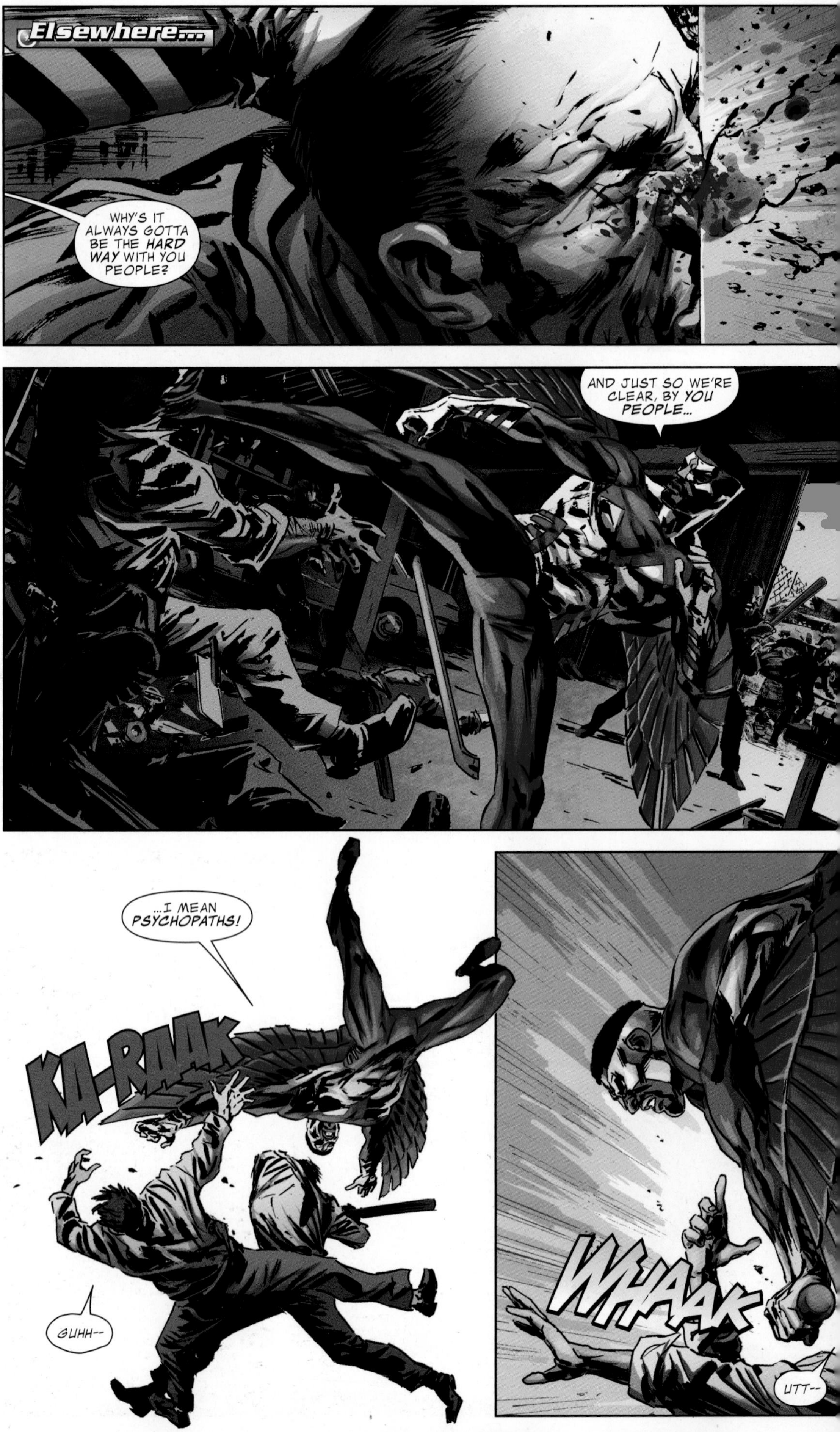
Elsewhere...
WHY'S IT ALWAYS GOTTA BE THE HARD WAY WITH YOU PEOPLE?
AND JUST SO WE'RE CLEAR, BY YOU PEOPLE...
...I MEAN PSYCHOPATHS!
KA-RAAK
GUHH--
WHAAK
UTT--

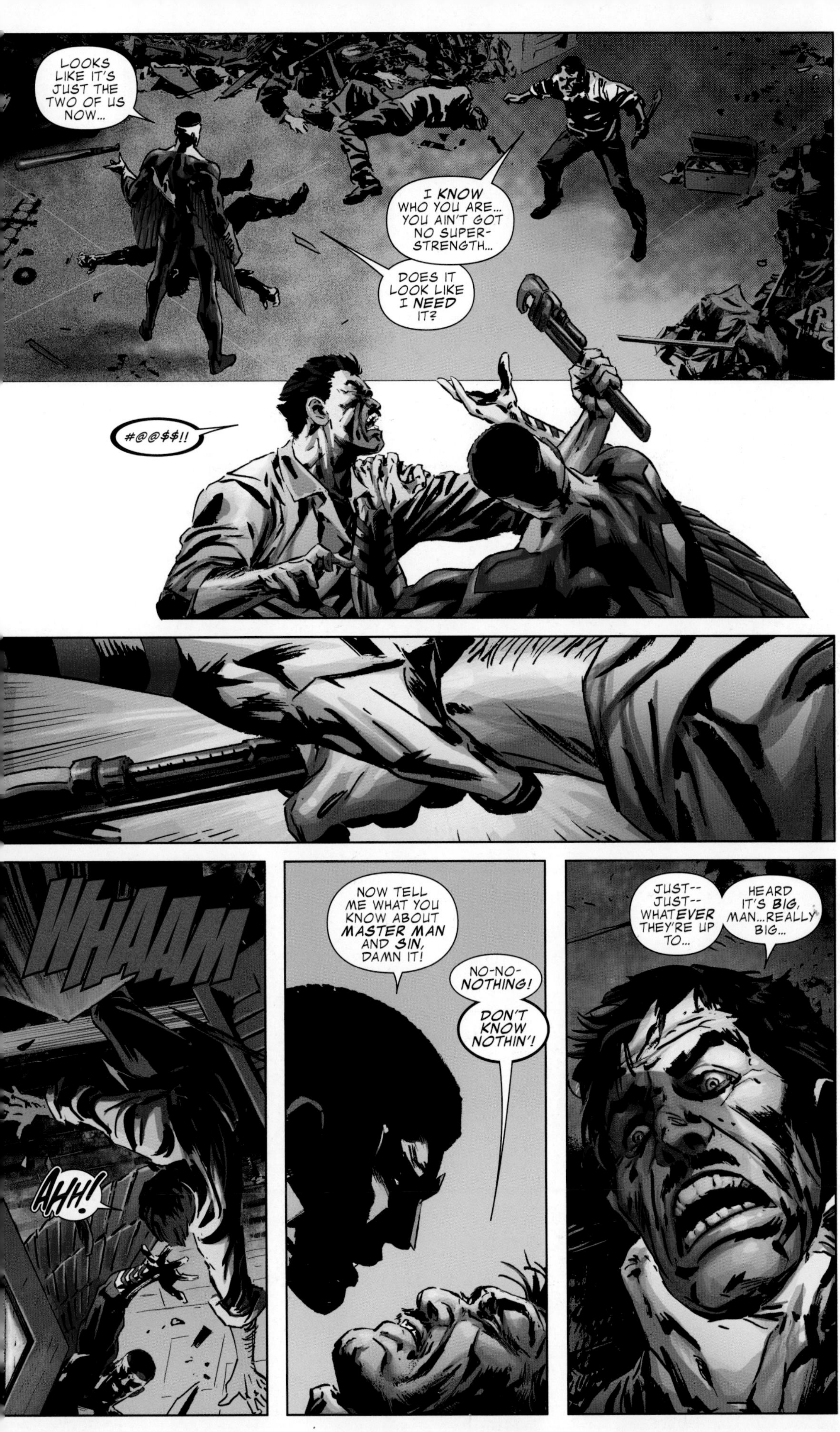
LOOKS LIKE IT'S JUST THE TWO OF US NOW...
I KNOW WHO YOU ARE... YOU AIN'T GOT NO SUPER-STRENGTH...
DOES IT LOOK LIKE I NEED IT?
#@@$$!!
WHAAM
AHH!
NOW TELL ME WHAT YOU KNOW ABOUT MASTER MAN AND SIN, DAMN IT!
NO-NO-NOTHING!
DON'T KNOW NOTHIN'!
JUST-- JUST-- WHATEVER THEY'RE UP TO...
HEARD IT'S BIG, MAN...REALLY BIG...

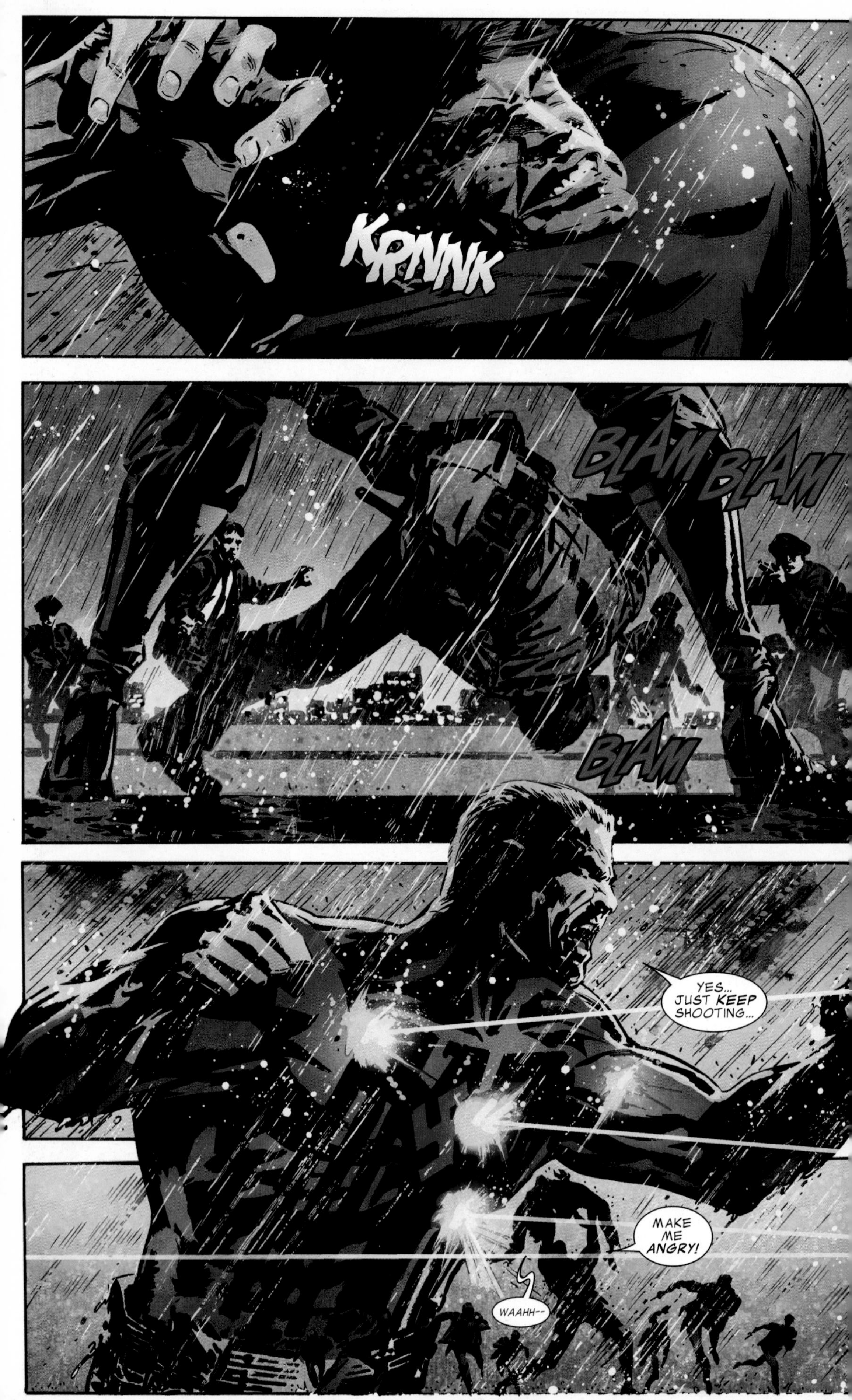
KRNNK
BLAM BLAM
BLAM
YES... JUST KEEP SHOOTING...
MAKE ME ANGRY!
WAAHH--

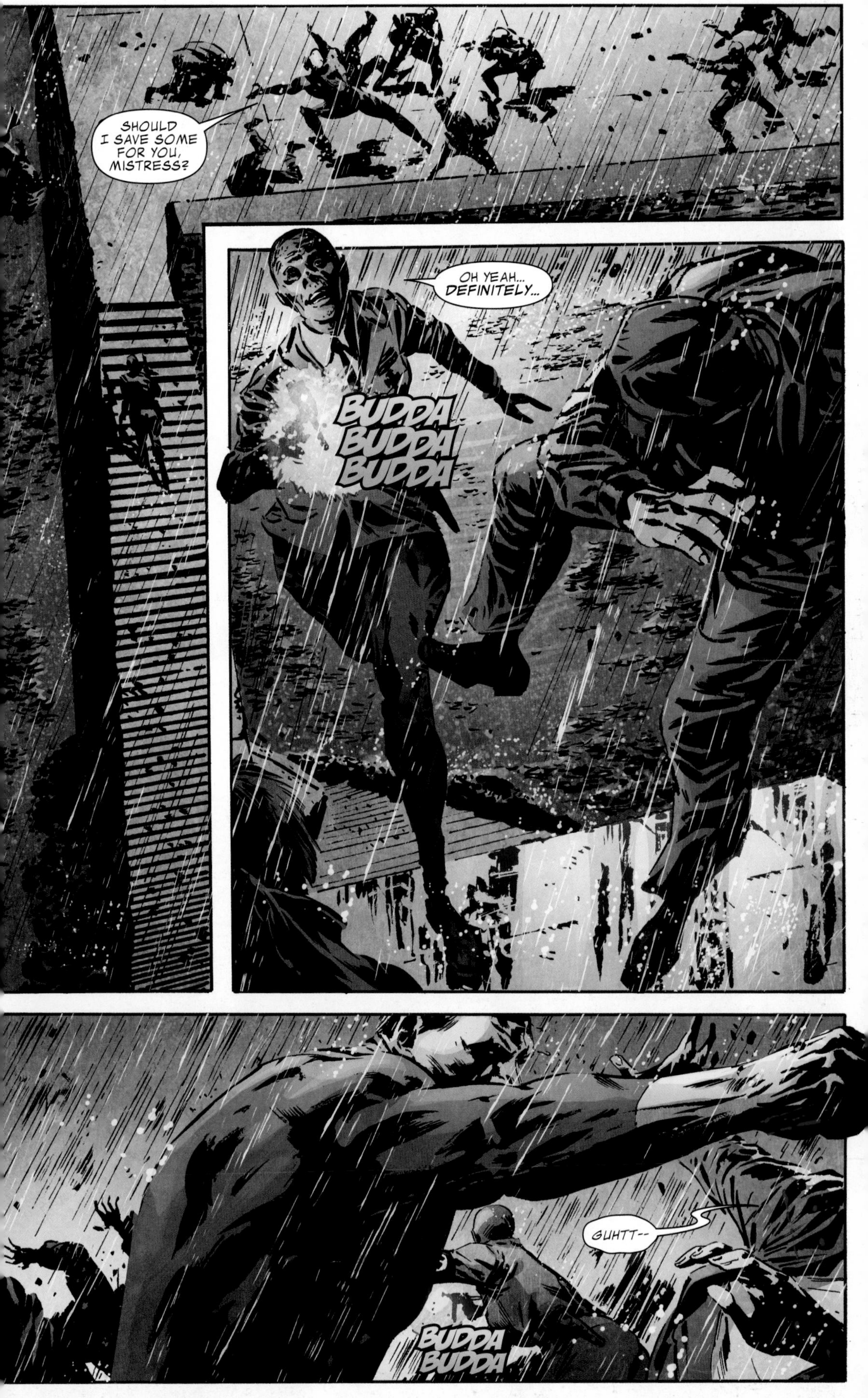
SHOULD I SAVE SOME FOR YOU, MISTRESS?
OH YEAH... DEFINITELY...
BUDDA BUDDA BUDDA
GUHTT--
BUDDA BUDDA

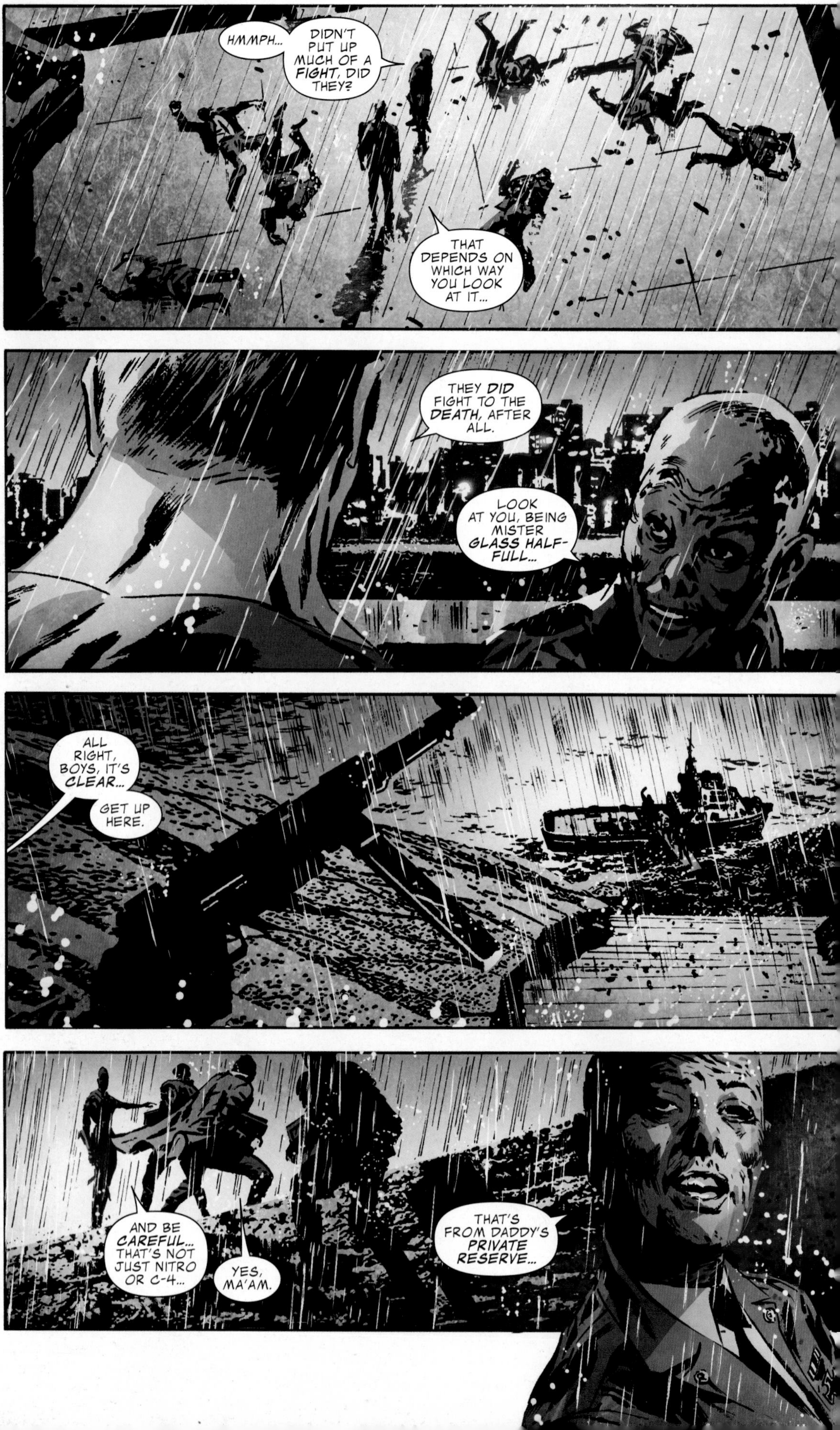
HMMPH...
DIDN'T PUT UP MUCH OF A FIGHT, DID THEY?
THAT DEPENDS ON WHICH WAY YOU LOOK AT IT...
THEY DID FIGHT TO THE DEATH, AFTER ALL.
LOOK AT YOU, BEING MISTER GLASS HALF-FULL...
ALL RIGHT, BOYS, IT'S CLEAR...
GET UP HERE.
AND BE CAREFUL... THAT'S NOT JUST NITRO OR C-4...
YES, MA'AM.
THAT'S FROM DADDY'S PRIVATE RESERVE...

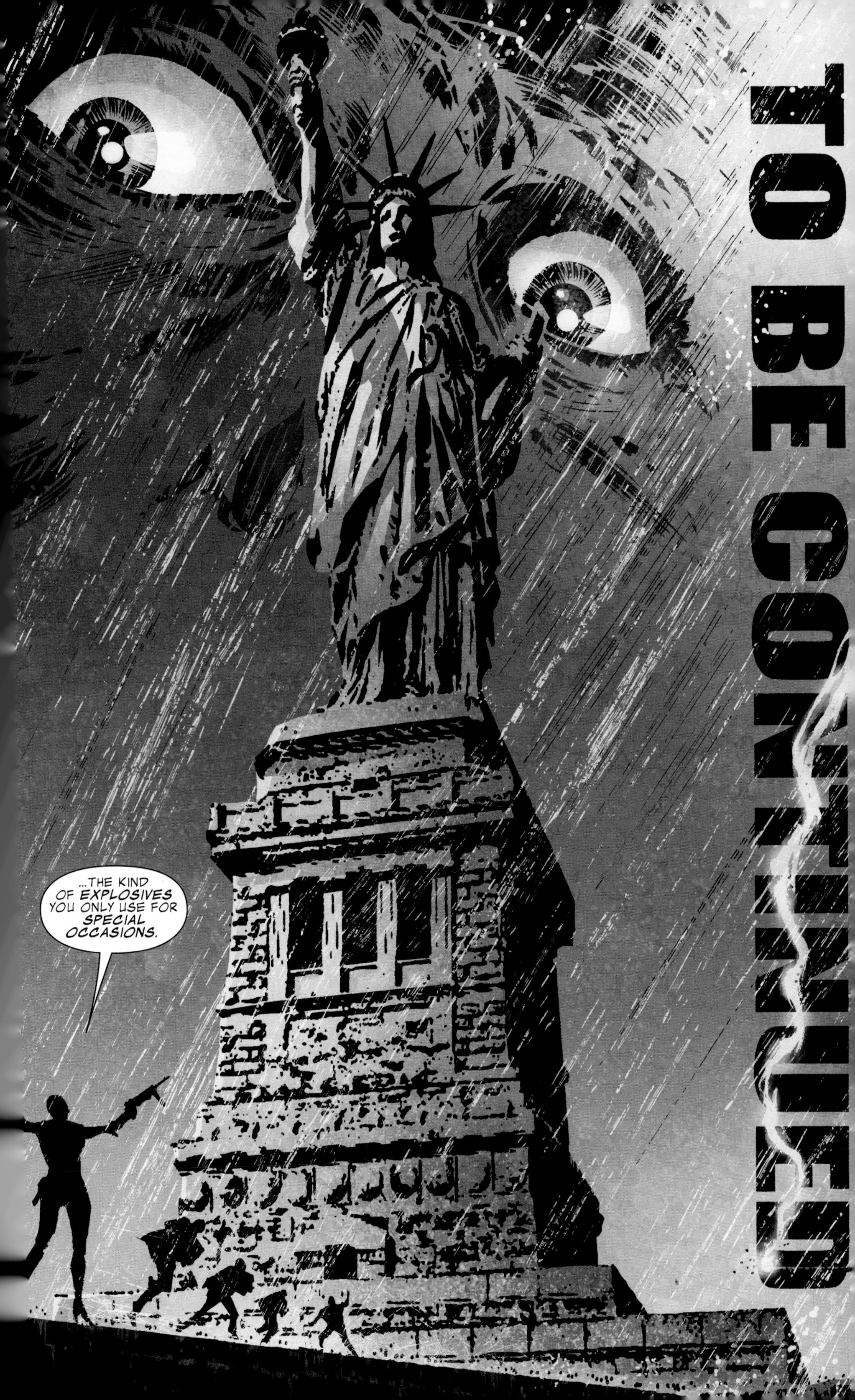
...THE KIND OF EXPLOSIVES YOU ONLY USE FOR SPECIAL OCCASIONS.
TO BE CONTINUED

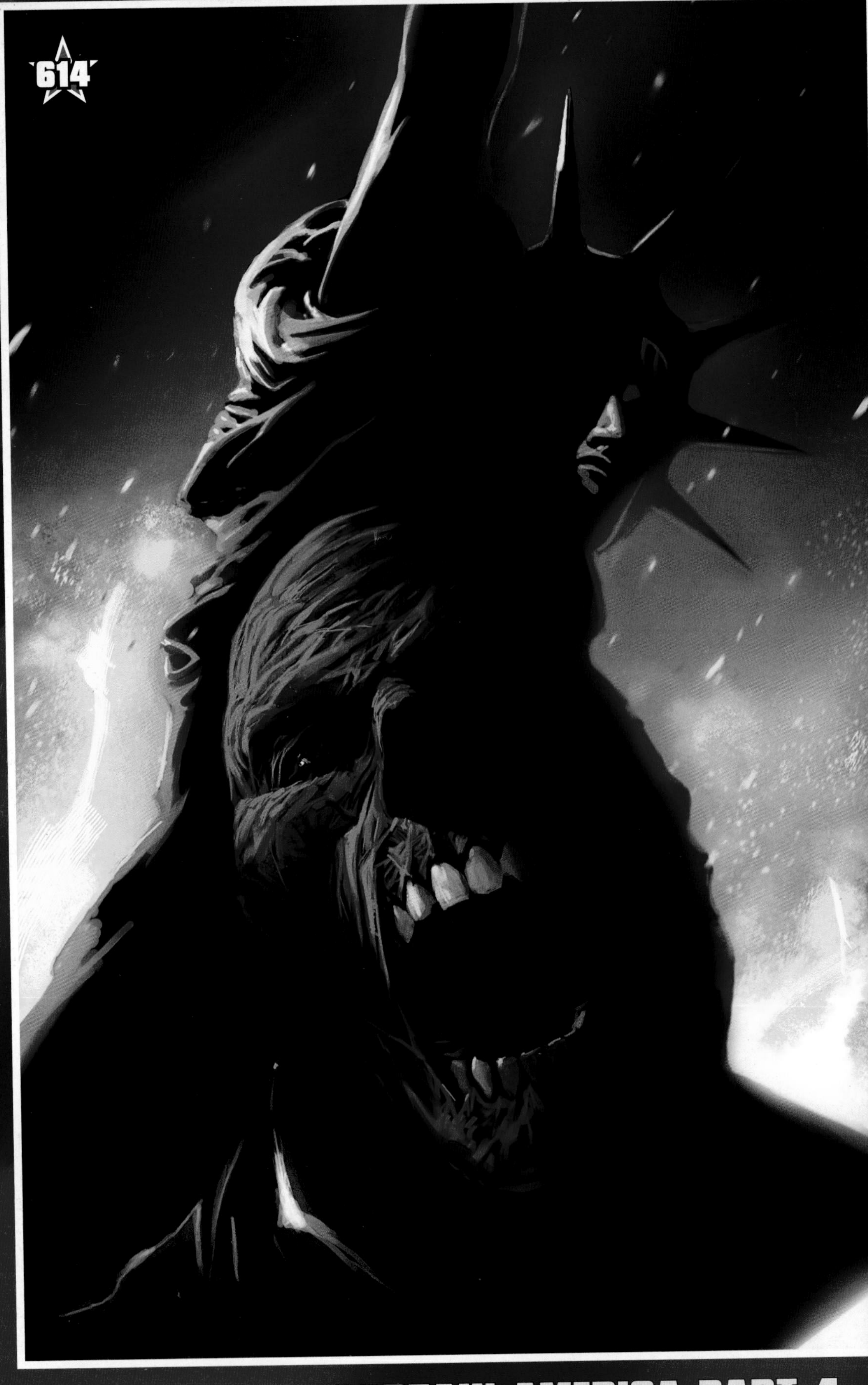
614

THE TRIAL OF CAPTAIN AMERICA PART 4

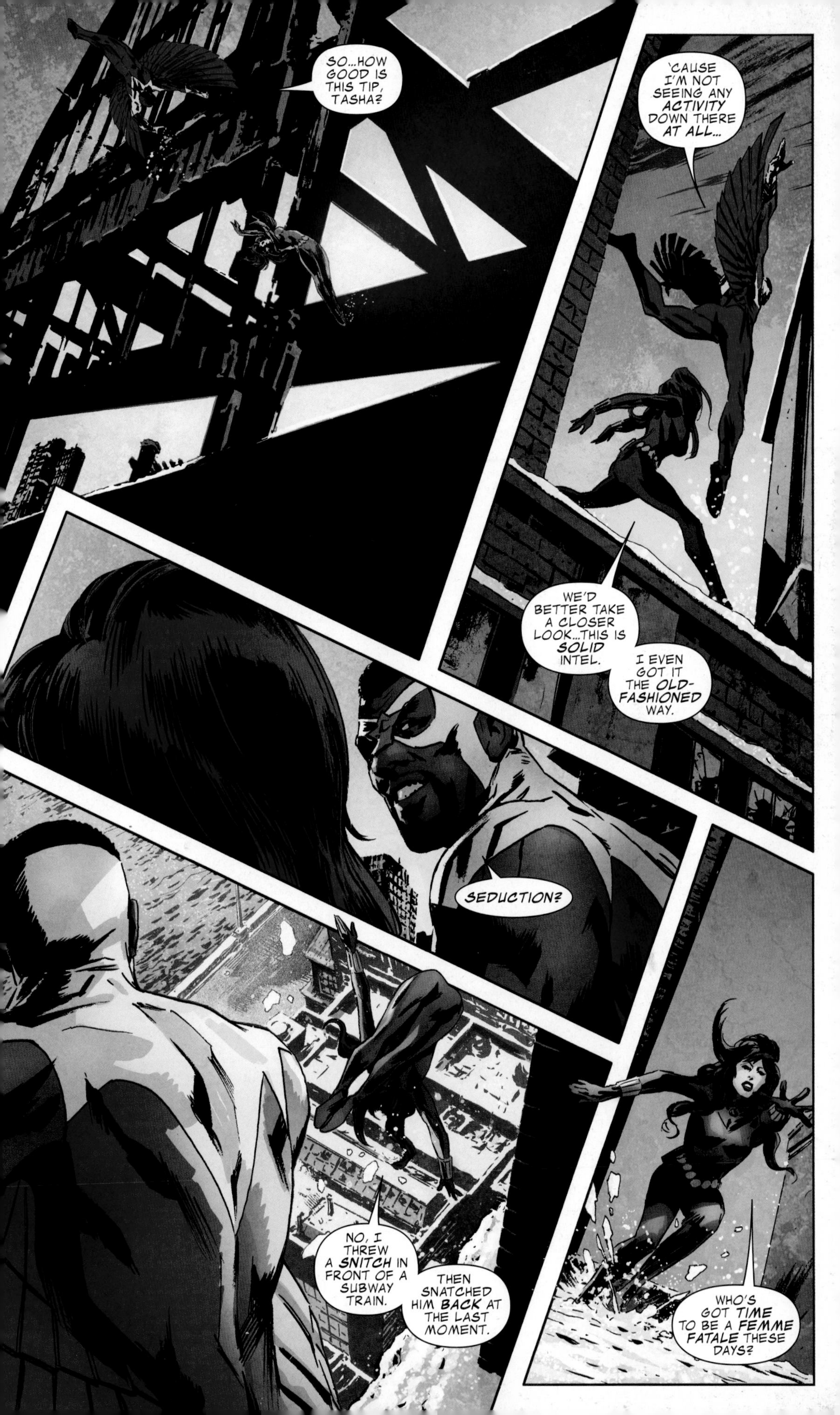

SO...HOW GOOD IS THIS TIP, TASHA?
'CAUSE I'M NOT SEEING ANY ACTIVITY DOWN THERE AT ALL...
WE'D BETTER TAKE A CLOSER LOOK...THIS IS SOLID INTEL.
I EVEN GOT IT THE OLD-FASHIONED WAY.
SEDUCTION?
NO, I THREW A SNITCH IN FRONT OF A SUBWAY TRAIN.
THEN SNATCHED HIM BACK AT THE LAST MOMENT.
WHO'S GOT TIME TO BE A FEMME FATALE THESE DAYS?

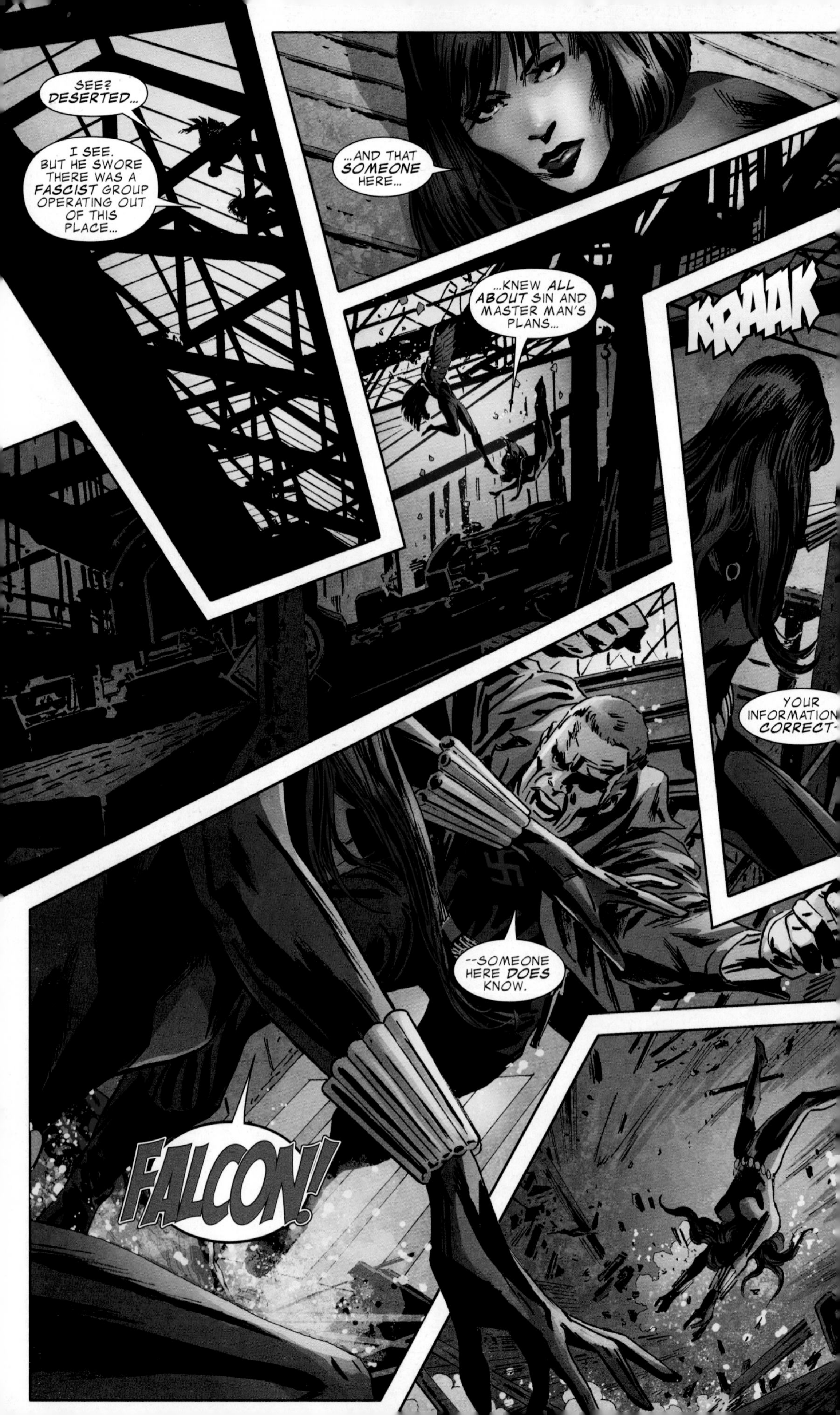
SEE? DESERTED...
I SEE. BUT HE SWORE THERE WAS A FASCIST GROUP OPERATING OUT OF THIS PLACE...
...AND THAT SOMEONE HERE...
...KNEW ALL ABOUT SIN AND MASTER MAN'S PLANS...
KRAAK
YOUR INFORMATION CORRECT-
--SOMEONE HERE DOES KNOW.
FALCON!

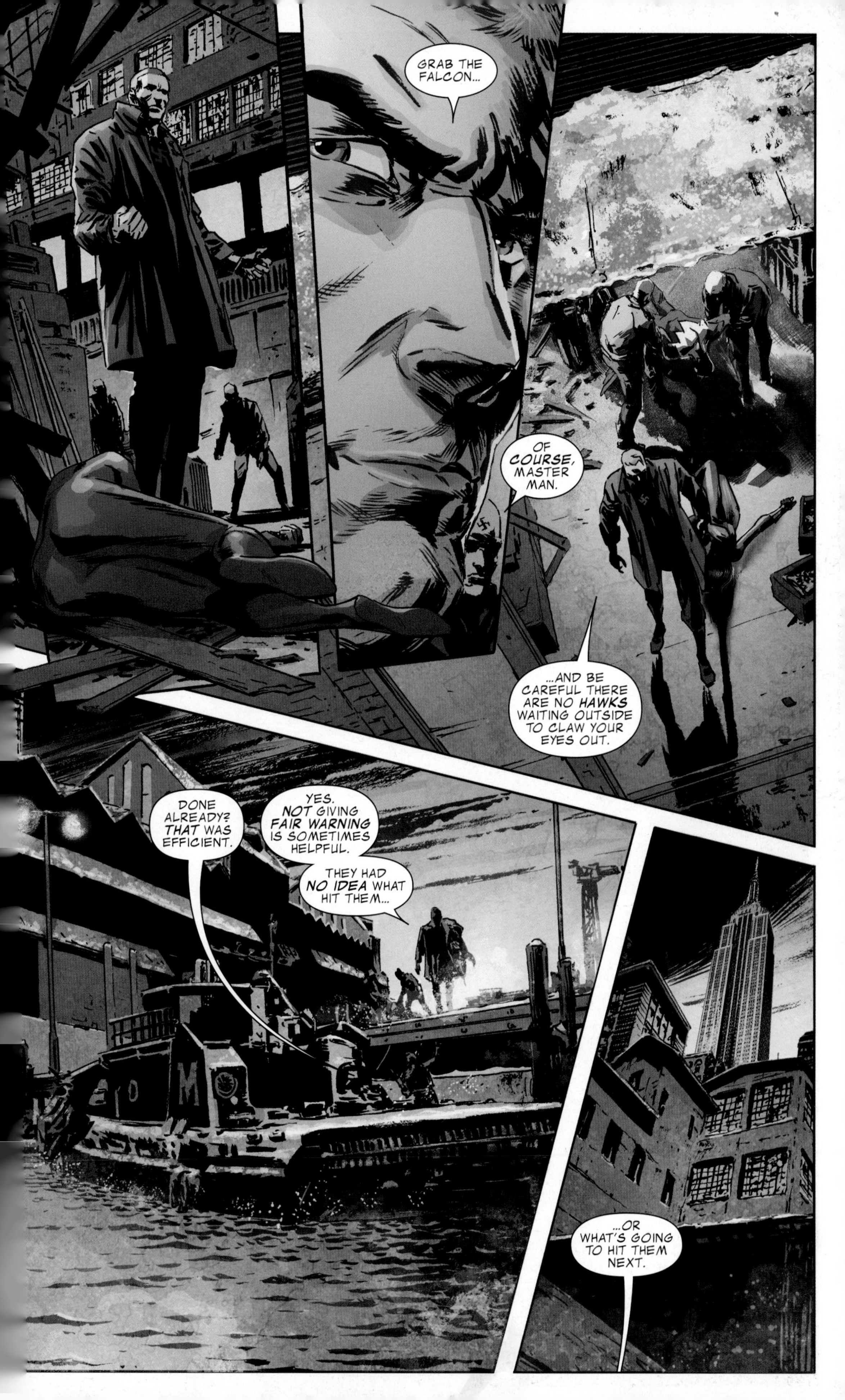
GRAB THE FALCON...
OF COURSE, MASTER MAN.
...AND BE CAREFUL THERE ARE NO HAWKS WAITING OUTSIDE TO CLAW YOUR EYES OUT.
DONE ALREADY? THAT WAS EFFICIENT.
YES. NOT GIVING FAIR WARNING IS SOMETIMES HELPFUL.
THEY HAD NO IDEA WHAT HIT THEM...
...OR WHAT'S GOING TO HIT THEM NEXT.

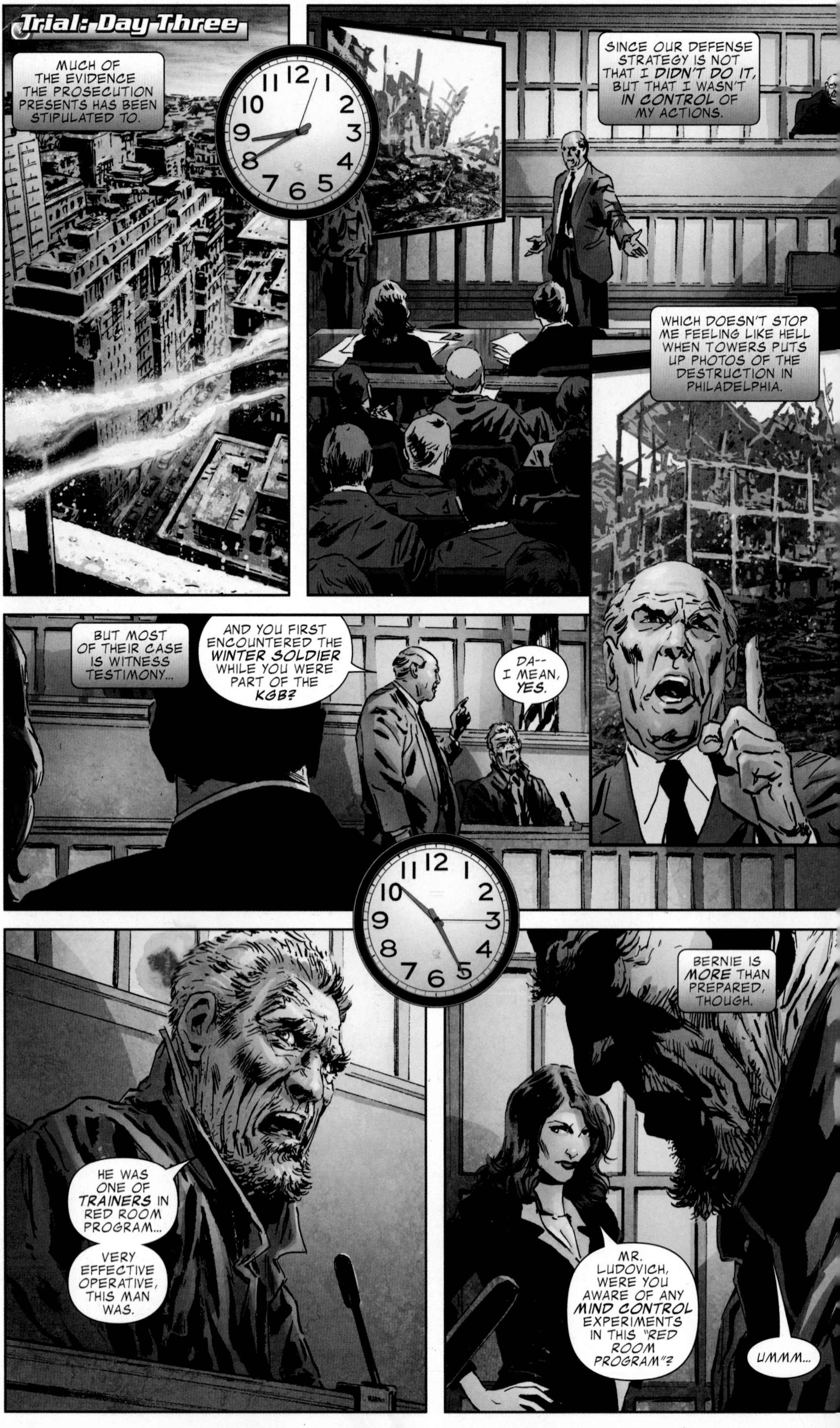
Trial: Day Three
MUCH OF THE EVIDENCE THE PROSECUTION PRESENTS HAS BEEN STIPULATED TO.
SINCE OUR DEFENSE STRATEGY IS NOT THAT I DIDN'T DO IT, BUT THAT I WASN'T IN CONTROL OF MY ACTIONS.
WHICH DOESN'T STOP ME FEELING LIKE HELL WHEN TOWERS PUTS UP PHOTOS OF THE DESTRUCTION IN PHILADELPHIA.
BUT MOST OF THEIR CASE IS WITNESS TESTIMONY...
AND YOU FIRST ENCOUNTERED THE WINTER SOLDIER WHILE YOU WERE PART OF THE KGB?
DA-- I MEAN, YES.
HE WAS ONE OF TRAINERS IN RED ROOM PROGRAM...
VERY EFFECTIVE OPERATIVE, THIS MAN WAS.
BERNIE IS MORE THAN PREPARED, THOUGH.
MR. LUDOVICH, WERE YOU AWARE OF ANY MIND CONTROL EXPERIMENTS IN THIS "RED ROOM PROGRAM"?
UMMM...

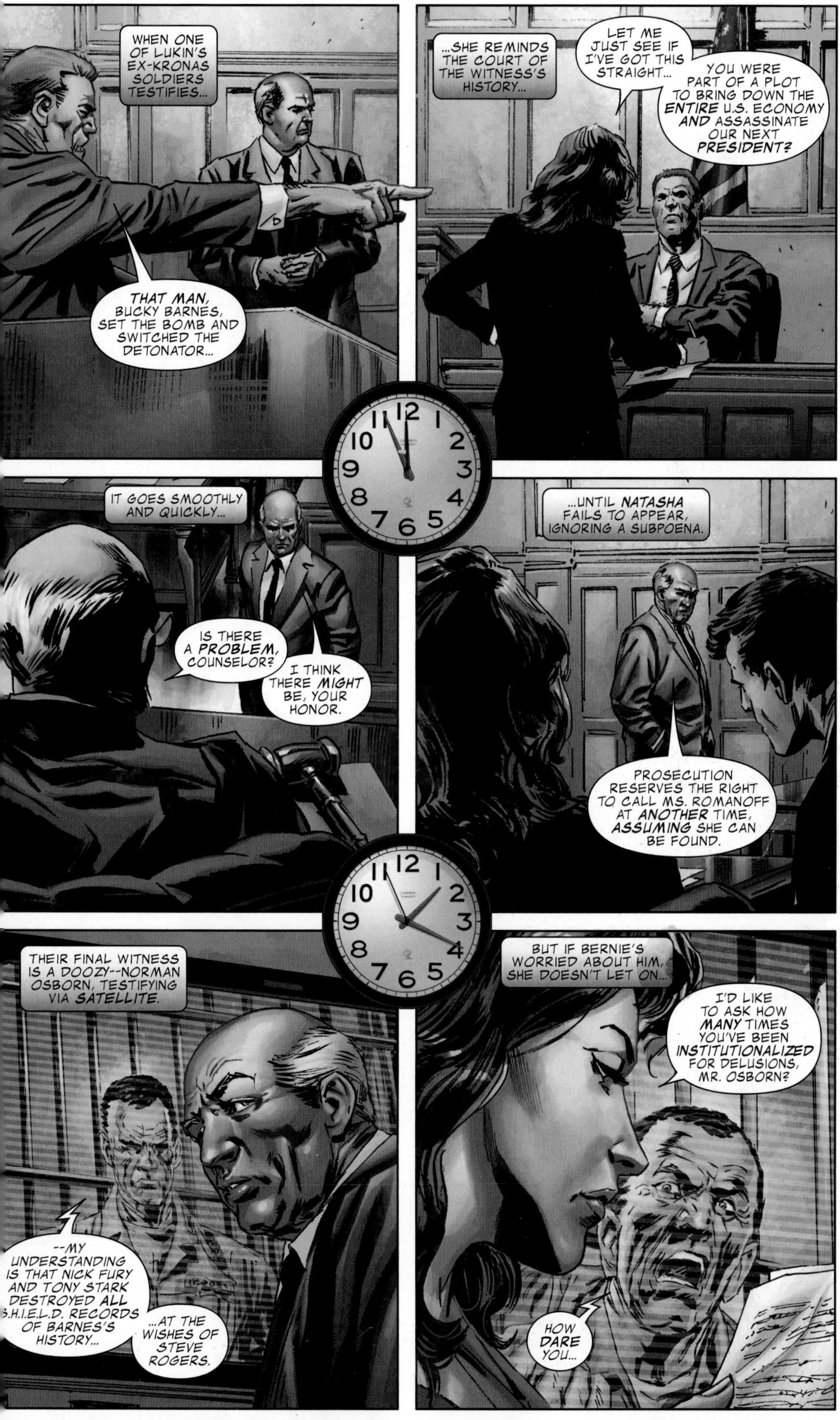
WHEN ONE OF LUKIN'S EX-KRONAS SOLDIERS TESTIFIES...
THAT MAN, BUCKY BARNES, SET THE BOMB AND SWITCHED THE DETONATOR...
...SHE REMINDS THE COURT OF THE WITNESS'S HISTORY...
LET ME JUST SEE IF I'VE GOT THIS STRAIGHT...
YOU WERE PART OF A PLOT TO BRING DOWN THE ENTIRE U.S. ECONOMY AND ASSASSINATE OUR NEXT PRESIDENT?
IT GOES SMOOTHLY AND QUICKLY...
IS THERE A PROBLEM, COUNSELOR?
I THINK THERE MIGHT BE, YOUR HONOR.
...UNTIL NATASHA FAILS TO APPEAR, IGNORING A SUBPOENA.
PROSECUTION RESERVES THE RIGHT TO CALL MS. ROMANOFF AT ANOTHER TIME, ASSUMING SHE CAN BE FOUND.
THEIR FINAL WITNESS IS A DOOZY--NORMAN OSBORN, TESTIFYING VIA SATELLITE.
--MY UNDERSTANDING IS THAT NICK FURY AND TONY STARK DESTROYED ALL S.H.I.E.L.D. RECORDS OF BARNES'S HISTORY...
...AT THE WISHES OF STEVE ROGERS.
BUT IF BERNIE'S WORRIED ABOUT HIM, SHE DOESN'T LET ON...
I'D LIKE TO ASK HOW MANY TIMES YOU'VE BEEN INSTITUTIONALIZED FOR DELUSIONS, MR. OSBORN?
HOW DARE YOU...

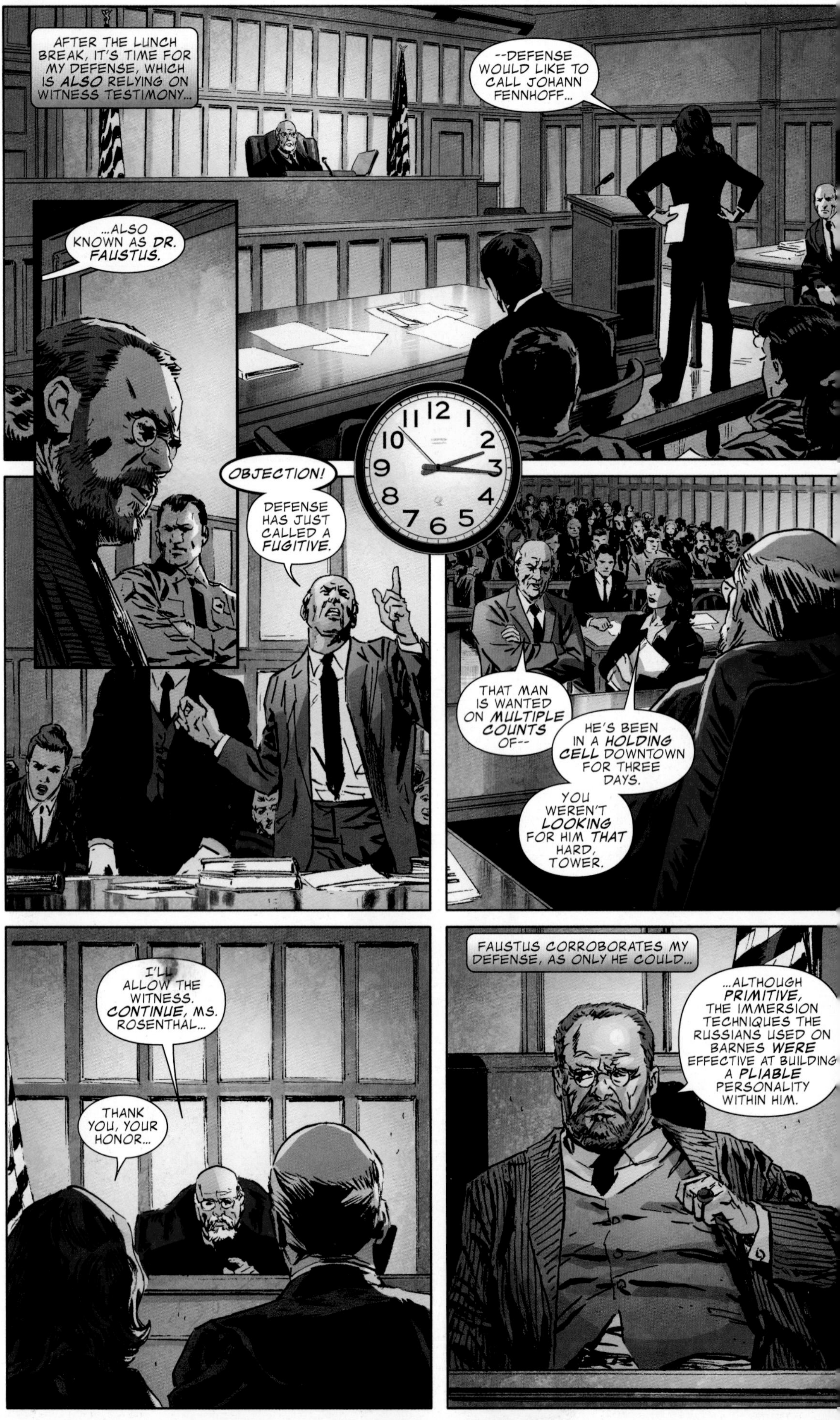
AFTER THE LUNCH BREAK, IT'S TIME FOR MY DEFENSE, WHICH IS ALSO RELYING ON WITNESS TESTIMONY...
--DEFENSE WOULD LIKE TO CALL JOHANN FENNHOFF...
...ALSO KNOWN AS DR. FAUSTUS.
OBJECTION!
DEFENSE HAS JUST CALLED A FUGITIVE.
THAT MAN IS WANTED ON MULTIPLE COUNTS OF--
HE'S BEEN IN A HOLDING CELL DOWNTOWN FOR THREE DAYS.
YOU WEREN'T LOOKING FOR HIM THAT HARD, TOWER.
I'LL ALLOW THE WITNESS. CONTINUE, MS. ROSENTHAL...
THANK YOU, YOUR HONOR...
FAUSTUS CORROBORATES MY DEFENSE, AS ONLY HE COULD...
...ALTHOUGH PRIMITIVE, THE IMMERSION TECHNIQUES THE RUSSIANS USED ON BARNES WERE EFFECTIVE AT BUILDING A PLIABLE PERSONALITY WITHIN HIM.

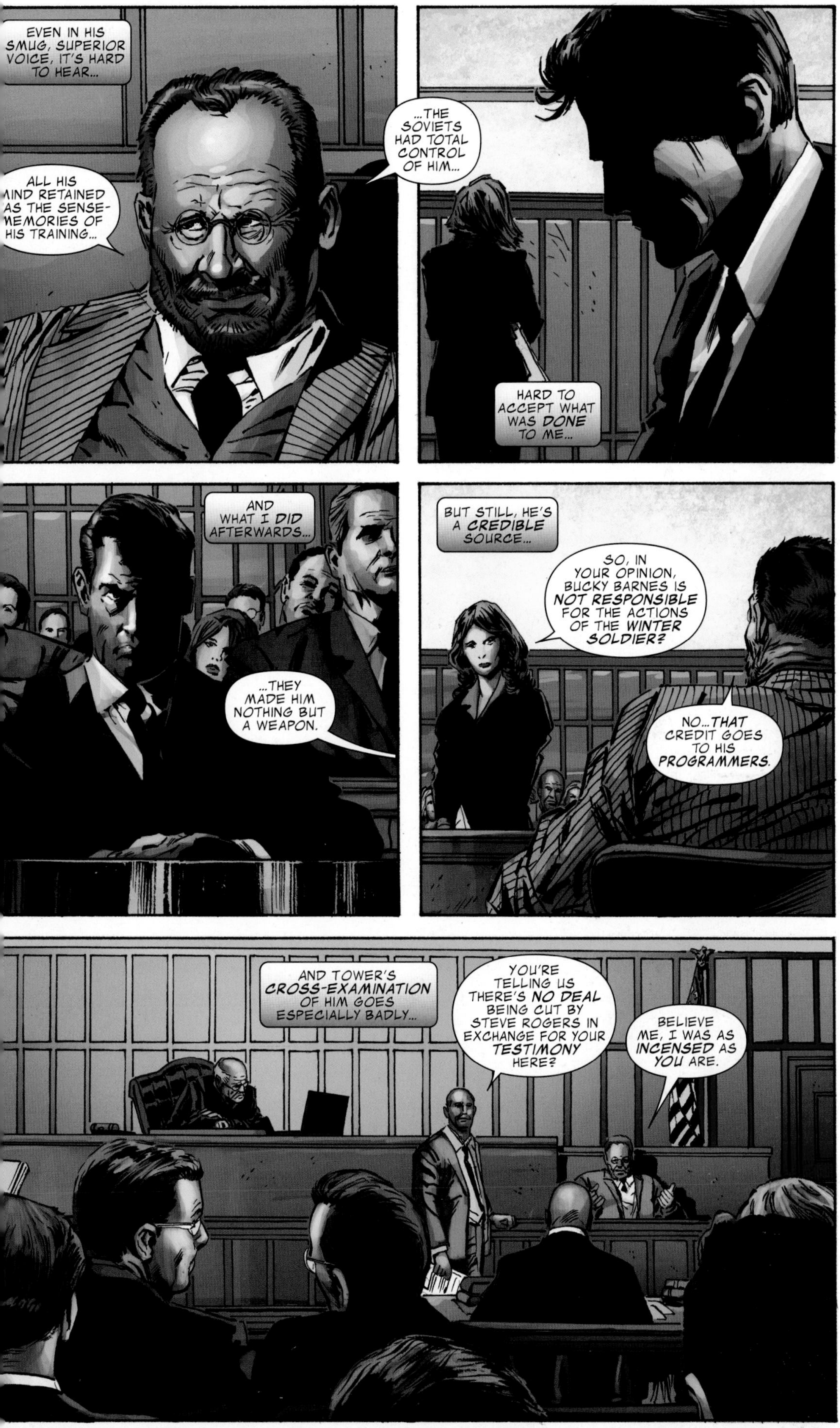
EVEN IN HIS SMUG, SUPERIOR VOICE, IT'S HARD TO HEAR...
ALL HIS MIND RETAINED WAS THE SENSE-MEMORIES OF HIS TRAINING...
...THE SOVIETS HAD TOTAL CONTROL OF HIM...
HARD TO ACCEPT WHAT WAS DONE TO ME...
AND WHAT I DID AFTERWARDS...
...THEY MADE HIM NOTHING BUT A WEAPON.
BUT STILL, HE'S A CREDIBLE SOURCE...
SO, IN YOUR OPINION, BUCKY BARNES IS NOT RESPONSIBLE FOR THE ACTIONS OF THE WINTER SOLDIER?
NO...THAT CREDIT GOES TO HIS PROGRAMMERS.
AND TOWER'S CROSS-EXAMINATION OF HIM GOES ESPECIALLY BADLY...
YOU'RE TELLING US THERE'S NO DEAL BEING CUT BY STEVE ROGERS IN EXCHANGE FOR YOUR TESTIMONY HERE?
BELIEVE ME, I WAS AS INCENSED AS YOU ARE.

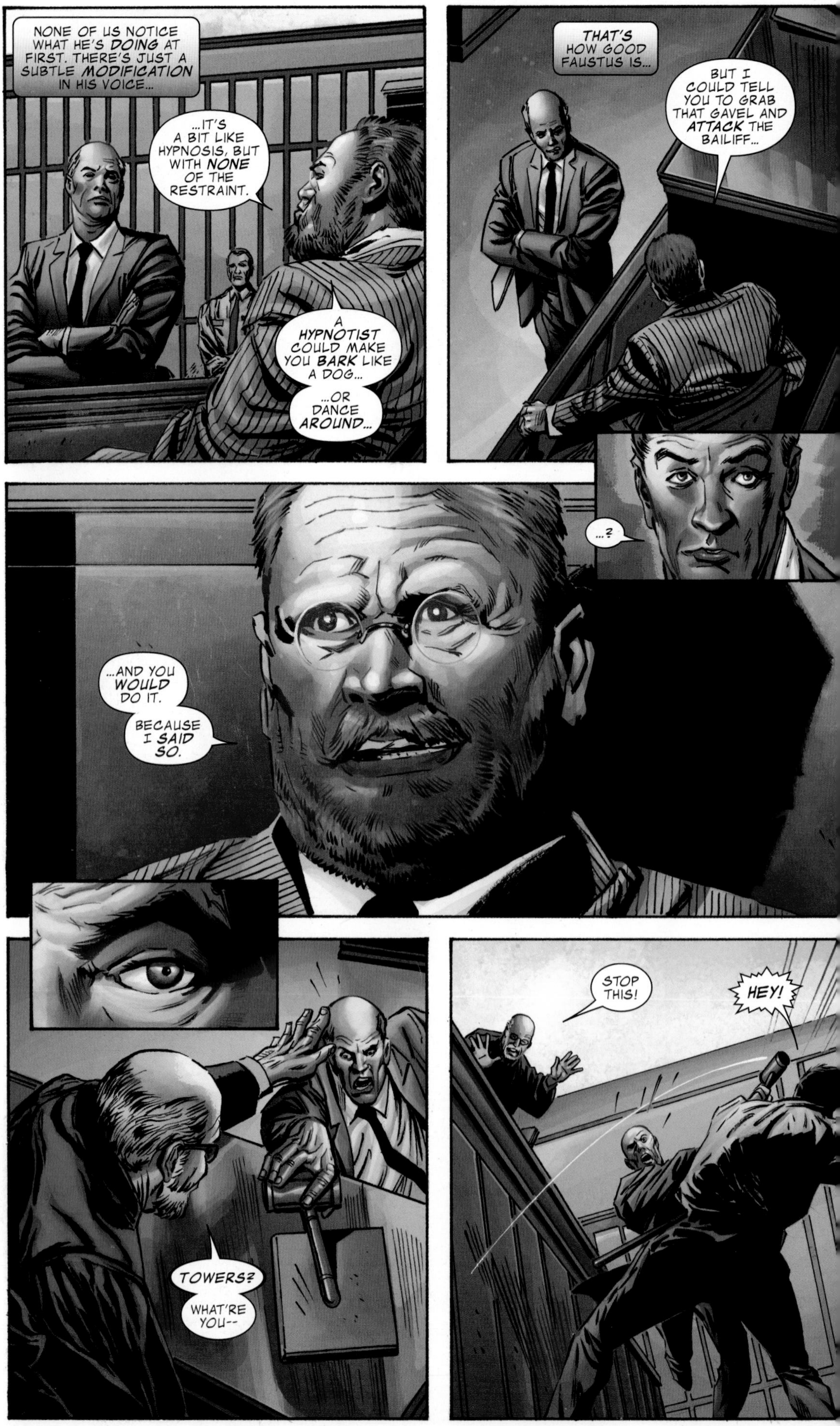
NONE OF US NOTICE WHAT HE'S DOING AT FIRST. THERE'S JUST A SUBTLE MODIFICATION IN HIS VOICE...
...IT'S A BIT LIKE HYPNOSIS, BUT WITH NONE OF THE RESTRAINT.
A HYPNOTIST COULD MAKE YOU BARK LIKE A DOG...
...OR DANCE AROUND...
THAT'S HOW GOOD FAUSTUS IS...
BUT I COULD TELL YOU TO GRAB THAT GAVEL AND ATTACK THE BAILIFF...
...?
...AND YOU WOULD DO IT.
BECAUSE I SAID SO.
TOWERS?
WHAT'RE YOU--
STOP THIS!
HEY!

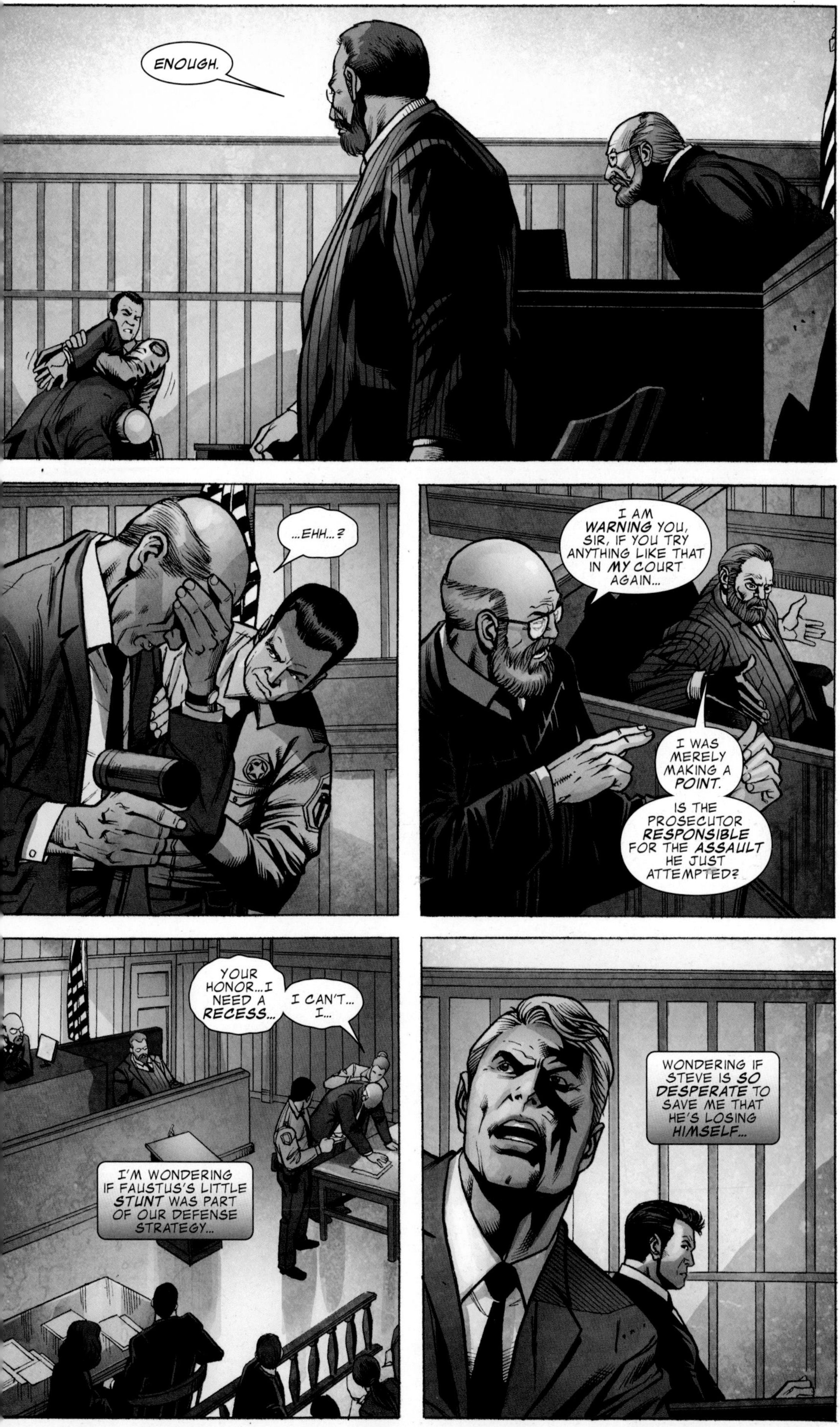
ENOUGH.
...EHH...?
I AM WARNING YOU, SIR, IF YOU TRY ANYTHING LIKE THAT IN MY COURT AGAIN...
I WAS MERELY MAKING A POINT.
IS THE PROSECUTOR RESPONSIBLE FOR THE ASSAULT HE JUST ATTEMPTED?
YOUR HONOR...I NEED A RECESS...
I CAN'T... I...
I'M WONDERING IF FAUSTUS'S LITTLE STUNT WAS PART OF OUR DEFENSE STRATEGY...
WONDERING IF STEVE IS SO DESPERATE TO SAVE ME THAT HE'S LOSING HIMSELF...

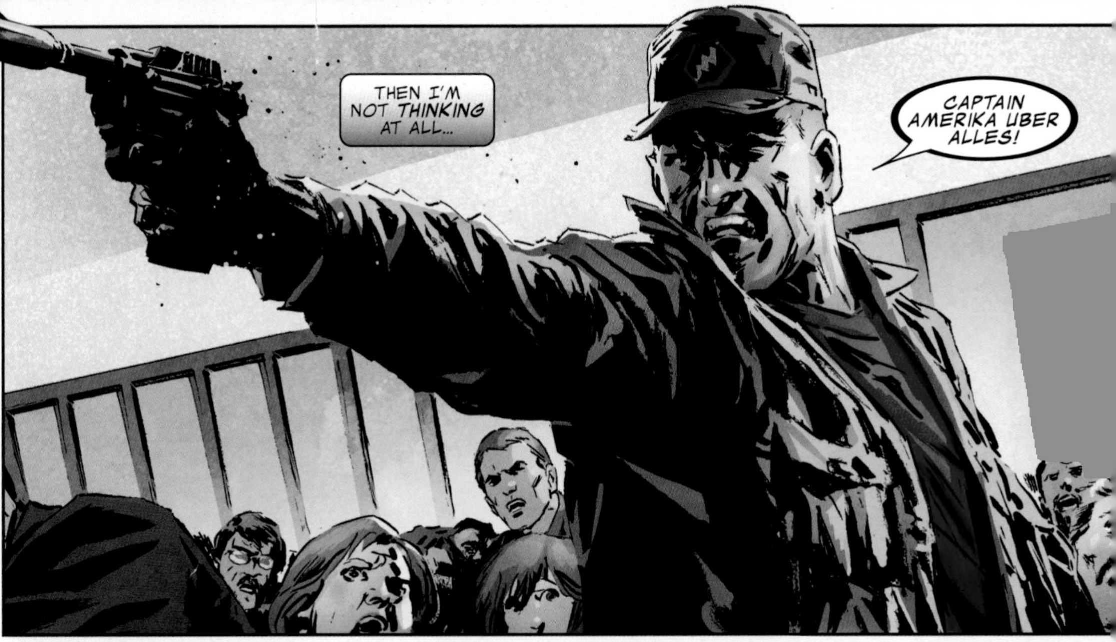
THEN I'M NOT THINKING AT ALL...
CAPTAIN AMERIKA UBER ALLES!

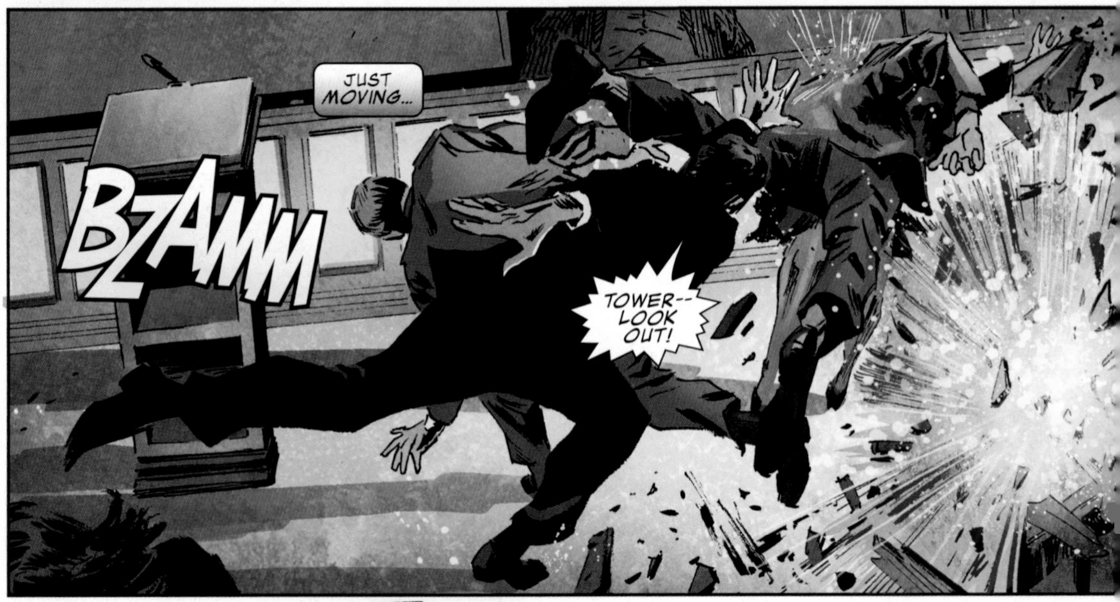
JUST MOVING...
BZAMM
TOWER-- LOOK OUT!

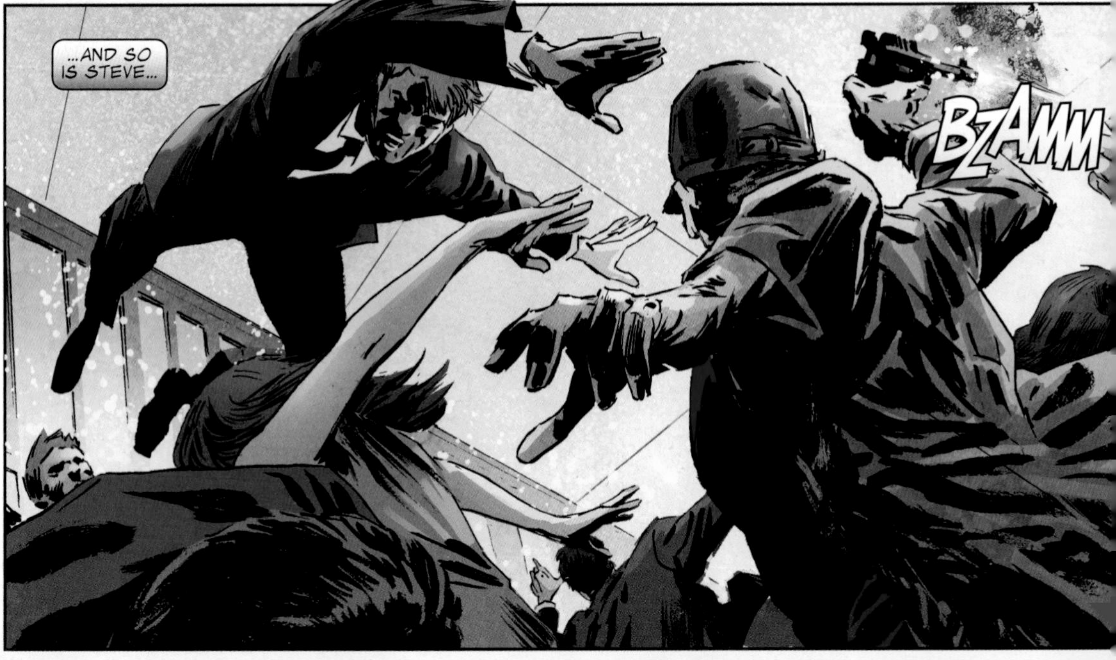
...AND SO IS STEVE...
BZAMM

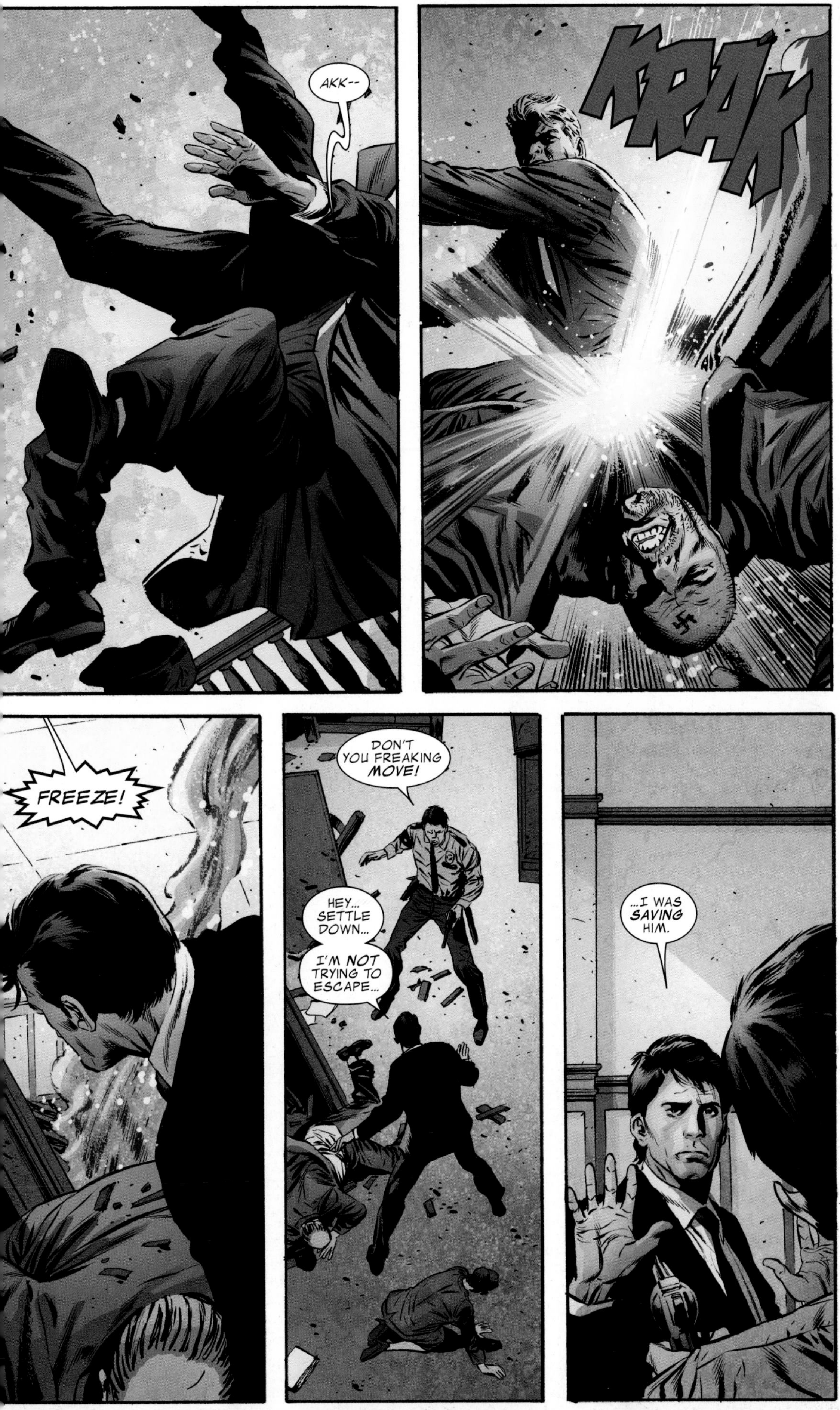
AKK--
KRAK
FREEZE!
DON'T YOU FREAKING MOVE!
HEY... SETTLE DOWN...
I'M NOT TRYING TO ESCAPE...
...I WAS SAVING HIM.

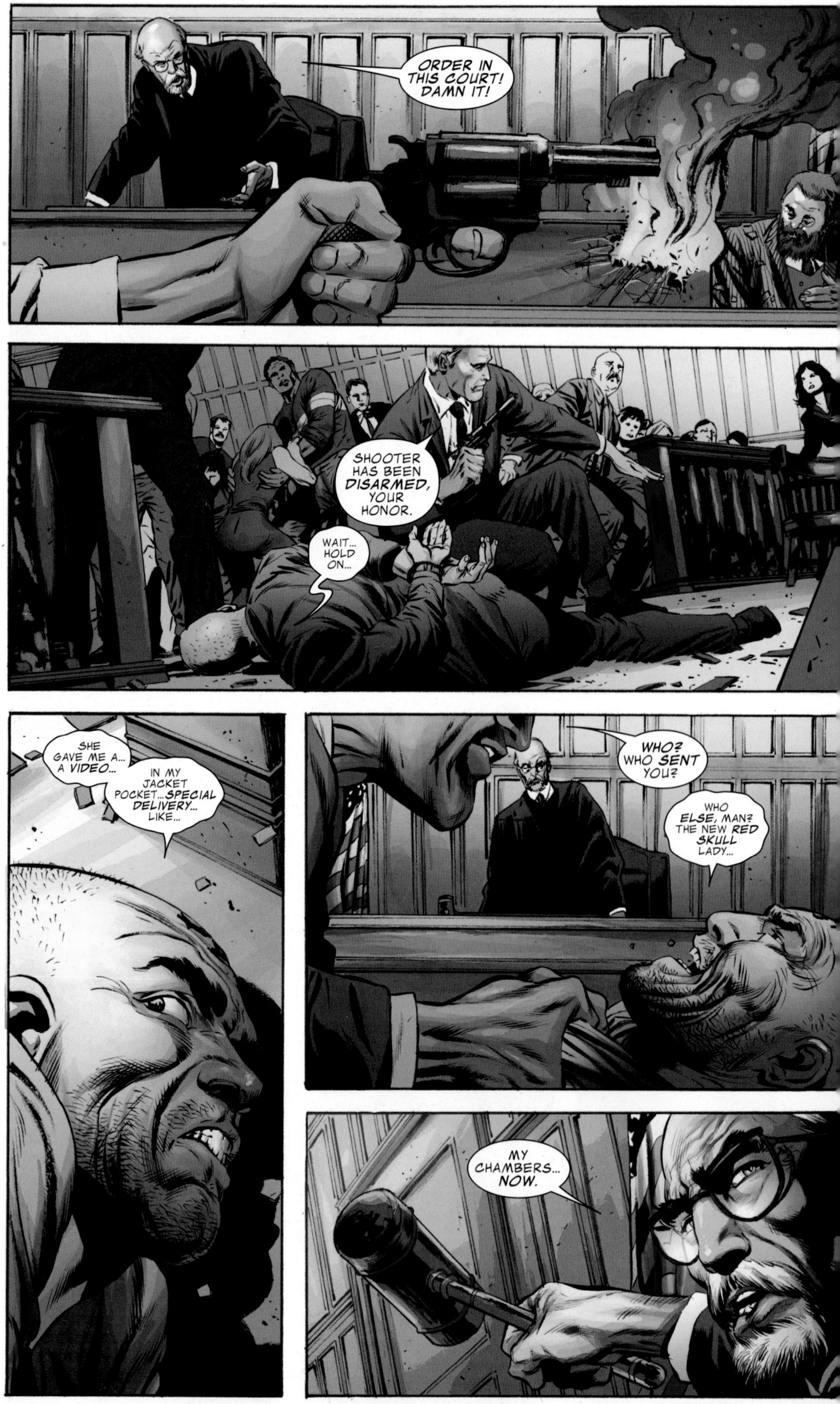
ORDER IN THIS COURT! DAMN IT!
SHOOTER HAS BEEN DISARMED, YOUR HONOR.
WAIT... HOLD ON...
SHE GAVE ME A... A VIDEO...
IN MY JACKET POCKET...SPECIAL DELIVERY... LIKE...
WHO? WHO SENT YOU?
WHO ELSE, MAN? THE NEW RED SKULL LADY...
MY CHAMBERS... NOW.

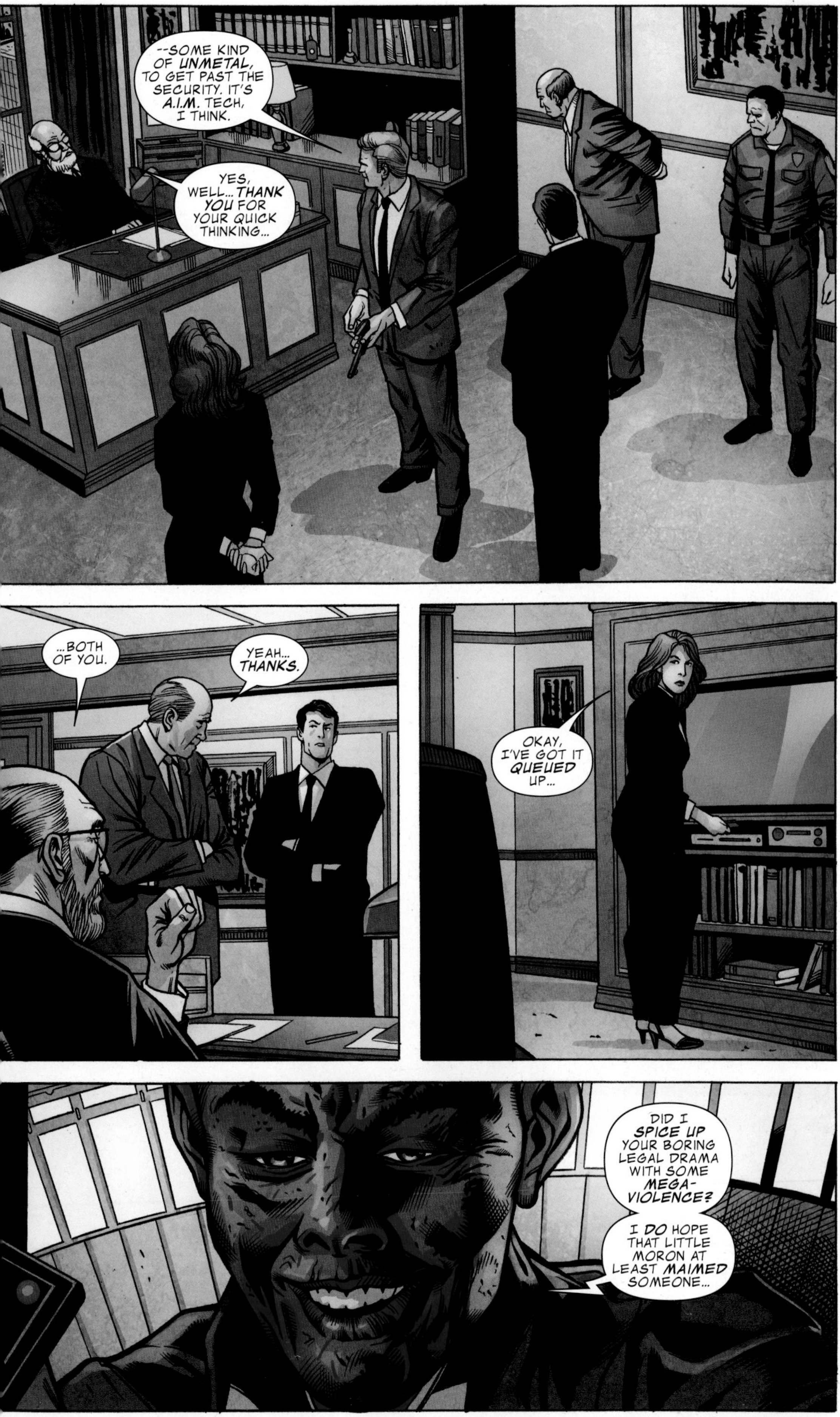
--SOME KIND OF UNMETAL, TO GET PAST THE SECURITY. IT'S A.I.M. TECH, I THINK.
YES, WELL... THANK YOU FOR YOUR QUICK THINKING...
...BOTH OF YOU.
YEAH... THANKS.
OKAY, I'VE GOT IT QUEUED UP...
DID I SPICE UP YOUR BORING LEGAL DRAMA WITH SOME MEGA-VIOLENCE?
I DO HOPE THAT LITTLE MORON AT LEAST MAIMED SOMEONE...

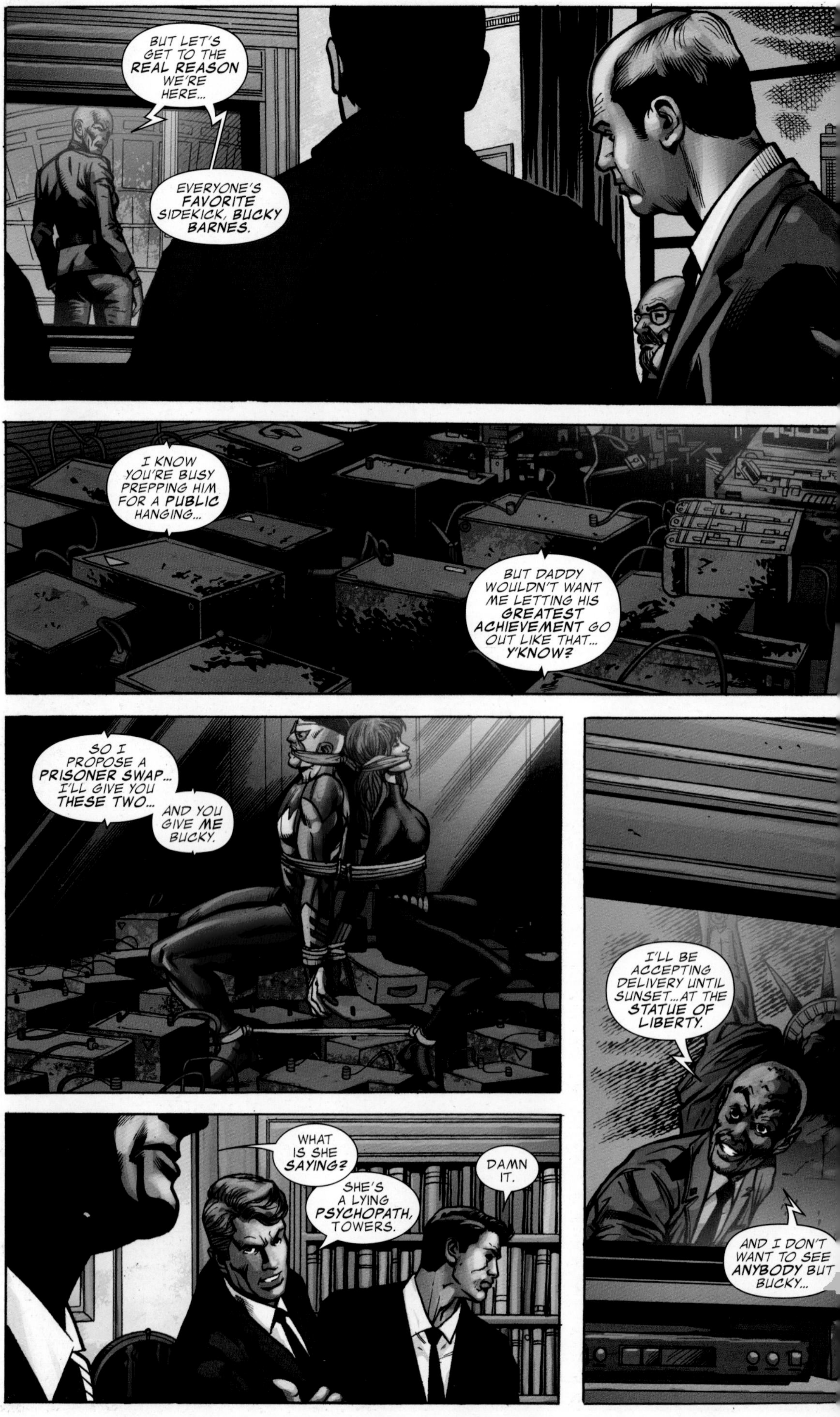
BUT LET'S GET TO THE REAL REASON WE'RE HERE...
EVERYONE'S FAVORITE SIDEKICK, BUCKY BARNES.
I KNOW YOU'RE BUSY PREPPING HIM FOR A PUBLIC HANGING...
BUT DADDY WOULDN'T WANT ME LETTING HIS GREATEST ACHIEVEMENT GO OUT LIKE THAT... Y'KNOW?
SO I PROPOSE A PRISONER SWAP... I'LL GIVE YOU THESE TWO...
AND YOU GIVE ME BUCKY.
I'LL BE ACCEPTING DELIVERY UNTIL SUNSET...AT THE STATUE OF LIBERTY.
AND I DON'T WANT TO SEE ANYBODY BUT BUCKY...
WHAT IS SHE SAYING?
SHE'S A LYING PSYCHOPATH, TOWERS.
DAMN IT.

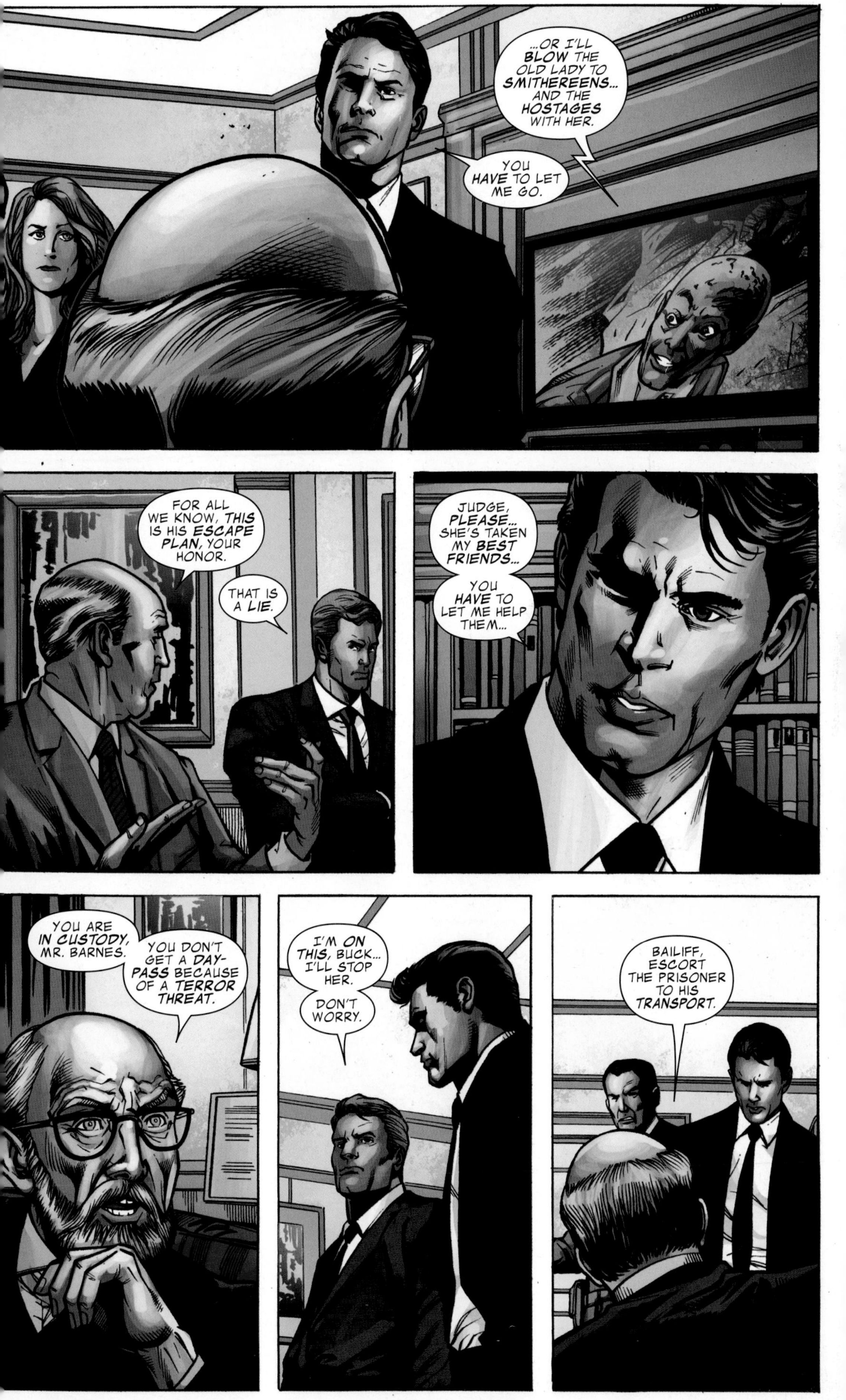
...OR I'LL BLOW THE OLD LADY TO SMITHEREENS... AND THE HOSTAGES WITH HER.
YOU HAVE TO LET ME GO.
FOR ALL WE KNOW, THIS IS HIS ESCAPE PLAN, YOUR HONOR.
THAT IS A LIE.
JUDGE, PLEASE... SHE'S TAKEN MY BEST FRIENDS...
YOU HAVE TO LET ME HELP THEM...
YOU ARE IN CUSTODY, MR. BARNES.
YOU DON'T GET A DAY-PASS BECAUSE OF A TERROR THREAT.
I'M ON THIS, BUCK... I'LL STOP HER.
DON'T WORRY.
BAILIFF, ESCORT THE PRISONER TO HIS TRANSPORT.

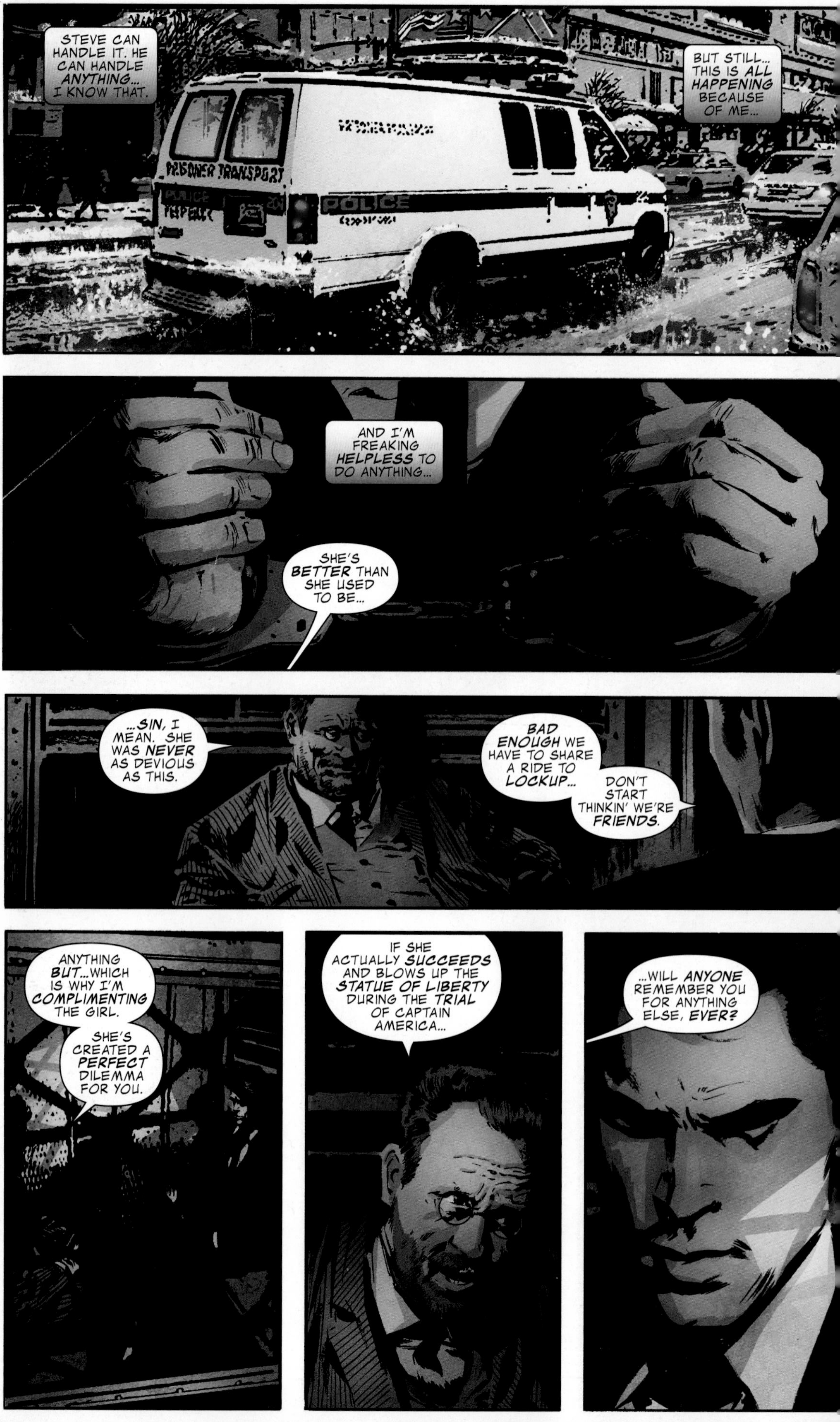
STEVE CAN HANDLE IT. HE CAN HANDLE ANYTHING... I KNOW THAT.
BUT STILL... THIS IS ALL HAPPENING BECAUSE OF ME...
PRISONER TRANSPORT
POLICE
AND I'M FREAKING HELPLESS TO DO ANYTHING...
SHE'S BETTER THAN SHE USED TO BE...
...SIN, I MEAN. SHE WAS NEVER AS DEVIOUS AS THIS.
BAD ENOUGH WE HAVE TO SHARE A RIDE TO LOCKUP...
DON'T START THINKIN' WE'RE FRIENDS.
ANYTHING BUT...WHICH IS WHY I'M COMPLIMENTING THE GIRL.
SHE'S CREATED A PERFECT DILEMMA FOR YOU.
IF SHE ACTUALLY SUCCEEDS AND BLOWS UP THE STATUE OF LIBERTY DURING THE TRIAL OF CAPTAIN AMERICA...
...WILL ANYONE REMEMBER YOU FOR ANYTHING ELSE, EVER?

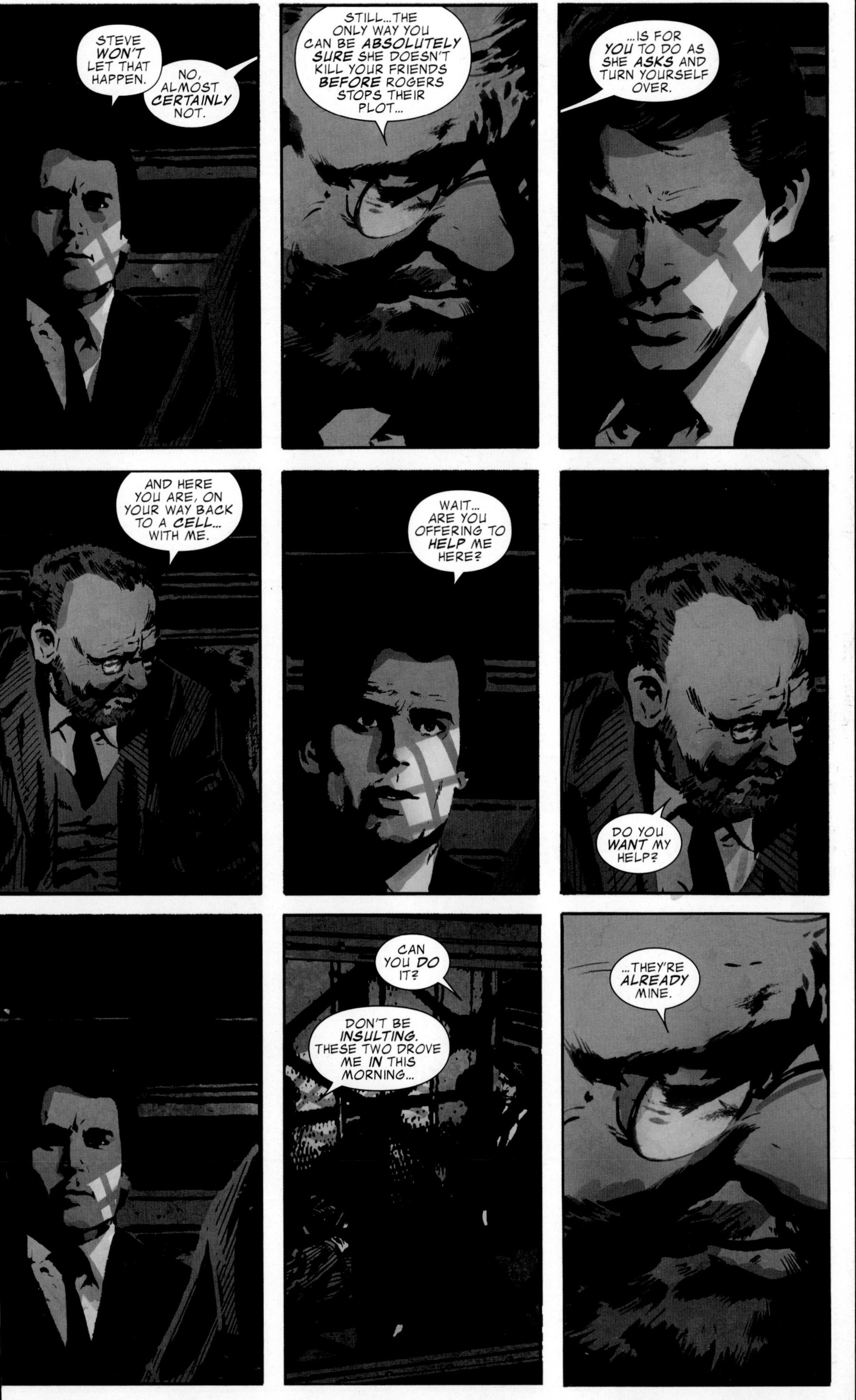
STEVE WON'T LET THAT HAPPEN.
NO, ALMOST CERTAINLY NOT.
STILL...THE ONLY WAY YOU CAN BE ABSOLUTELY SURE SHE DOESN'T KILL YOUR FRIENDS BEFORE ROGERS STOPS THEIR PLOT...
...IS FOR YOU TO DO AS SHE ASKS AND TURN YOURSELF OVER.
AND HERE YOU ARE, ON YOUR WAY BACK TO A CELL... WITH ME.
WAIT... ARE YOU OFFERING TO HELP ME HERE?
DO YOU WANT MY HELP?
CAN YOU DO IT?
DON'T BE INSULTING. THESE TWO DROVE ME IN THIS MORNING...
...THEY'RE ALREADY MINE.

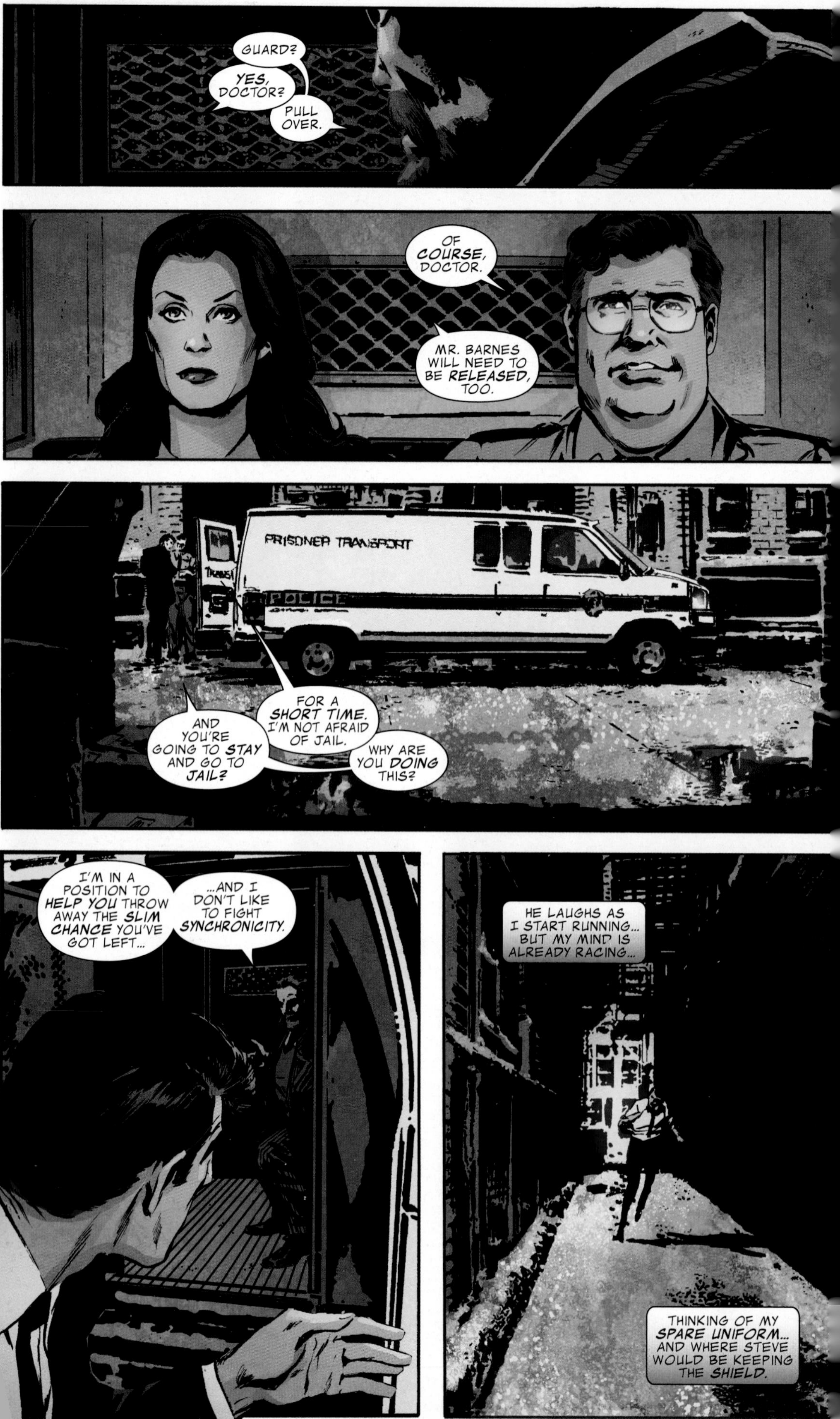

GUARD?
YES, DOCTOR?
PULL OVER.
OF COURSE, DOCTOR.
MR. BARNES WILL NEED TO BE RELEASED, TOO.
PRISONER TRANSPORT
POLICE
AND YOU'RE GOING TO STAY AND GO TO JAIL?
FOR A SHORT TIME. I'M NOT AFRAID OF JAIL.
WHY ARE YOU DOING THIS?
I'M IN A POSITION TO HELP YOU THROW AWAY THE SLIM CHANCE YOU'VE GOT LEFT...
...AND I DON'T LIKE TO FIGHT SYNCHRONICITY.
HE LAUGHS AS I START RUNNING... BUT MY MIND IS ALREADY RACING...
THINKING OF MY SPARE UNIFORM... AND WHERE STEVE WOULD BE KEEPING THE SHIELD.

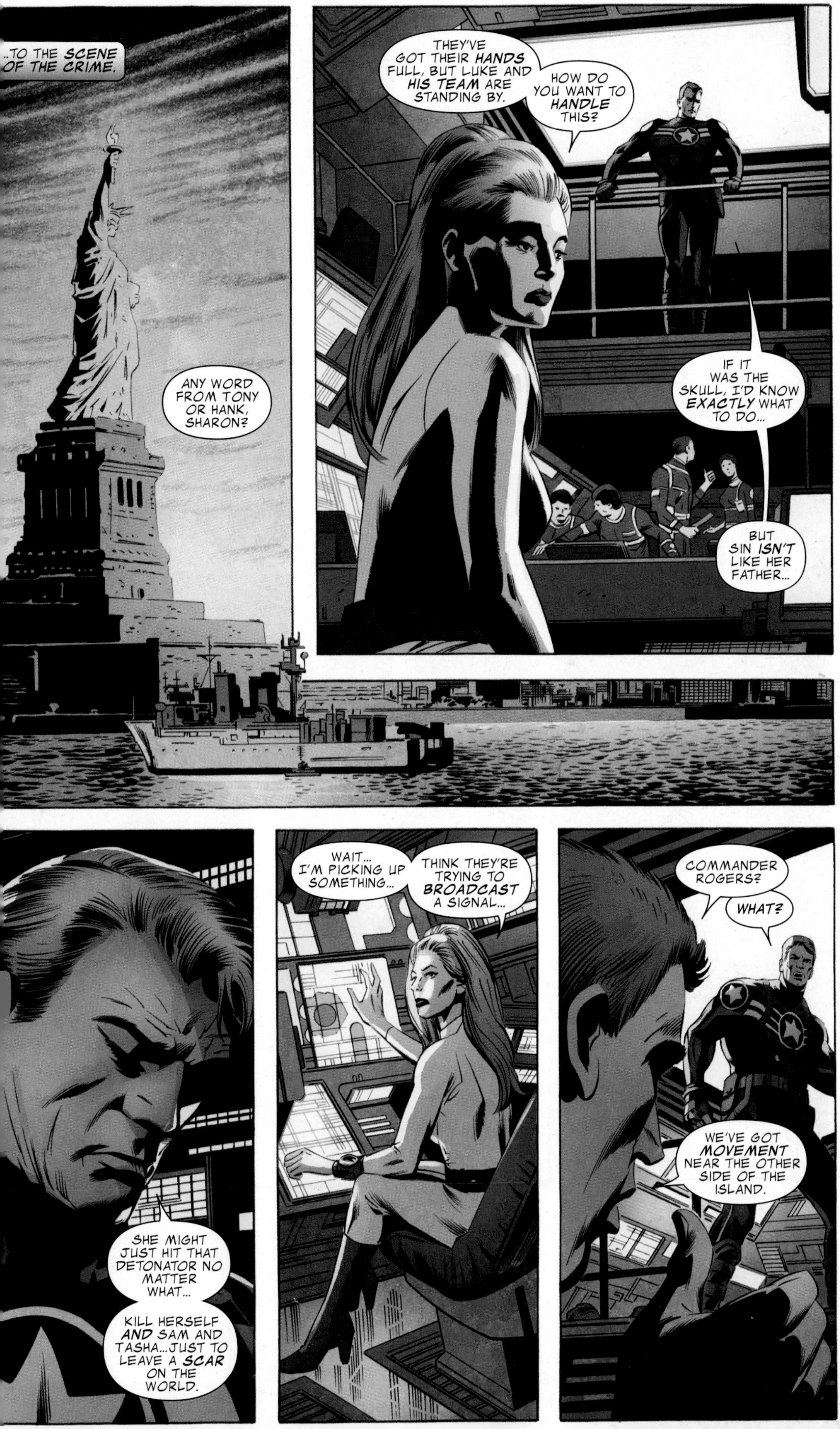
..TO THE SCENE OF THE CRIME.
ANY WORD FROM TONY OR HANK, SHARON?
THEY'VE GOT THEIR HANDS FULL, BUT LUKE AND HIS TEAM ARE STANDING BY.
HOW DO YOU WANT TO HANDLE THIS?
IF IT WAS THE SKULL, I'D KNOW EXACTLY WHAT TO DO...
BUT SIN ISN'T LIKE HER FATHER...
SHE MIGHT JUST HIT THAT DETONATOR NO MATTER WHAT...
KILL HERSELF AND SAM AND TASHA...JUST TO LEAVE A SCAR ON THE WORLD.
WAIT... I'M PICKING UP SOMETHING...
THINK THEY'RE TRYING TO BROADCAST A SIGNAL...
COMMANDER ROGERS?
WHAT?
WE'VE GOT MOVEMENT NEAR THE OTHER SIDE OF THE ISLAND.

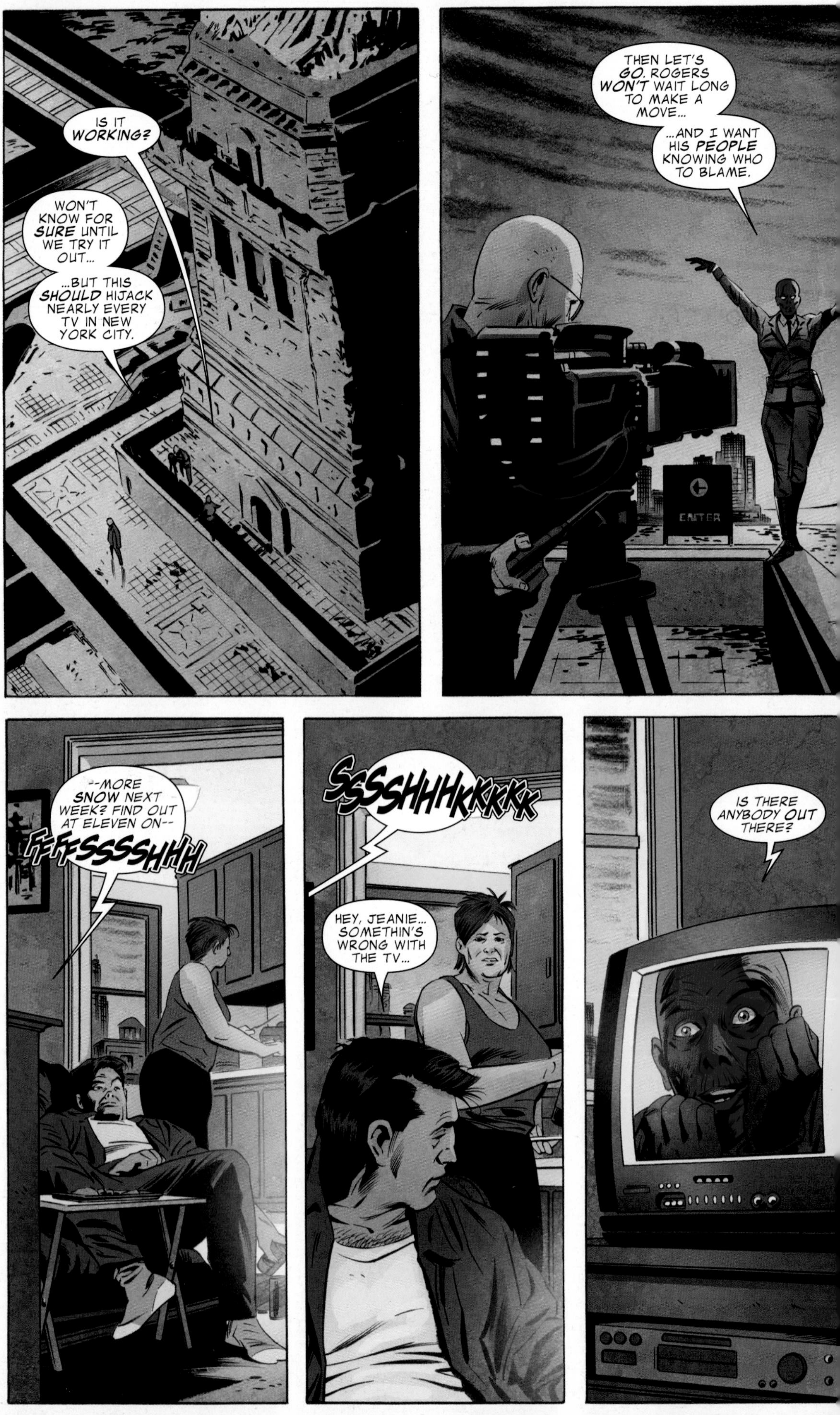
IS IT WORKING?
WON'T KNOW FOR SURE UNTIL WE TRY IT OUT...
...BUT THIS SHOULD HIJACK NEARLY EVERY TV IN NEW YORK CITY.
THEN LET'S GO. ROGERS WON'T WAIT LONG TO MAKE A MOVE...
...AND I WANT HIS PEOPLE KNOWING WHO TO BLAME.
ENTER
--MORE SNOW NEXT WEEK? FIND OUT AT ELEVEN ON--
FFFFSSSSSHHH
SSSSHHHKKKKK
HEY, JEANIE... SOMETHIN'S WRONG WITH THE TV...
IS THERE ANYBODY OUT THERE?

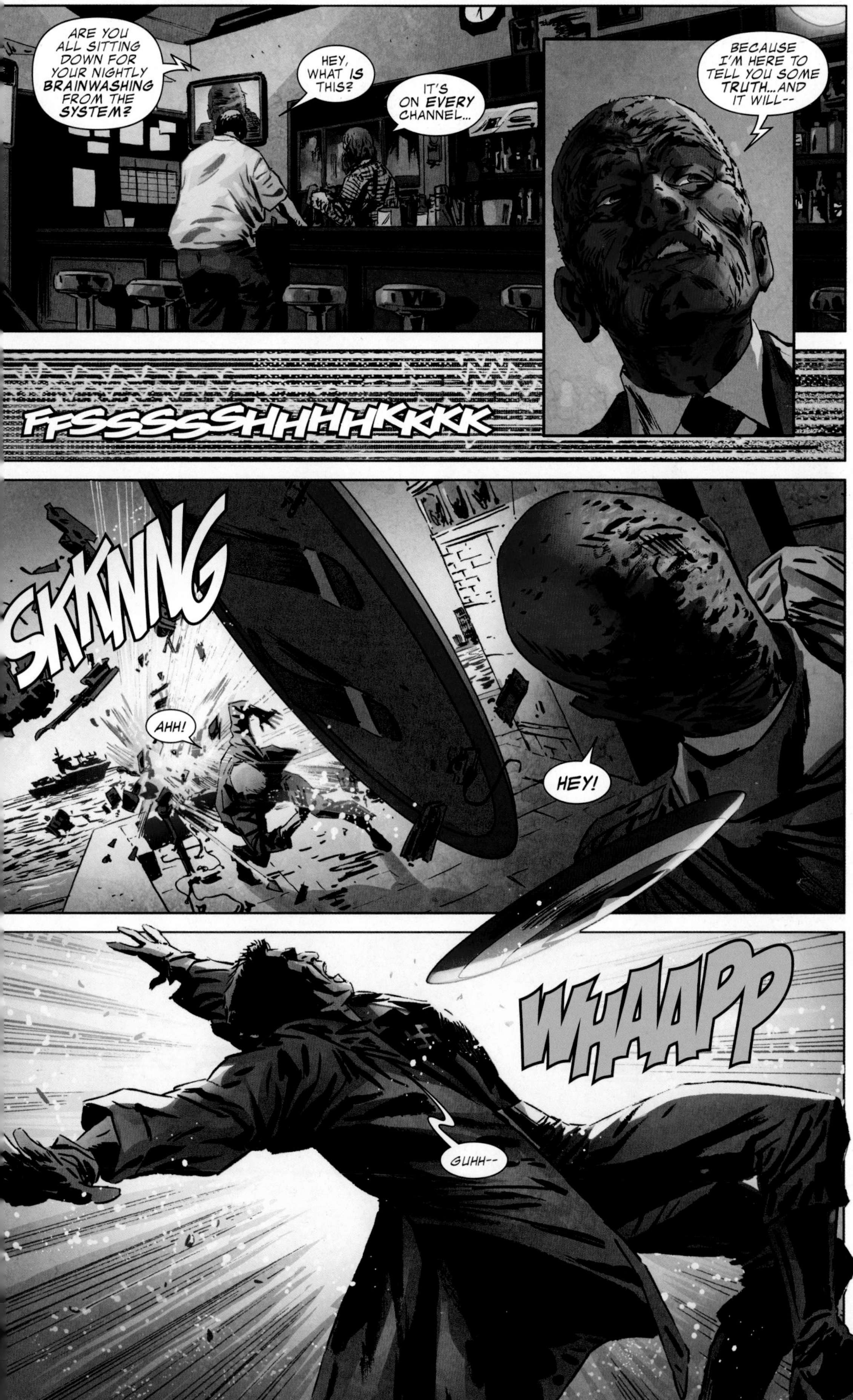

ARE YOU ALL SITTING DOWN FOR YOUR NIGHTLY BRAINWASHING FROM THE SYSTEM?
HEY, WHAT IS THIS?
IT'S ON EVERY CHANNEL...
BECAUSE I'M HERE TO TELL YOU SOME TRUTH...AND IT WILL--
FFSSSSSHHHHKKKK
SKKNNG
AHH!
HEY!
WHAAPP
GUHH--

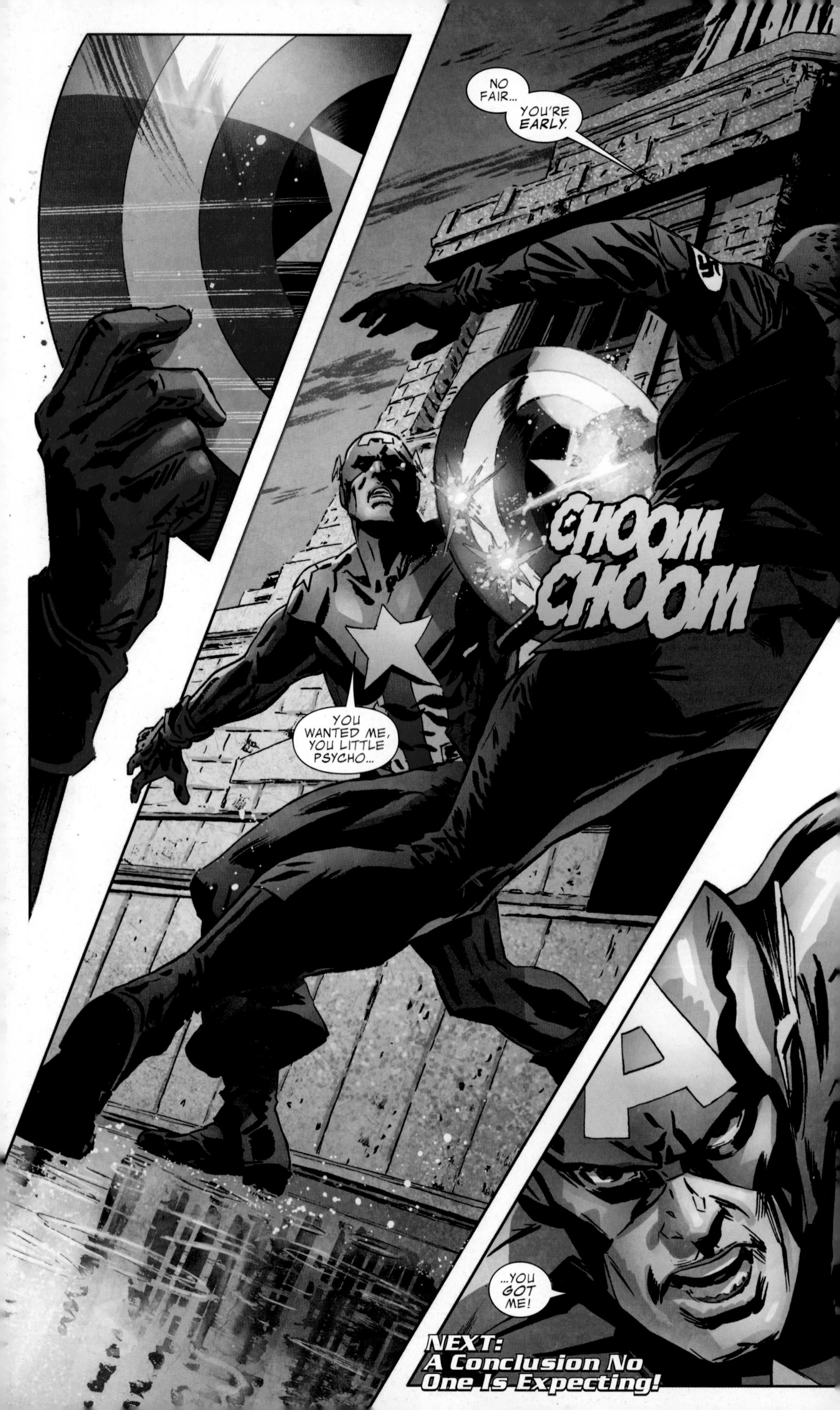
NO FAIR... YOU'RE EARLY.
CHOOM CHOOM
YOU WANTED ME, YOU LITTLE PSYCHO...
...YOU GOT ME!
NEXT: A Conclusion No One Is Expecting!

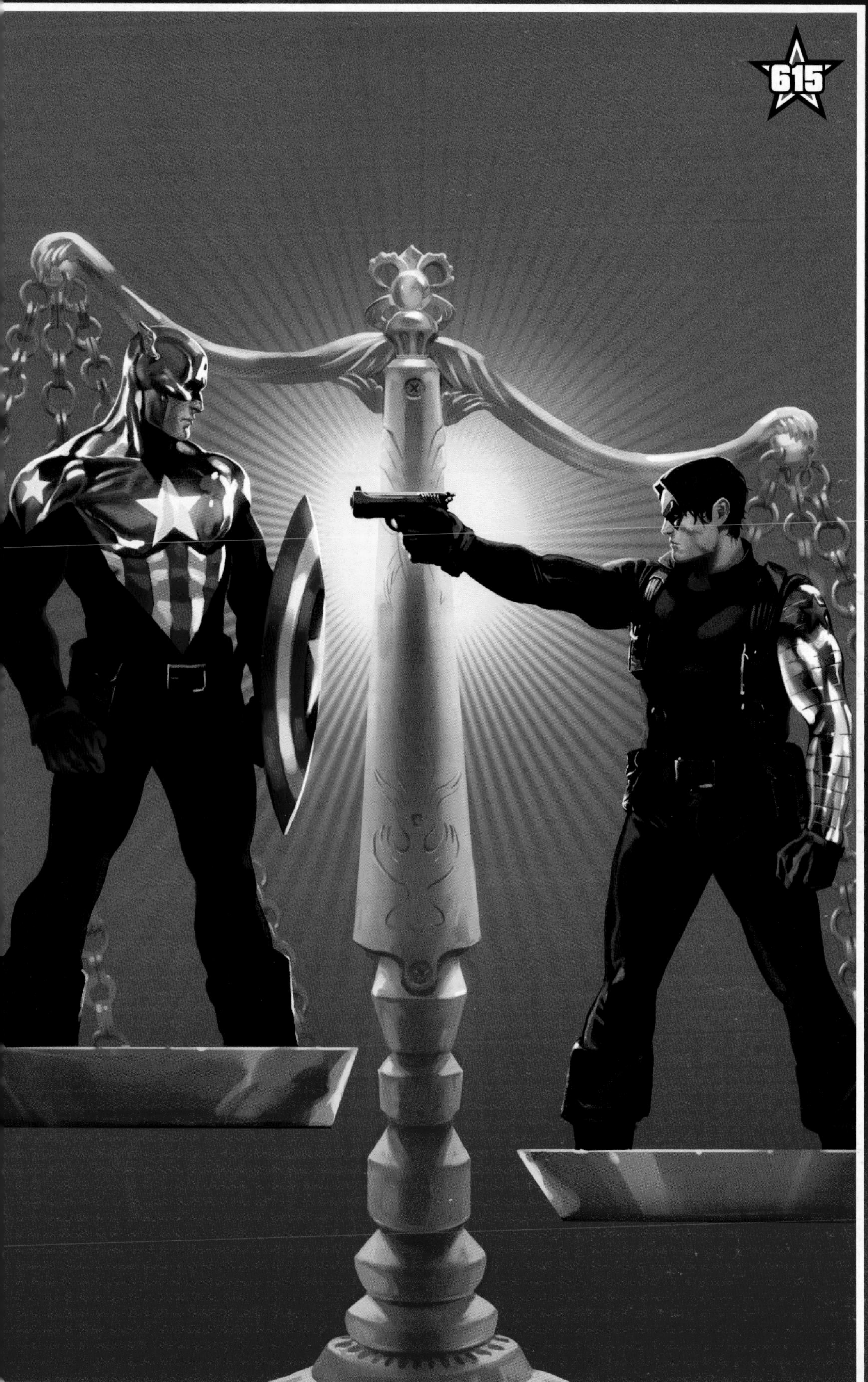
615

THE TRIAL OF CAPTAIN AMERICA PART 5

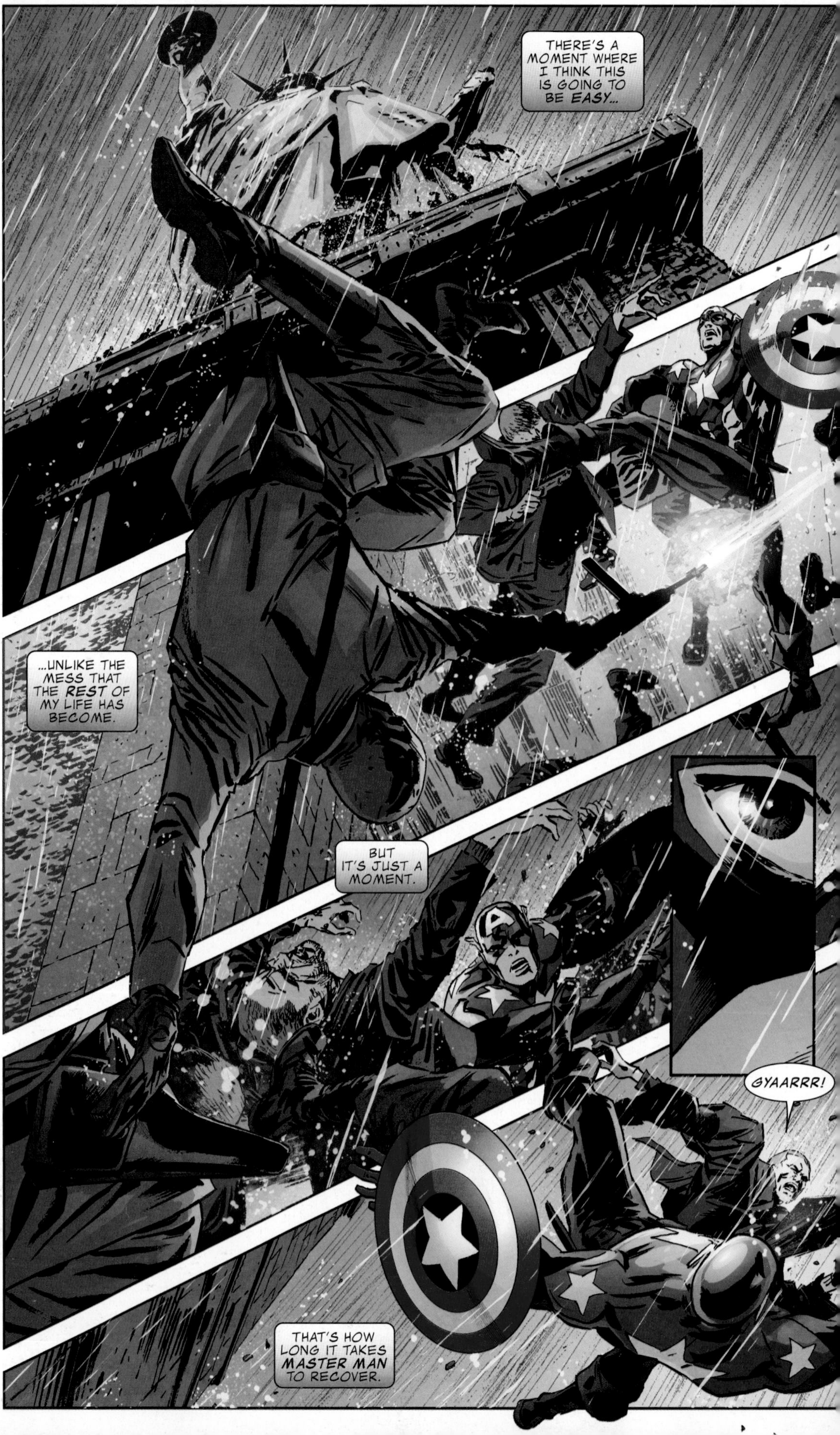
THERE'S A MOMENT WHERE I THINK THIS IS GOING TO BE EASY...
...UNLIKE THE MESS THAT THE REST OF MY LIFE HAS BECOME.
BUT IT'S JUST A MOMENT.
GYAARRR!
THAT'S HOW LONG IT TAKES MASTER MAN TO RECOVER.

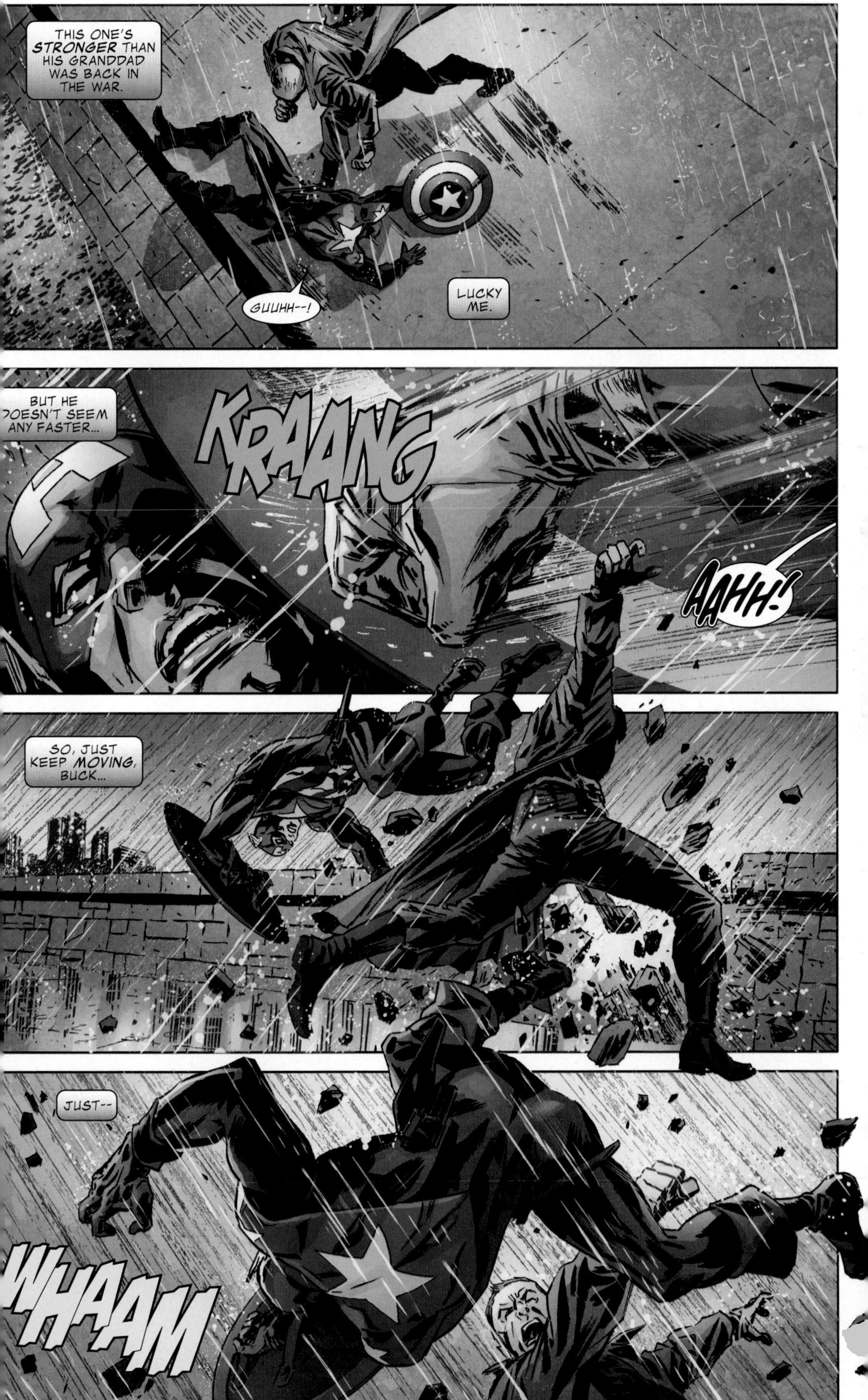
THIS ONE'S STRONGER THAN HIS GRANDDAD WAS BACK IN THE WAR.
GUUHH--!
LUCKY ME.
BUT HE DOESN'T SEEM ANY FASTER...
KRAANG
AAHH!
SO, JUST KEEP MOVING, BUCK...
JUST--
WHAAM

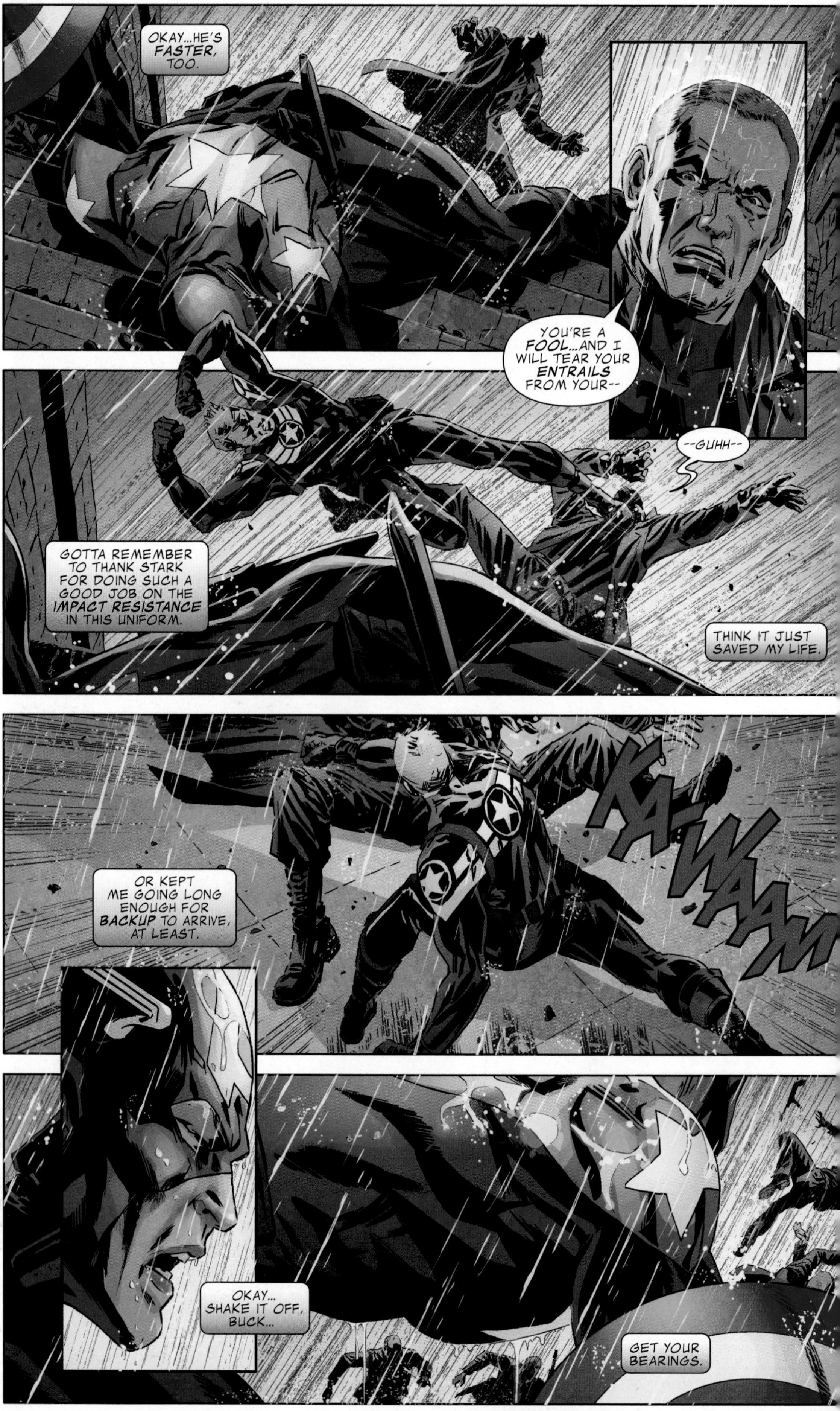
OKAY...HE'S FASTER, TOO.
YOU'RE A FOOL...AND I WILL TEAR YOUR ENTRAILS FROM YOUR--
--GUHH--
GOTTA REMEMBER TO THANK STARK FOR DOING SUCH A GOOD JOB ON THE IMPACT RESISTANCE IN THIS UNIFORM.
THINK IT JUST SAVED MY LIFE.
KA-WAAMM
OR KEPT ME GOING LONG ENOUGH FOR BACKUP TO ARRIVE, AT LEAST.
OKAY... SHAKE IT OFF, BUCK...
GET YOUR BEARINGS.

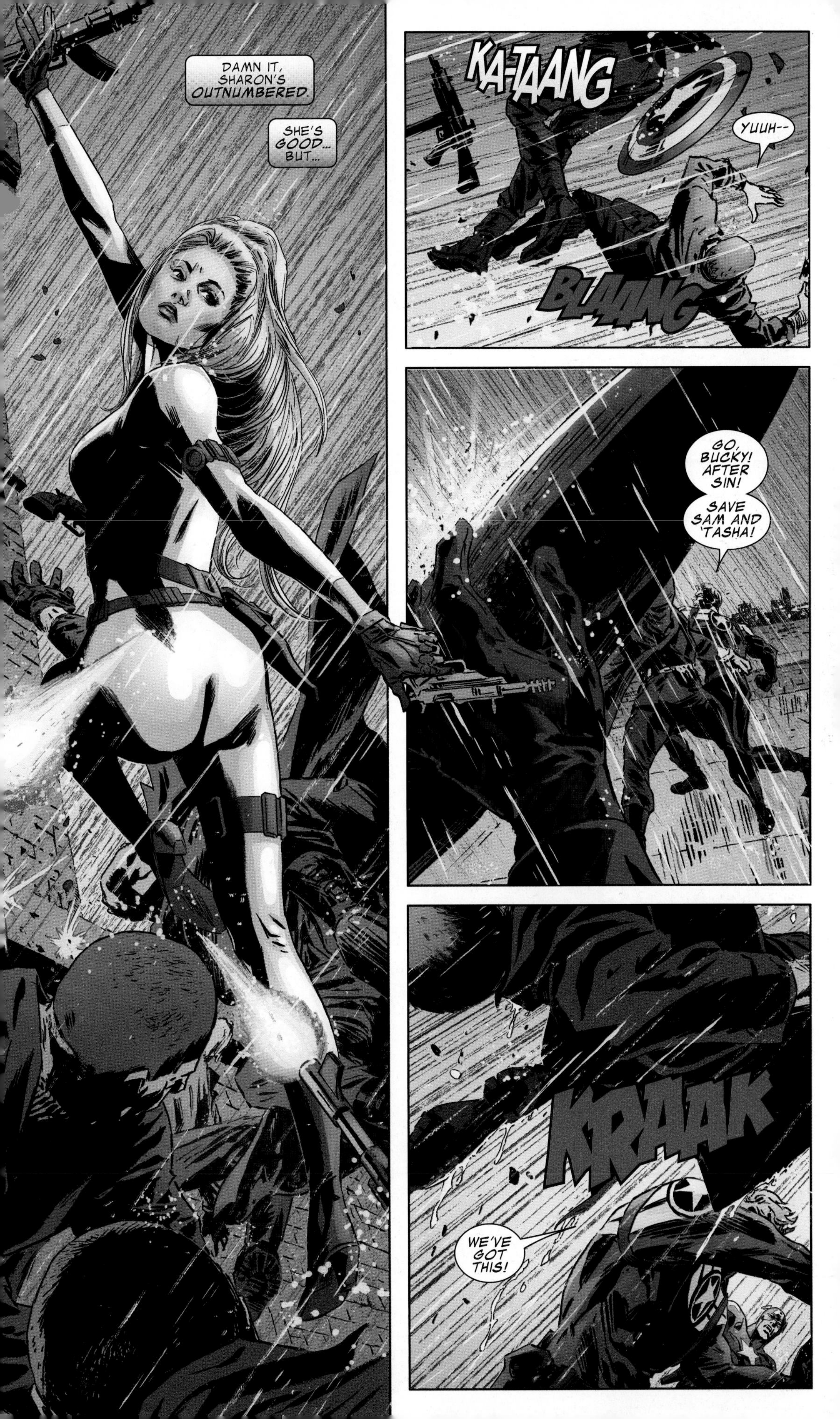
DAMN IT, SHARON'S OUTNUMBERED.
SHE'S GOOD... BUT...
KA-TAANG
YUUH--
BLAAANG
GO, BUCKY! AFTER SIN!
SAVE SAM AND 'TASHA!
KRAAK
WE'VE GOT THIS!

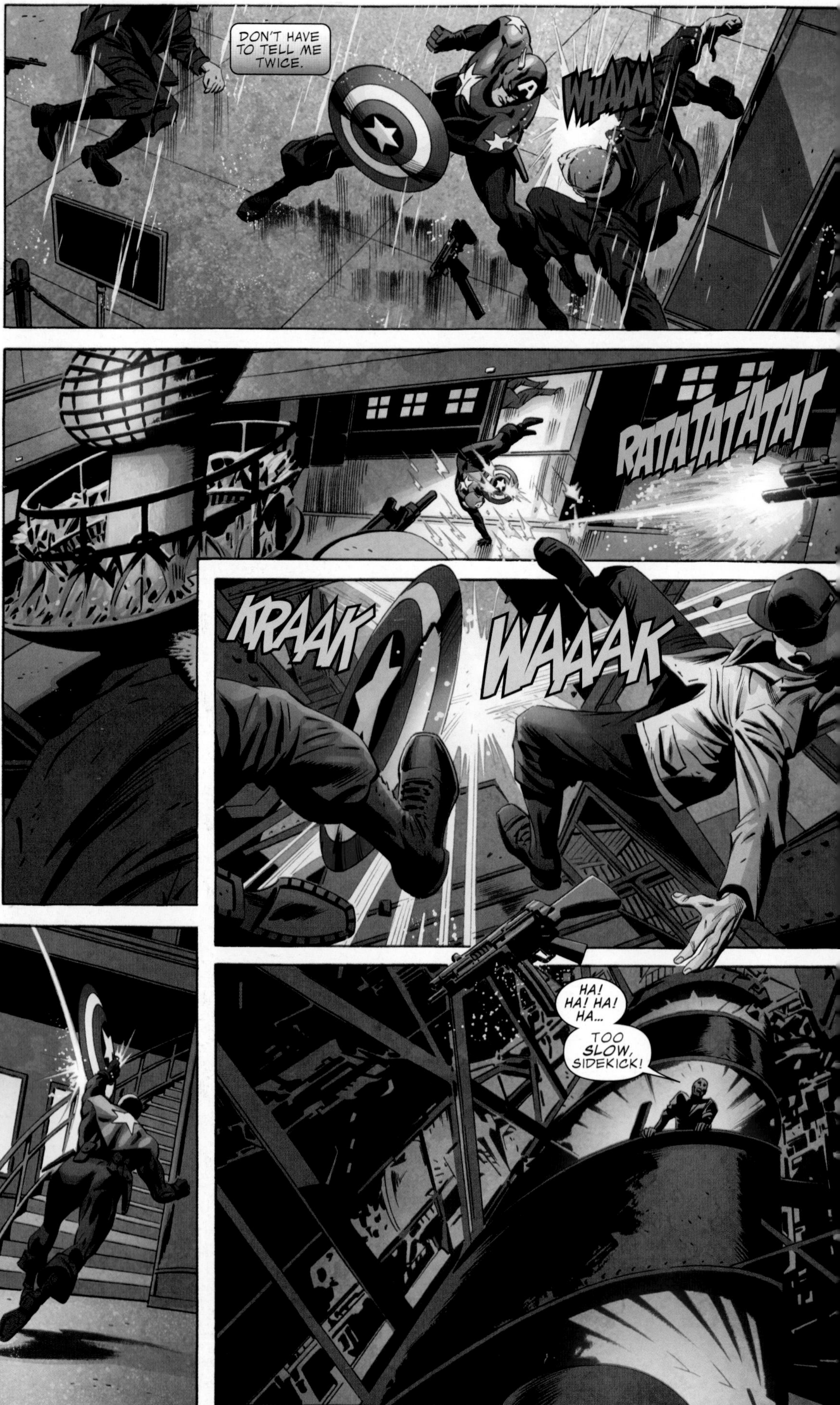
DON'T HAVE TO TELL ME TWICE.
WHAAM
RATATATATAT
KRAAK
WAAAK
HA! HA! HA! HA...
TOO SLOW, SIDEKICK!

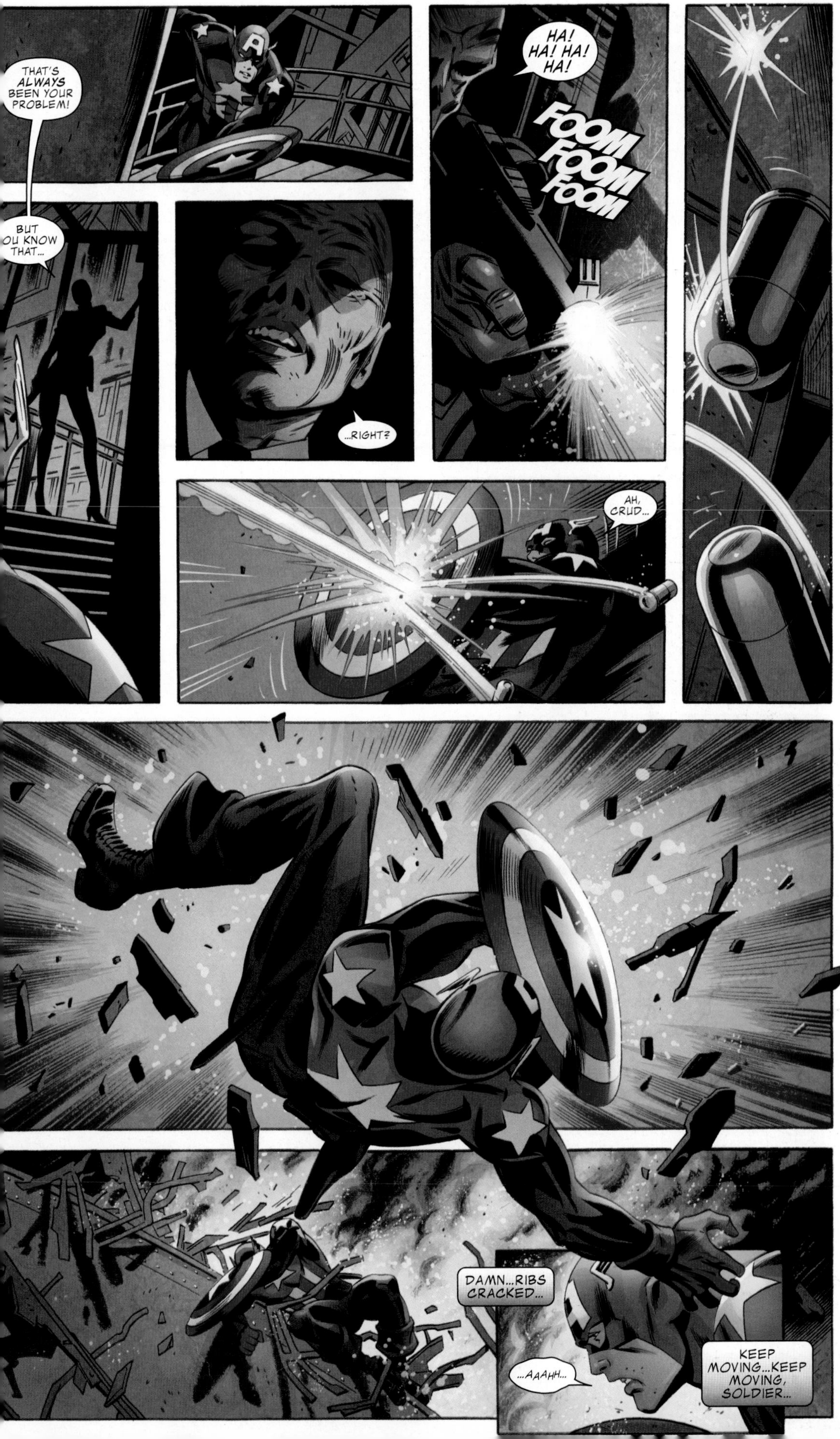
THAT'S ALWAYS BEEN YOUR PROBLEM!
BUT OU KNOW THAT...
...RIGHT?
HA! HA! HA! HA!
FOOM FOOM FOOM
AH, CRUD...
DAMN...RIBS CRACKED...
...AAAHH...
KEEP MOVING...KEEP MOVING, SOLDIER...

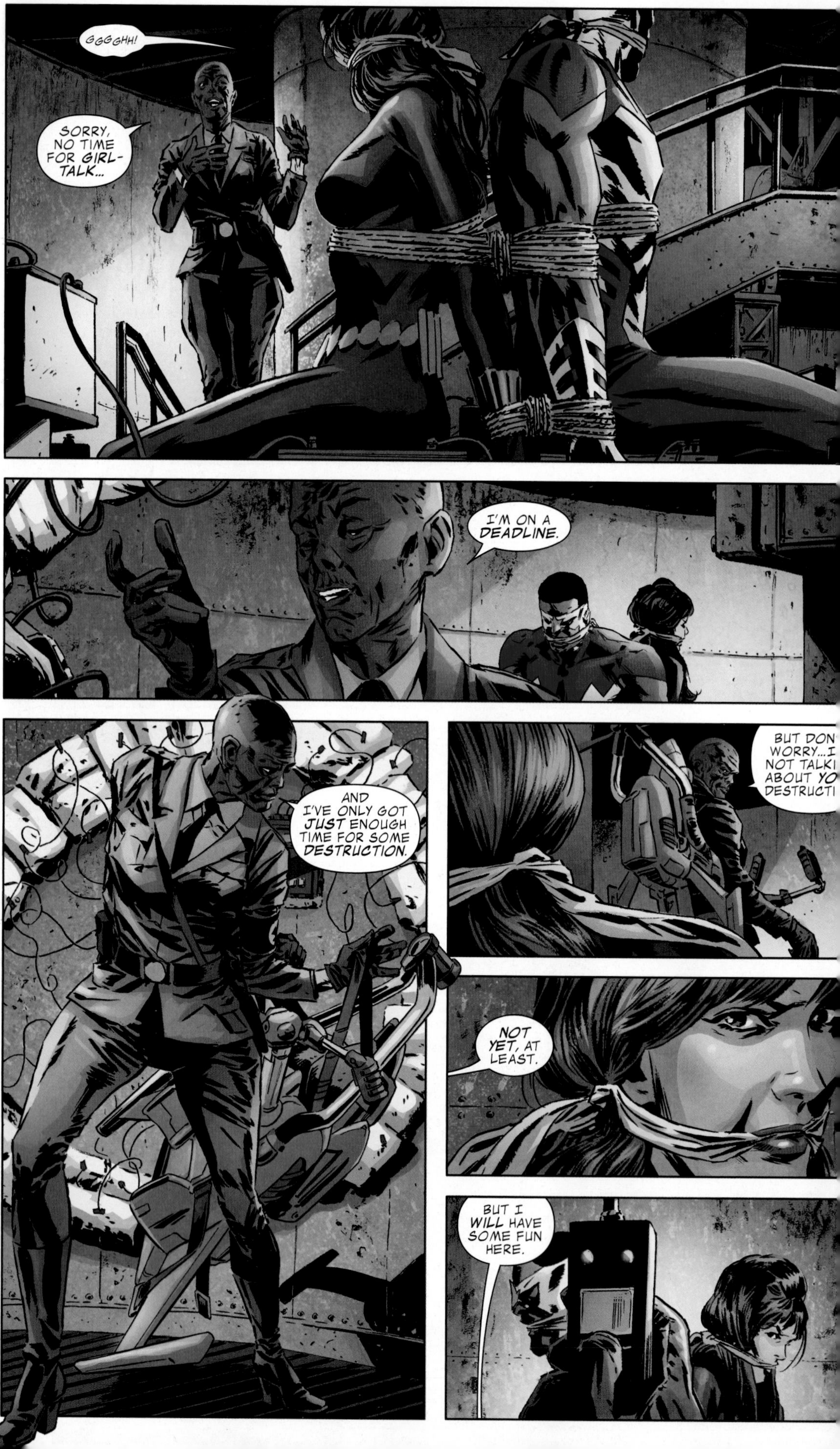
GGGGHH!
SORRY, NO TIME FOR GIRL-TALK...
I'M ON A DEADLINE.
AND I'VE ONLY GOT JUST ENOUGH TIME FOR SOME DESTRUCTION.
BUT DON WORRY...I NOT TALKI ABOUT YO DESTRUCTI
NOT YET, AT LEAST.
BUT I WILL HAVE SOME FUN HERE.

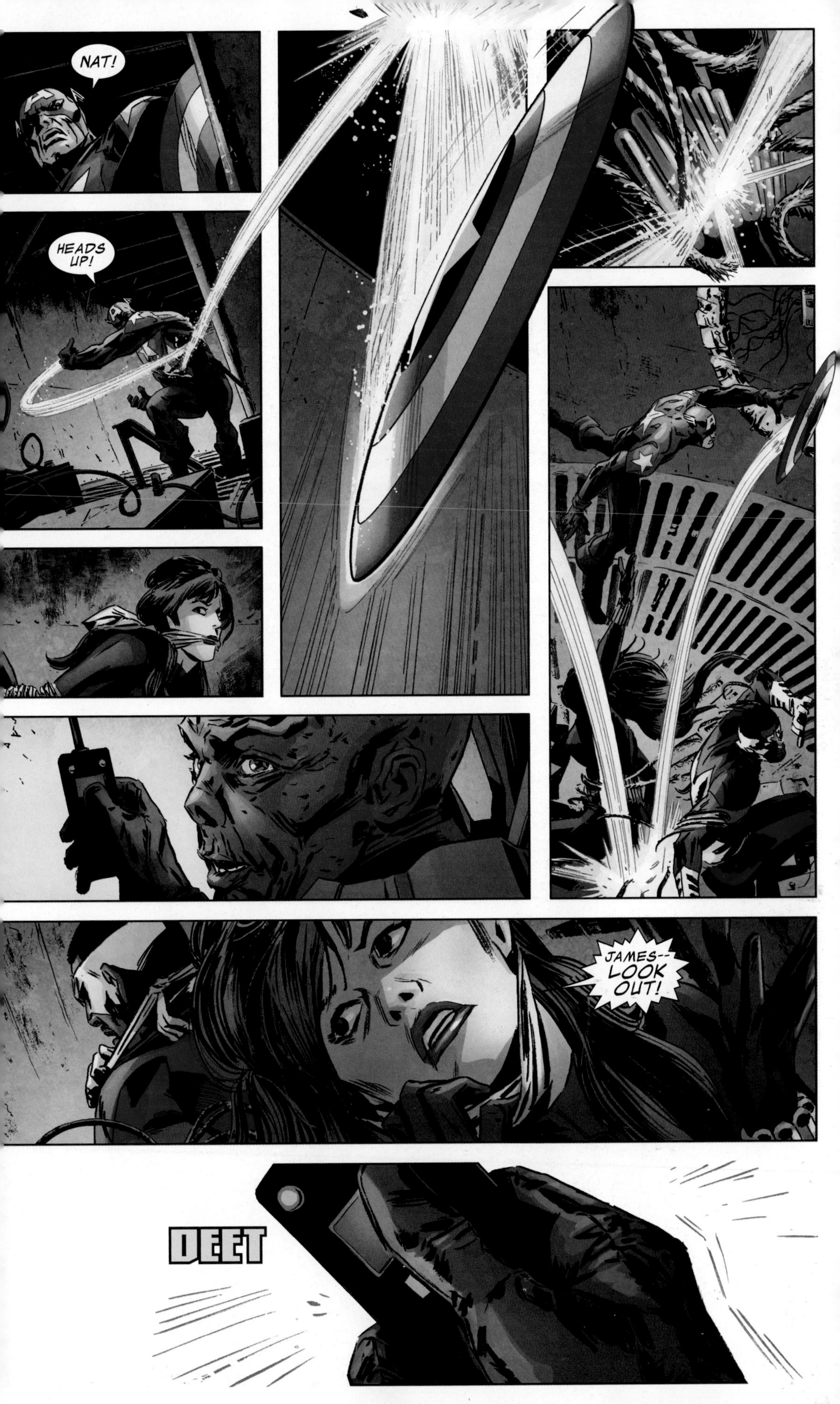
NAT!
HEADS UP!
JAMES-- LOOK OUT!
DEET

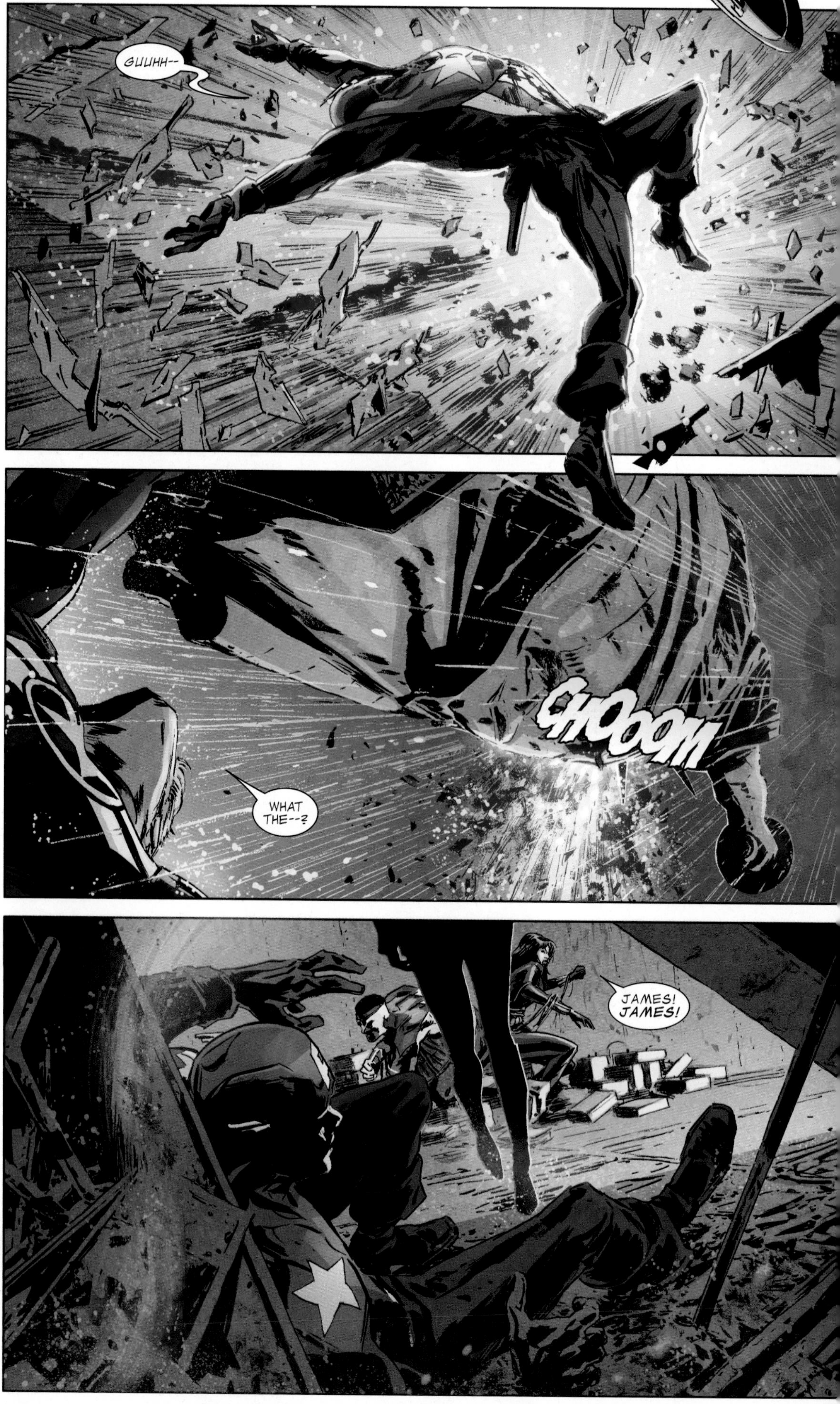
GUUHH--
CHOOOM
WHAT THE--?
JAMES! JAMES!

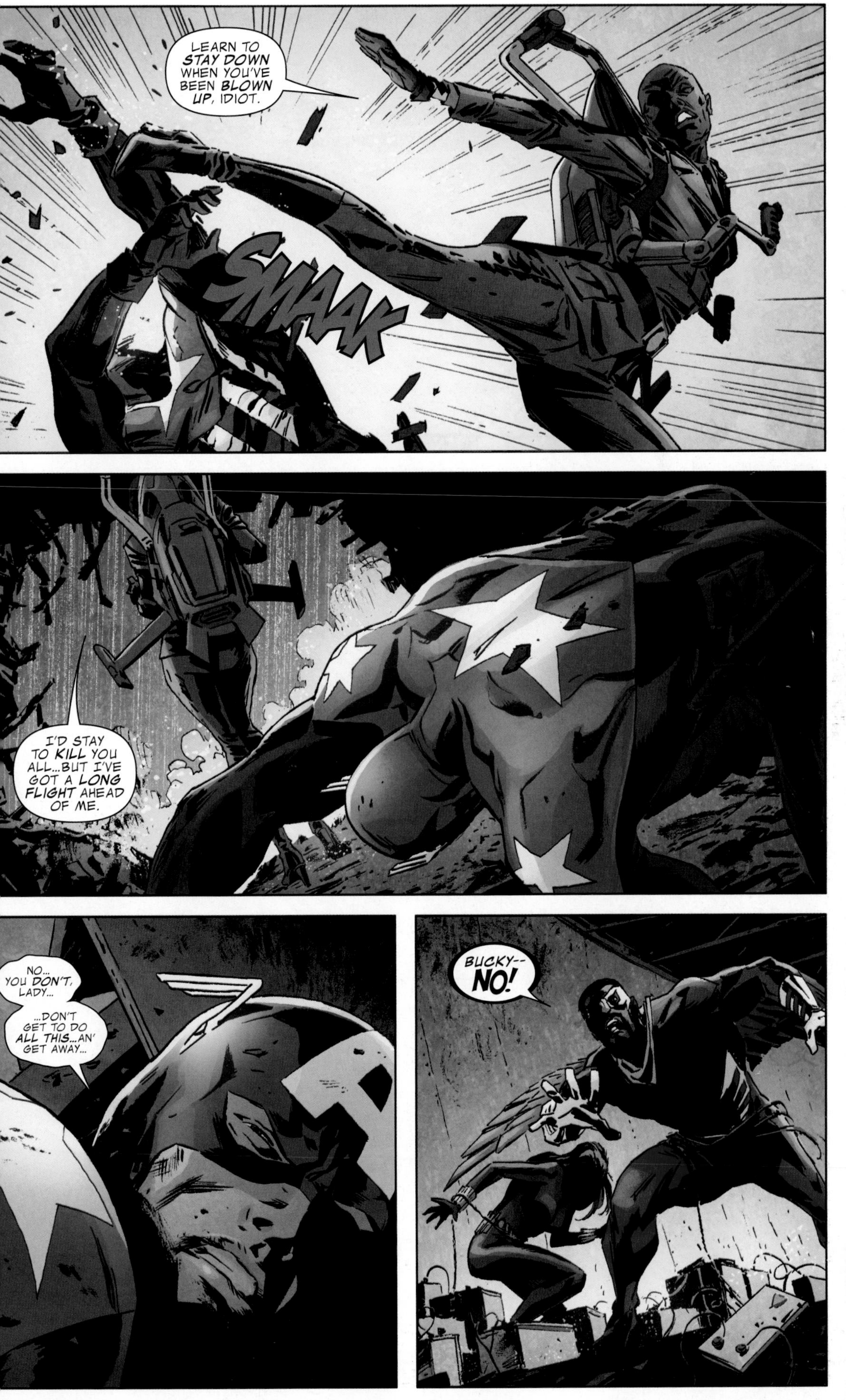
LEARN TO STAY DOWN WHEN YOU'VE BEEN BLOWN UP, IDIOT.
SMAAK
I'D STAY TO KILL YOU ALL...BUT I'VE GOT A LONG FLIGHT AHEAD OF ME.
NO... YOU DON'T, LADY...
...DON'T GET TO DO ALL THIS...AN' GET AWAY...
BUCKY-- NO!

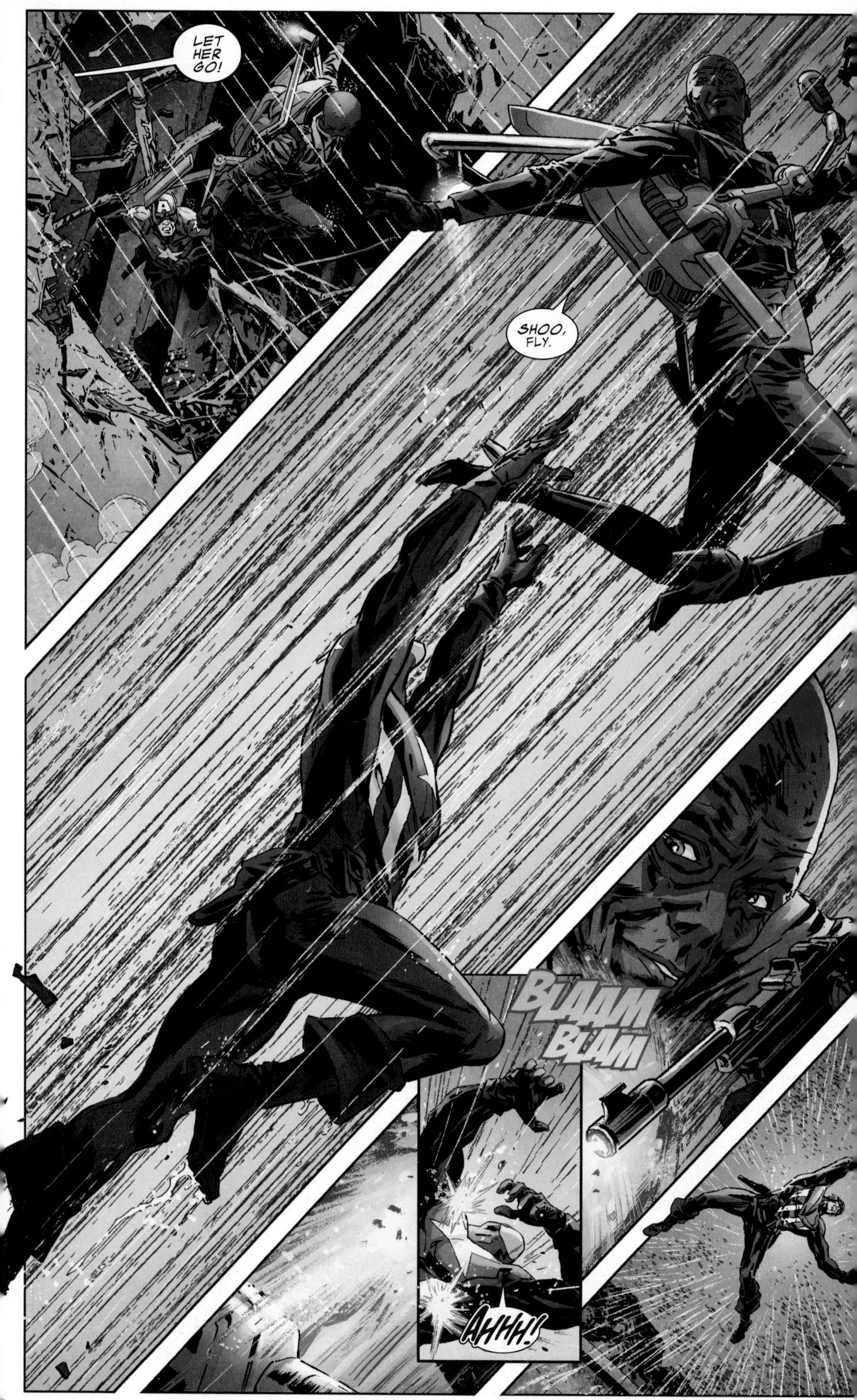
LET HER GO!
SHOO, FLY.
BLAAM
BLAM
AHHH!

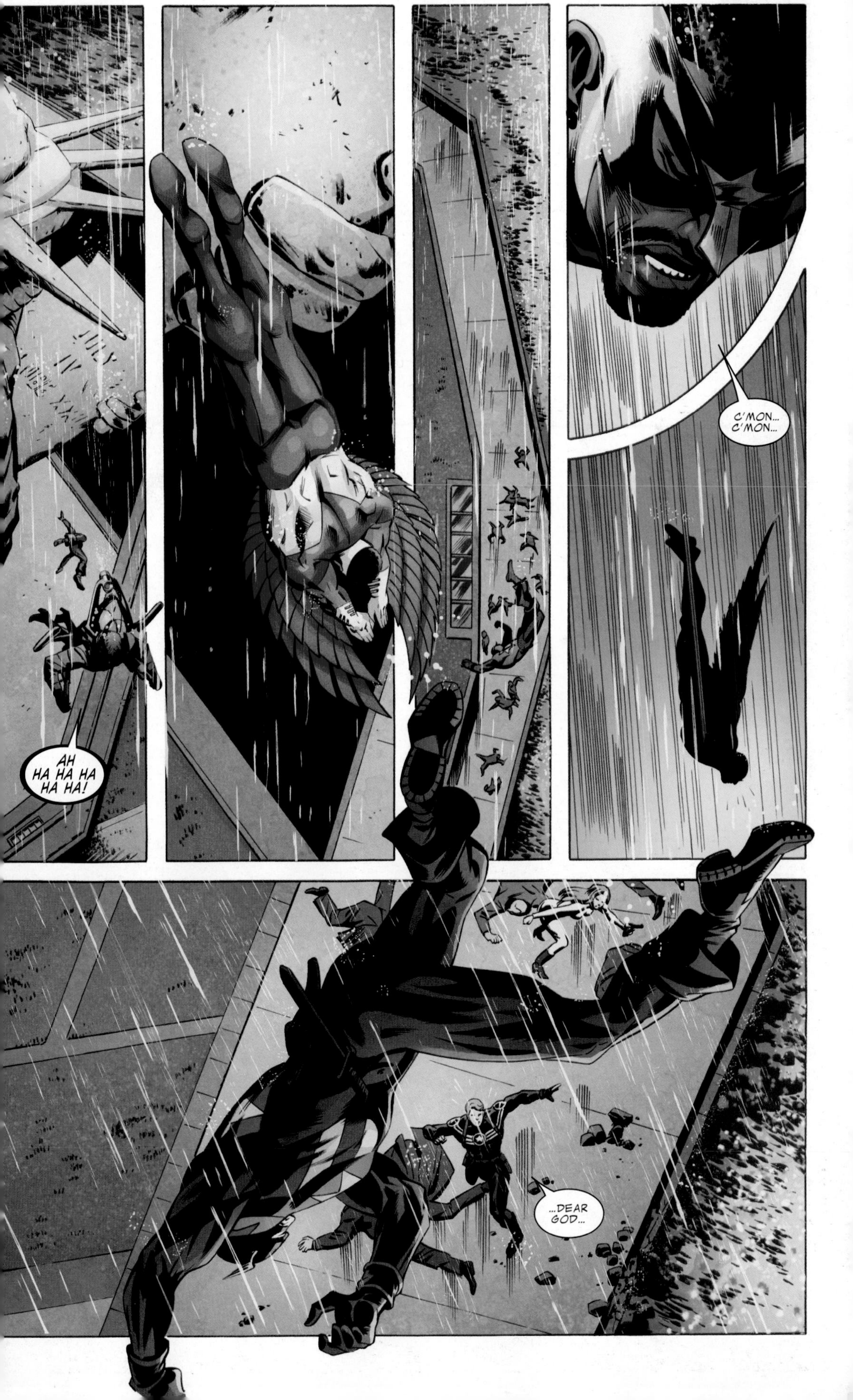
AH HA HA HA HA HA!
C'MON... C'MON...
...DEAR GOD...

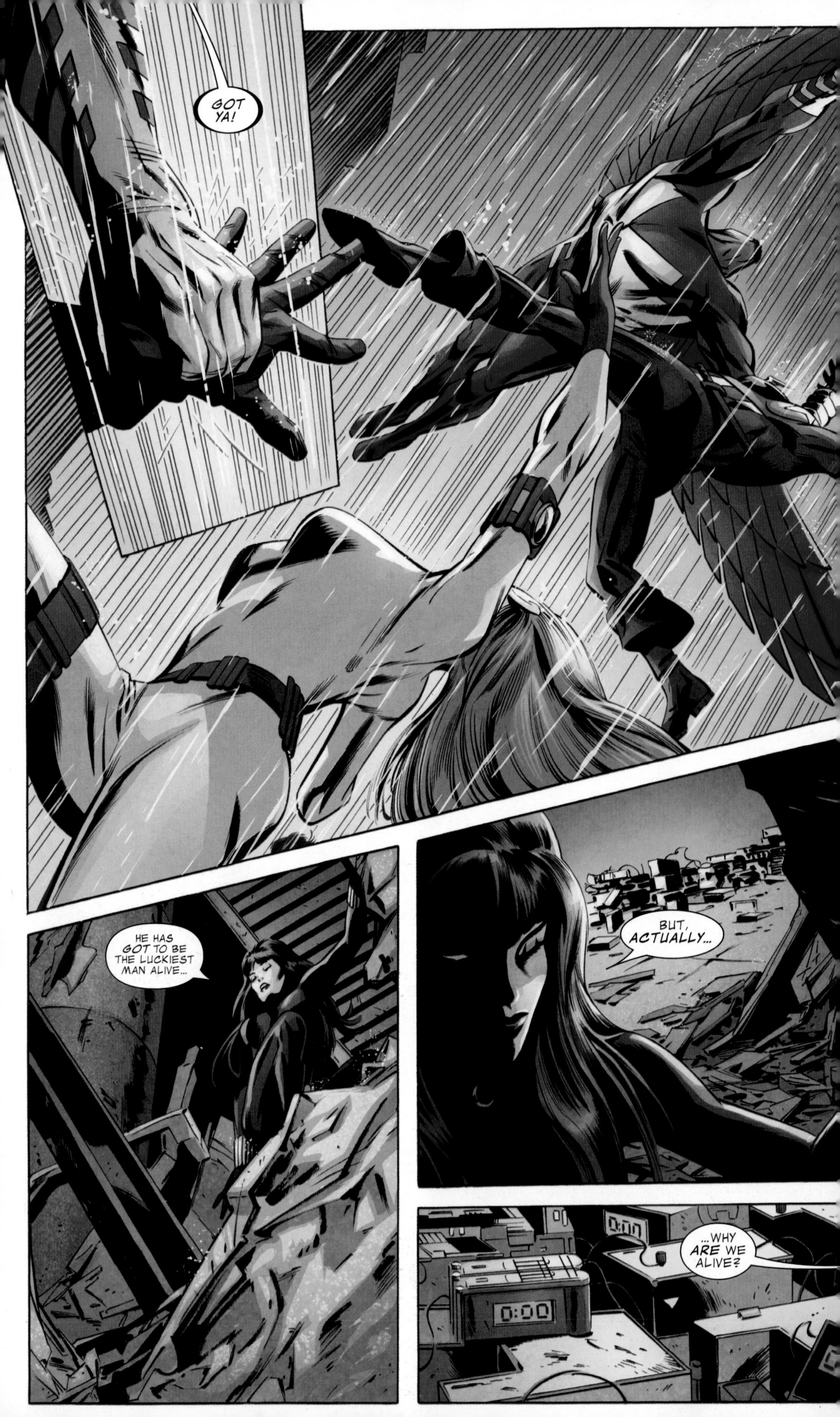
GOT YA!
HE HAS GOT TO BE THE LUCKIEST MAN ALIVE...
BUT, ACTUALLY...
...WHY ARE WE ALIVE?
0:00

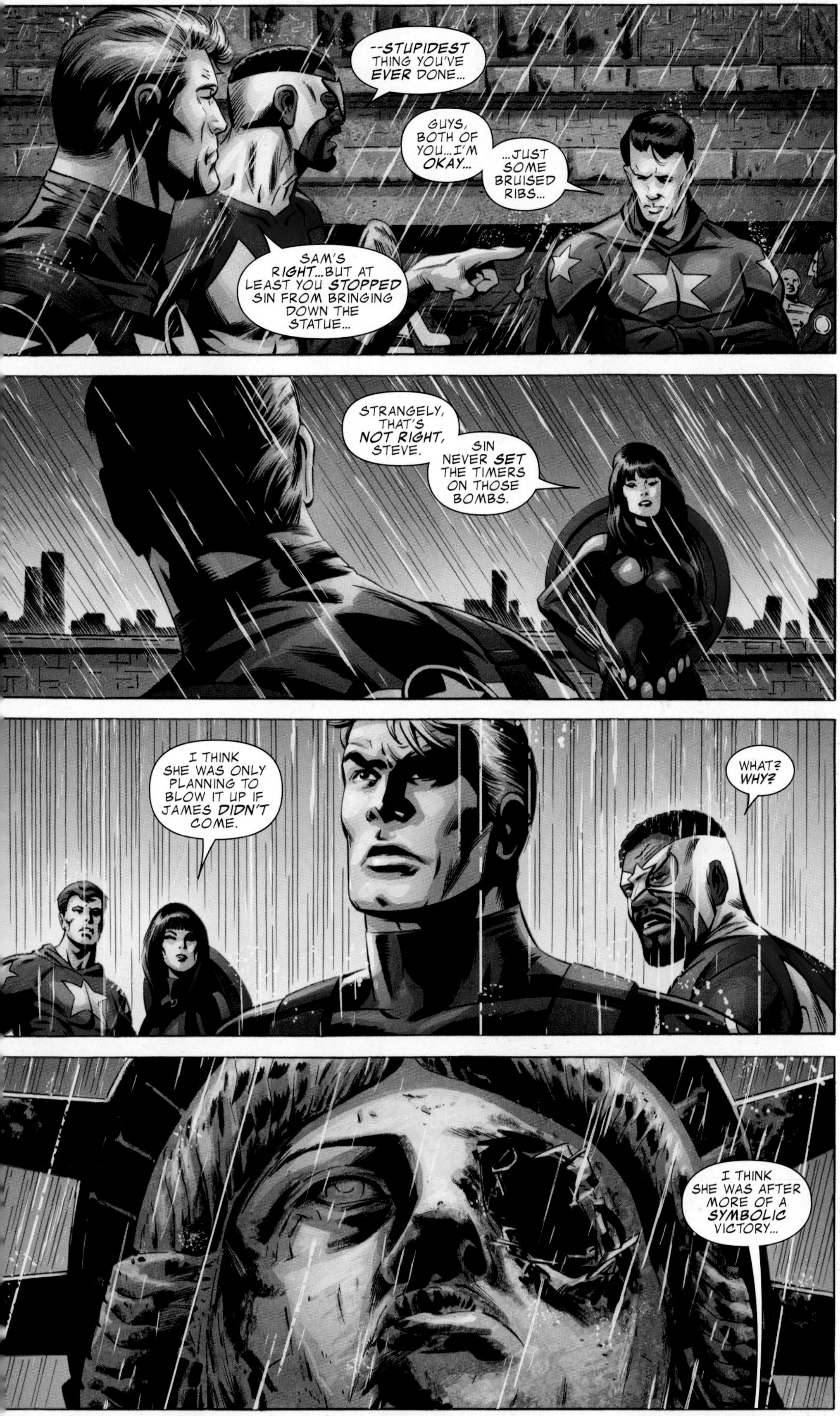
--STUPIDEST THING YOU'VE EVER DONE...
GUYS, BOTH OF YOU...I'M OKAY...
...JUST SOME BRUISED RIBS...
SAM'S RIGHT...BUT AT LEAST YOU STOPPED SIN FROM BRINGING DOWN THE STATUE...
STRANGELY, THAT'S NOT RIGHT, STEVE.
SIN NEVER SET THE TIMERS ON THOSE BOMBS.
I THINK SHE WAS ONLY PLANNING TO BLOW IT UP IF JAMES DIDN'T COME.
WHAT? WHY?
I THINK SHE WAS AFTER MORE OF A SYMBOLIC VICTORY...

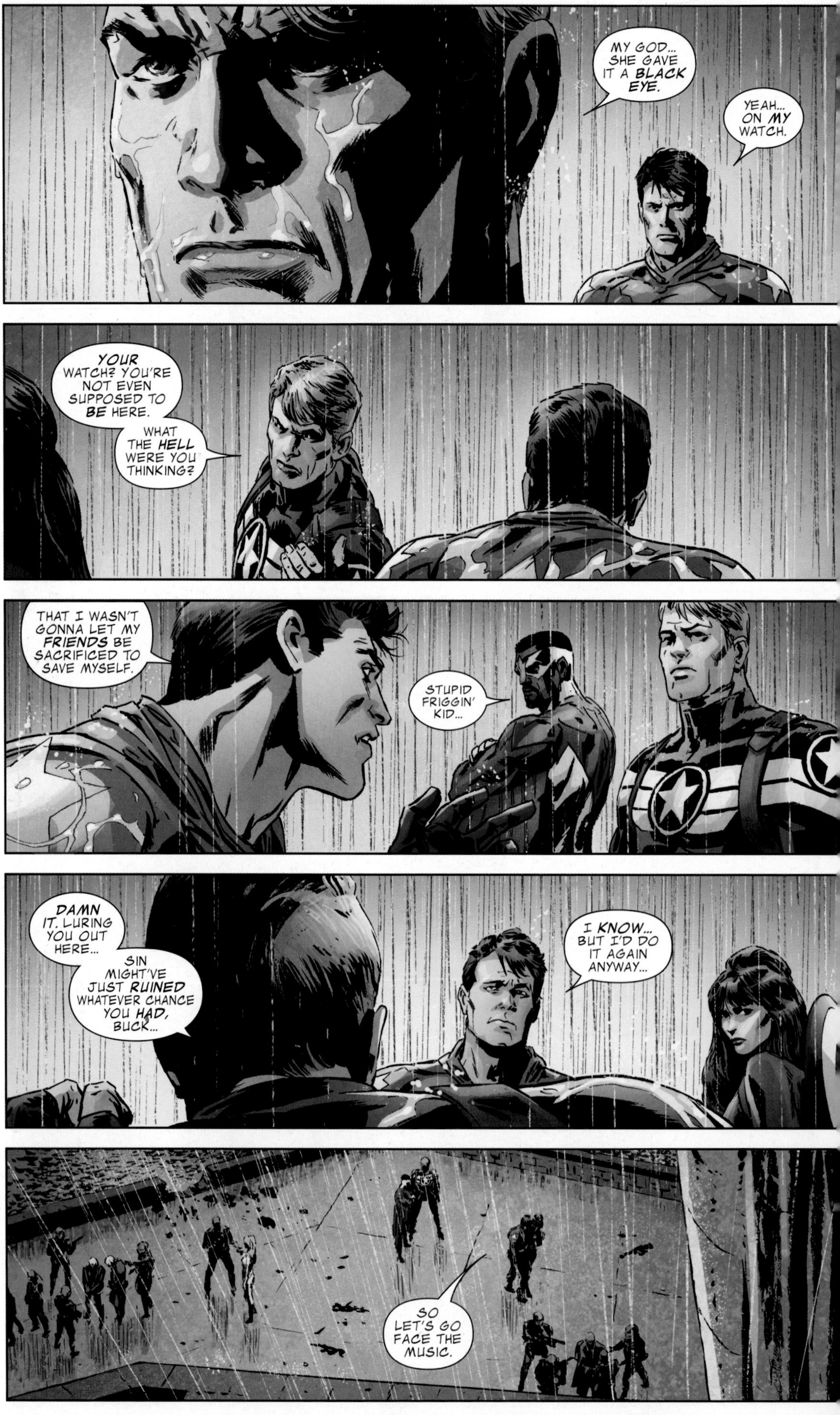
MY GOD... SHE GAVE IT A BLACK EYE.
YEAH... ON MY WATCH.
YOUR WATCH? YOU'RE NOT EVEN SUPPOSED TO BE HERE.
WHAT THE HELL WERE YOU THINKING?
THAT I WASN'T GONNA LET MY FRIENDS BE SACRIFICED TO SAVE MYSELF.
STUPID FRIGGIN' KID...
DAMN IT. LURING YOU OUT HERE...
SIN MIGHT'VE JUST RUINED WHATEVER CHANCE YOU HAD, BUCK...
I KNOW... BUT I'D DO IT AGAIN ANYWAY...
SO LET'S GO FACE THE MUSIC.

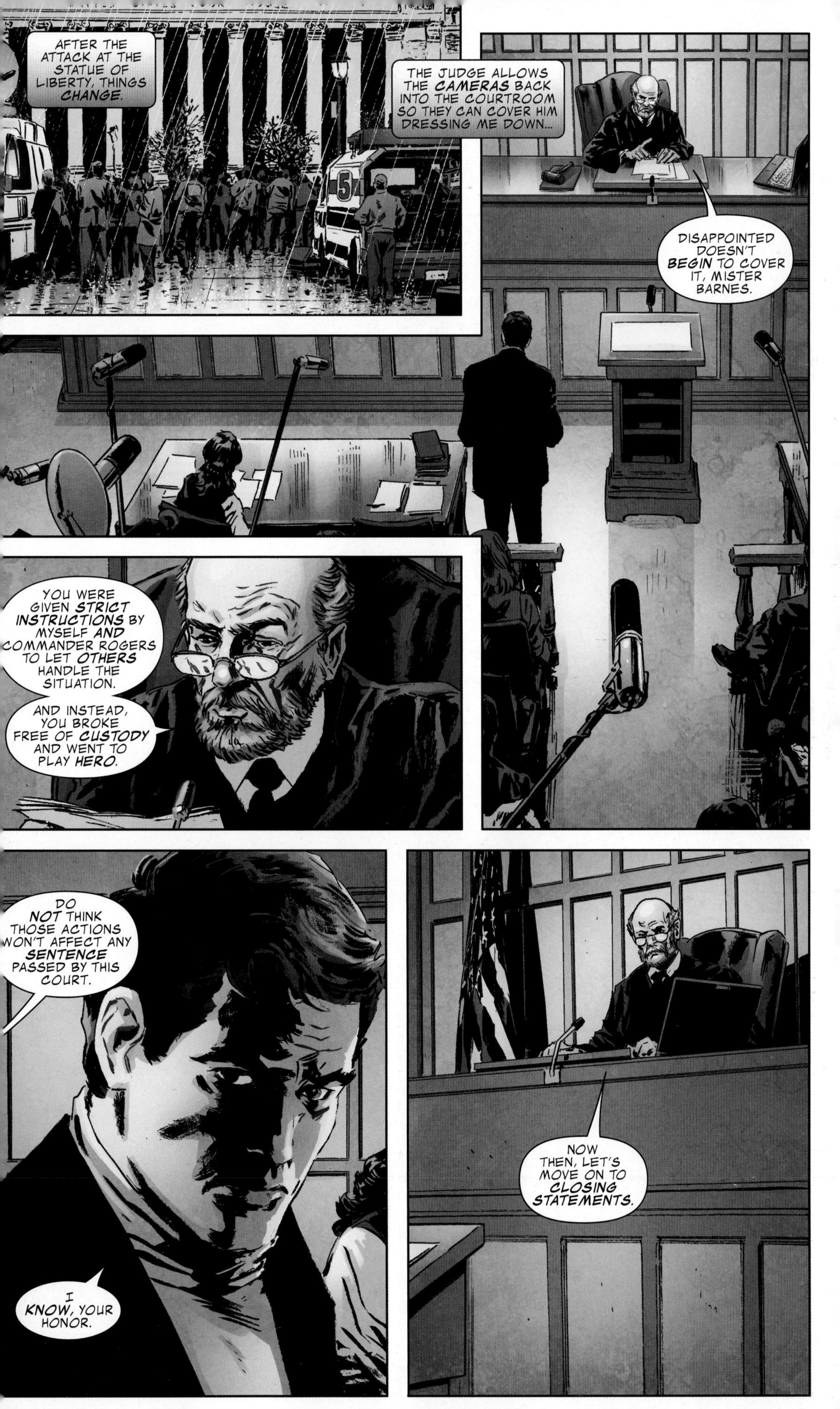
AFTER THE ATTACK AT THE STATUE OF LIBERTY, THINGS CHANGE.
THE JUDGE ALLOWS THE CAMERAS BACK INTO THE COURTROOM SO THEY CAN COVER HIM DRESSING ME DOWN...
DISAPPOINTED DOESN'T BEGIN TO COVER IT, MISTER BARNES.
YOU WERE GIVEN STRICT INSTRUCTIONS BY MYSELF AND COMMANDER ROGERS TO LET OTHERS HANDLE THE SITUATION.
AND INSTEAD, YOU BROKE FREE OF CUSTODY AND WENT TO PLAY HERO.
DO NOT THINK THOSE ACTIONS WON'T AFFECT ANY SENTENCE PASSED BY THIS COURT.
I KNOW, YOUR HONOR.
NOW THEN, LET'S MOVE ON TO CLOSING STATEMENTS.

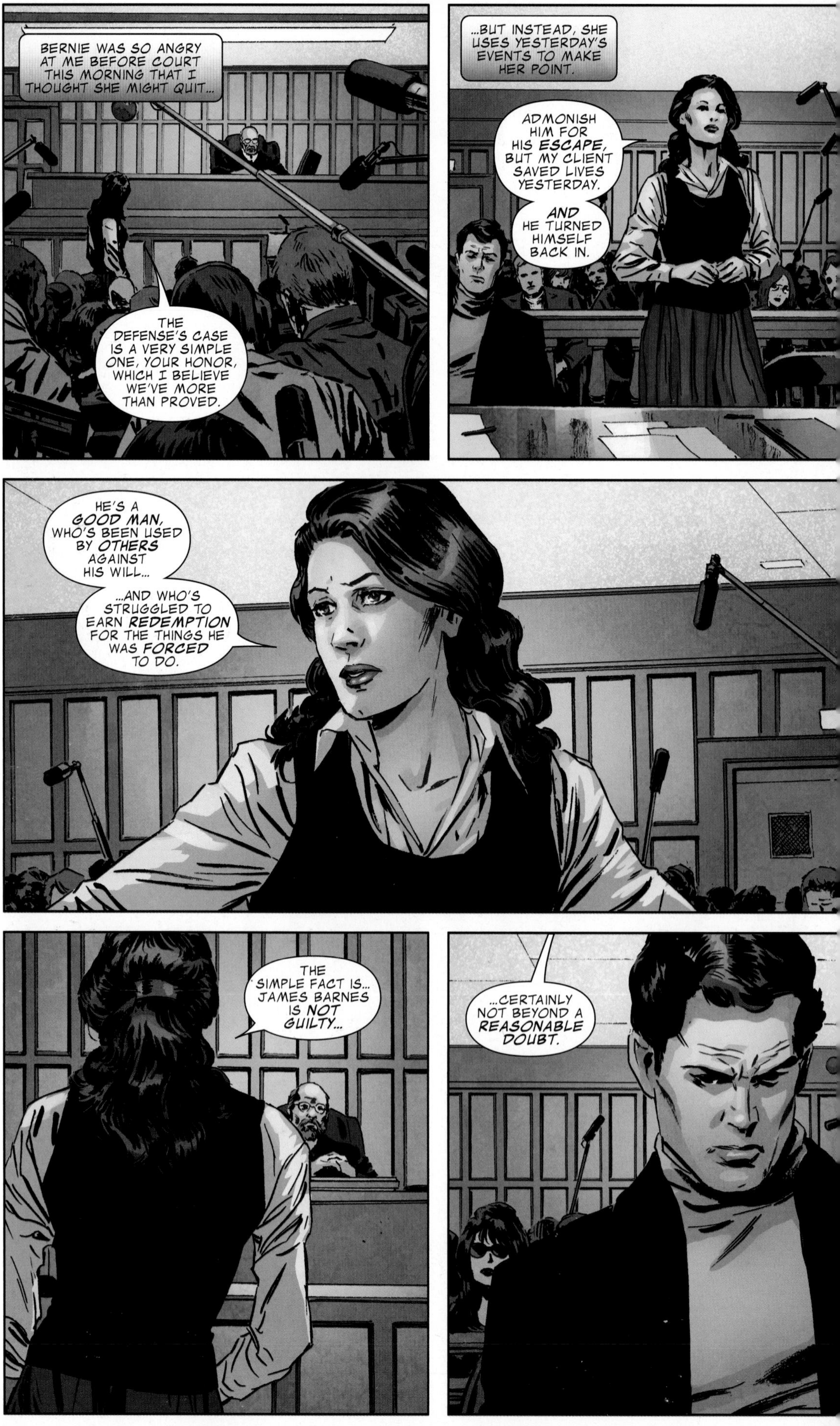
BERNIE WAS SO ANGRY AT ME BEFORE COURT THIS MORNING THAT I THOUGHT SHE MIGHT QUIT...
THE DEFENSE'S CASE IS A VERY SIMPLE ONE, YOUR HONOR, WHICH I BELIEVE WE'VE MORE THAN PROVED.
...BUT INSTEAD, SHE USES YESTERDAY'S EVENTS TO MAKE HER POINT.
ADMONISH HIM FOR HIS ESCAPE, BUT MY CLIENT SAVED LIVES YESTERDAY.
AND HE TURNED HIMSELF BACK IN.
HE'S A GOOD MAN, WHO'S BEEN USED BY OTHERS AGAINST HIS WILL...
...AND WHO'S STRUGGLED TO EARN REDEMPTION FOR THE THINGS HE WAS FORCED TO DO.
THE SIMPLE FACT IS... JAMES BARNES IS NOT GUILTY...
...CERTAINLY NOT BEYOND A REASONABLE DOUBT.

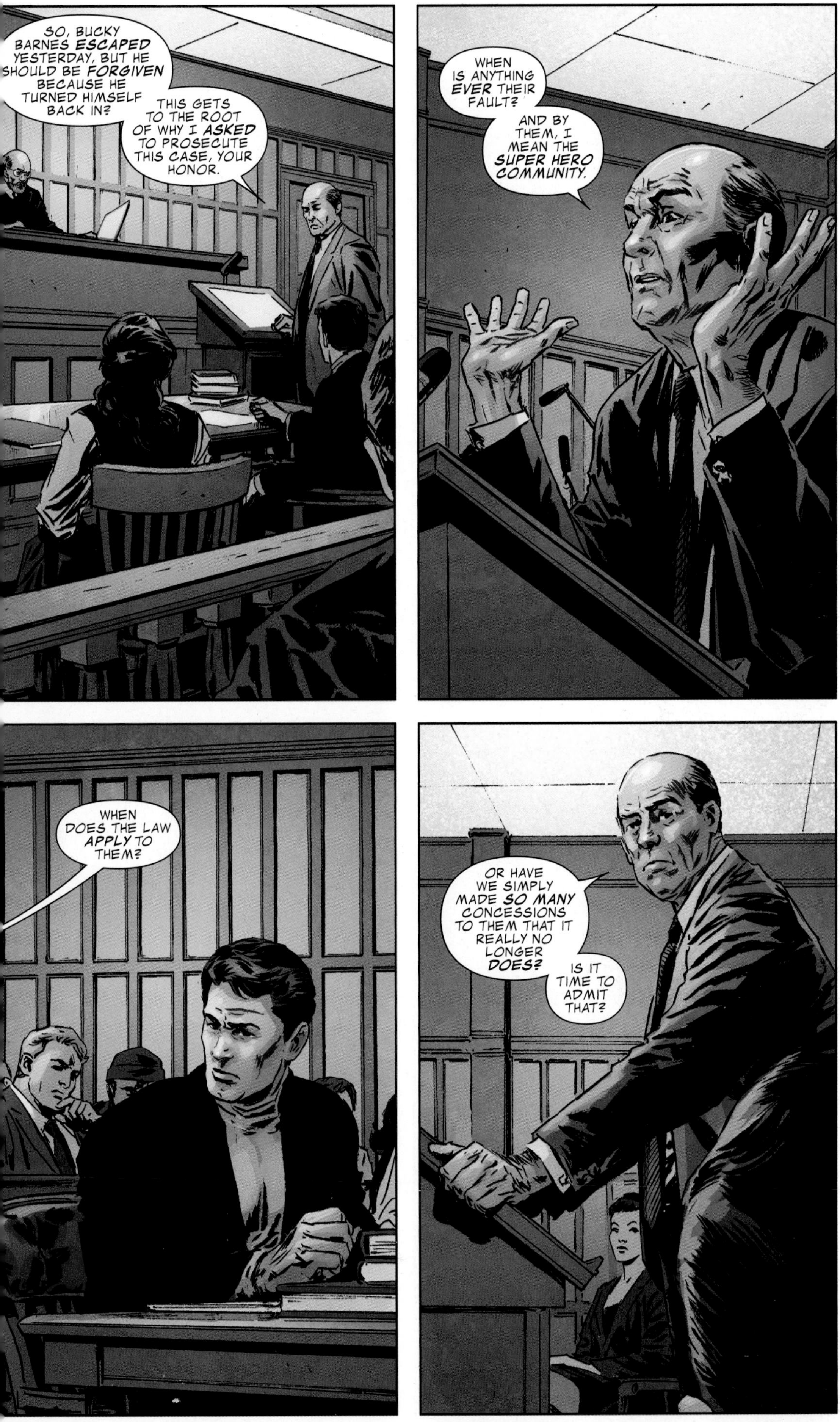
SO, BUCKY BARNES ESCAPED YESTERDAY, BUT HE SHOULD BE FORGIVEN BECAUSE HE TURNED HIMSELF BACK IN?
THIS GETS TO THE ROOT OF WHY I ASKED TO PROSECUTE THIS CASE, YOUR HONOR.
WHEN IS ANYTHING EVER THEIR FAULT?
AND BY THEM, I MEAN THE SUPER HERO COMMUNITY.
WHEN DOES THE LAW APPLY TO THEM?
OR HAVE WE SIMPLY MADE SO MANY CONCESSIONS TO THEM THAT IT REALLY NO LONGER DOES?
IS IT TIME TO ADMIT THAT?

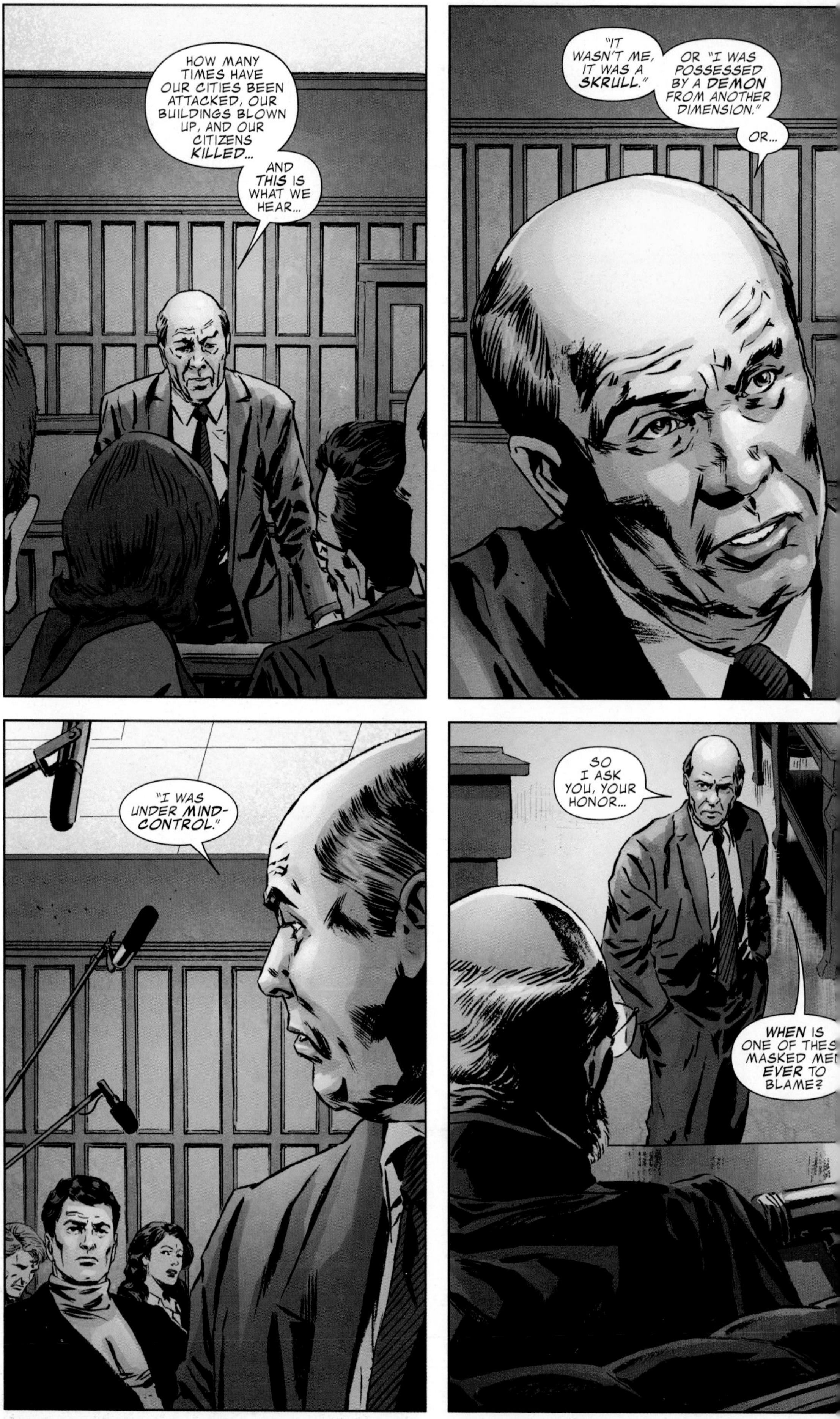
HOW MANY TIMES HAVE OUR CITIES BEEN ATTACKED, OUR BUILDINGS BLOWN UP, AND OUR CITIZENS KILLED...
AND THIS IS WHAT WE HEAR...
"IT WASN'T ME, IT WAS A SKRULL."
OR "I WAS POSSESSED BY A DEMON FROM ANOTHER DIMENSION."
OR...
"I WAS UNDER MIND-CONTROL."
SO I ASK YOU, YOUR HONOR...
WHEN IS ONE OF THES MASKED ME EVER TO BLAME?

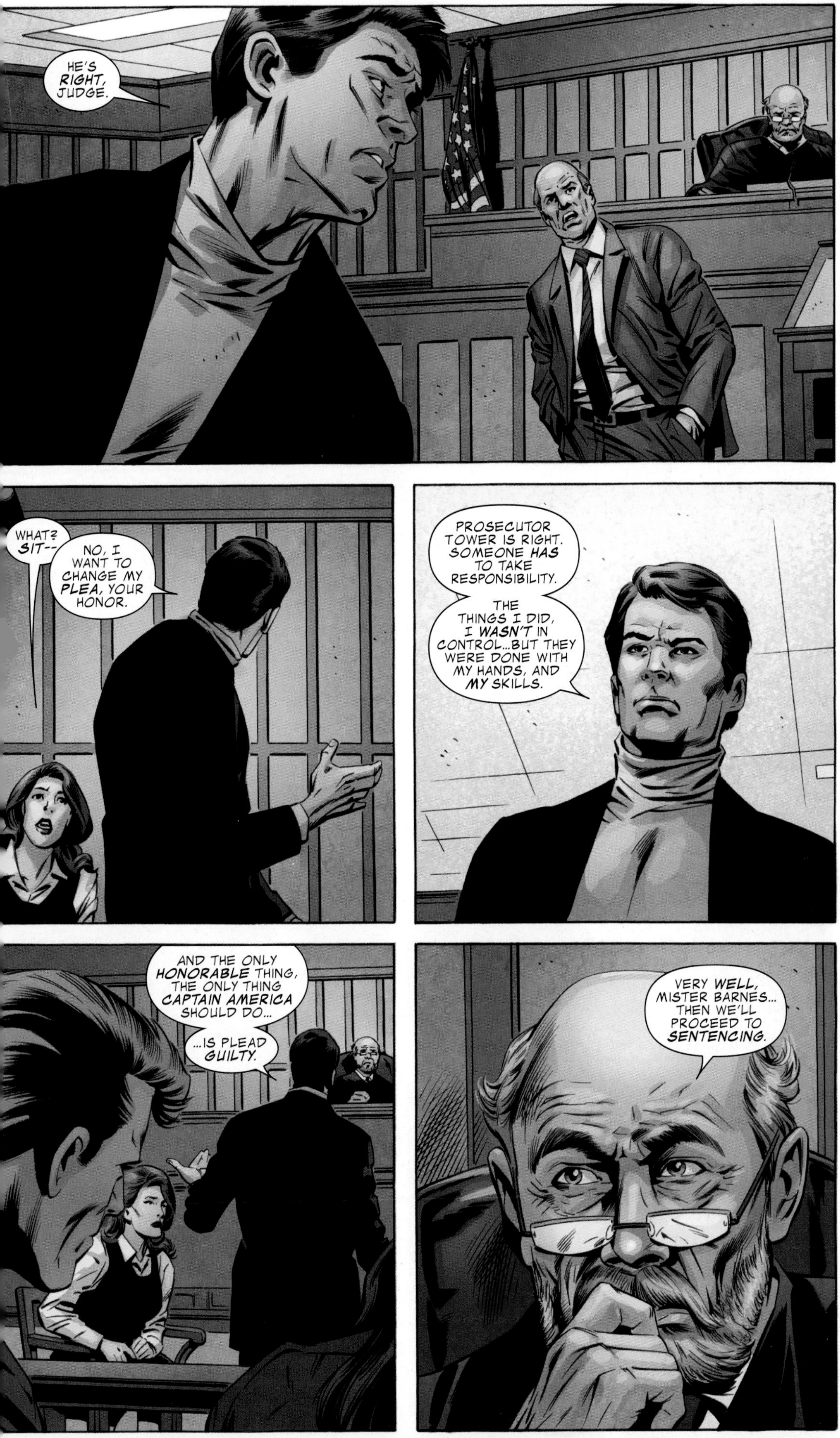
HE'S RIGHT, JUDGE.
WHAT? SIT--
NO, I WANT TO CHANGE MY PLEA, YOUR HONOR.
PROSECUTOR TOWER IS RIGHT. SOMEONE HAS TO TAKE RESPONSIBILITY.
THE THINGS I DID, I WASN'T IN CONTROL...BUT THEY WERE DONE WITH MY HANDS, AND MY SKILLS.
AND THE ONLY HONORABLE THING, THE ONLY THING CAPTAIN AMERICA SHOULD DO...
...IS PLEAD GUILTY.
VERY WELL, MISTER BARNES... THEN WE'LL PROCEED TO SENTENCING.

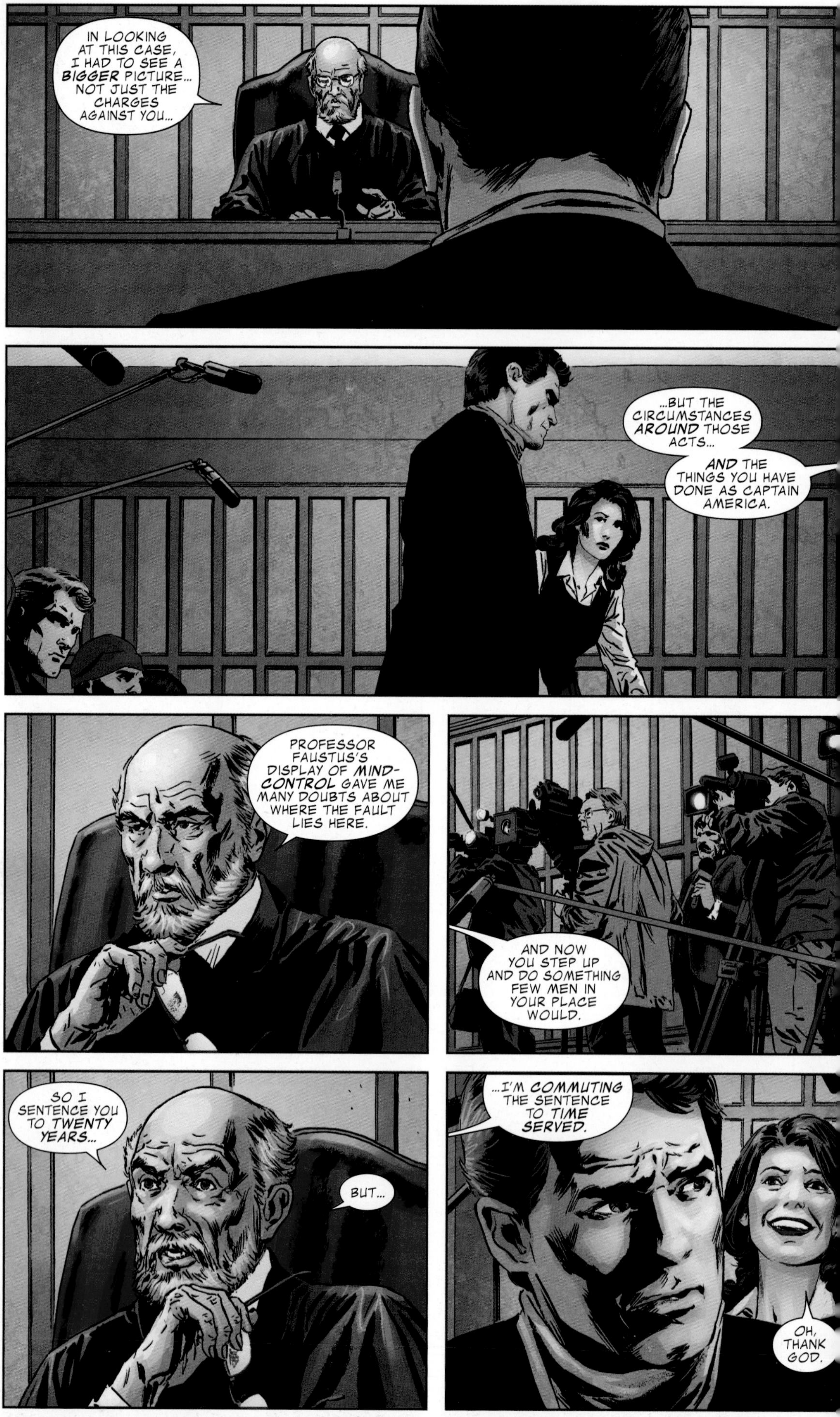
IN LOOKING AT THIS CASE, I HAD TO SEE A BIGGER PICTURE... NOT JUST THE CHARGES AGAINST YOU...
...BUT THE CIRCUMSTANCES AROUND THOSE ACTS...
AND THE THINGS YOU HAVE DONE AS CAPTAIN AMERICA.
PROFESSOR FAUSTUS'S DISPLAY OF MIND-CONTROL GAVE ME MANY DOUBTS ABOUT WHERE THE FAULT LIES HERE.
AND NOW YOU STEP UP AND DO SOMETHING FEW MEN IN YOUR PLACE WOULD.
SO I SENTENCE YOU TO TWENTY YEARS...
BUT...
...I'M COMMUTING THE SENTENCE TO TIME SERVED.
OH, THANK GOD.

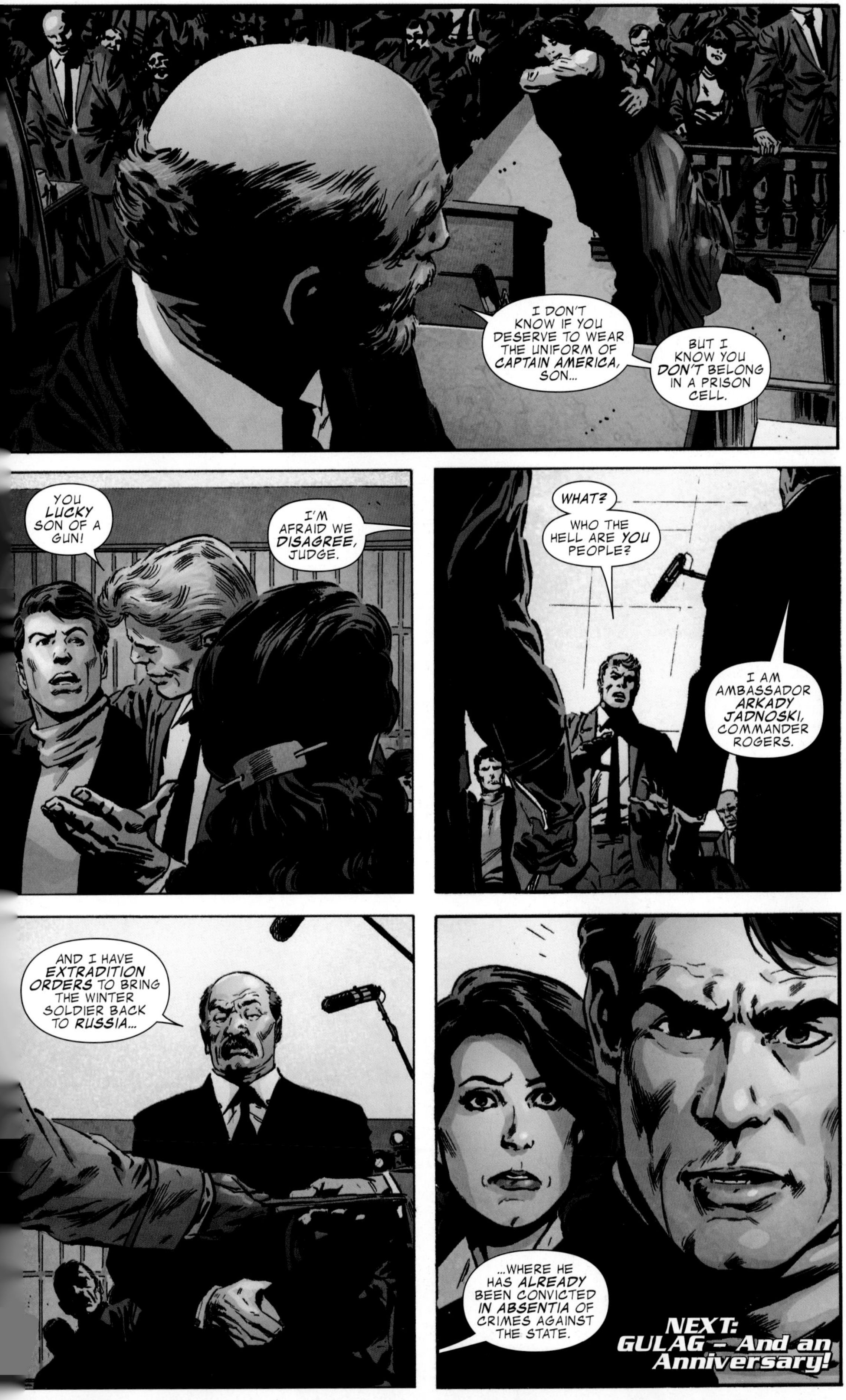
I DON'T KNOW IF YOU DESERVE TO WEAR THE UNIFORM OF CAPTAIN AMERICA, SON...
BUT I KNOW YOU DON'T BELONG IN A PRISON CELL.
YOU LUCKY SON OF A GUN!
I'M AFRAID WE DISAGREE, JUDGE.
WHAT?
WHO THE HELL ARE YOU PEOPLE?
I AM AMBASSADOR ARKADY JADNOSKI, COMMANDER ROGERS.
AND I HAVE EXTRADITION ORDERS TO BRING THE WINTER SOLDIER BACK TO RUSSIA...
...WHERE HE HAS ALREADY BEEN CONVICTED IN ABSENTIA OF CRIMES AGAINST THE STATE.
NEXT: GULAG – And an Anniversary!

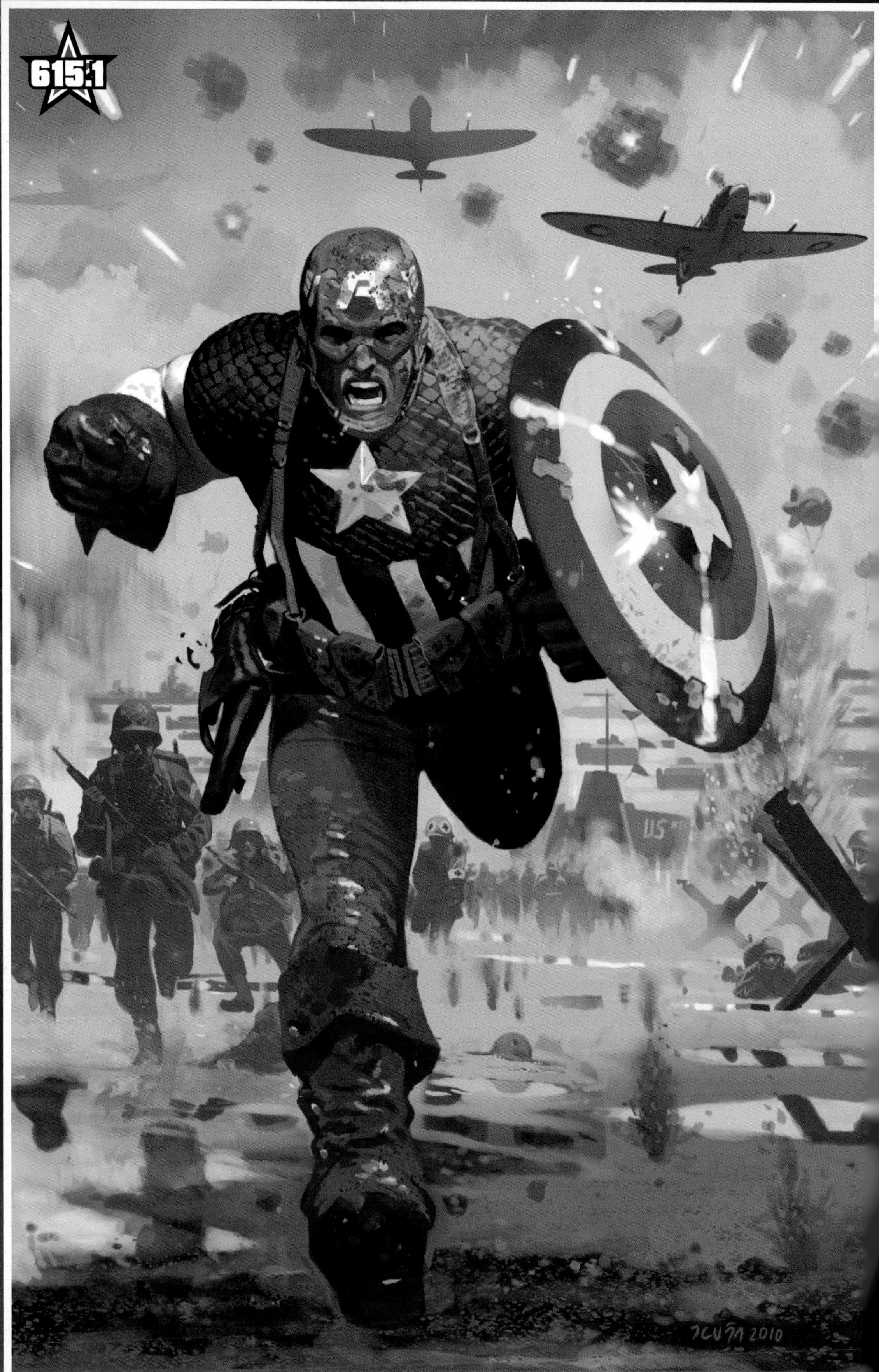
615.1
US
JCUJM 2010

AROUND AND ROUND

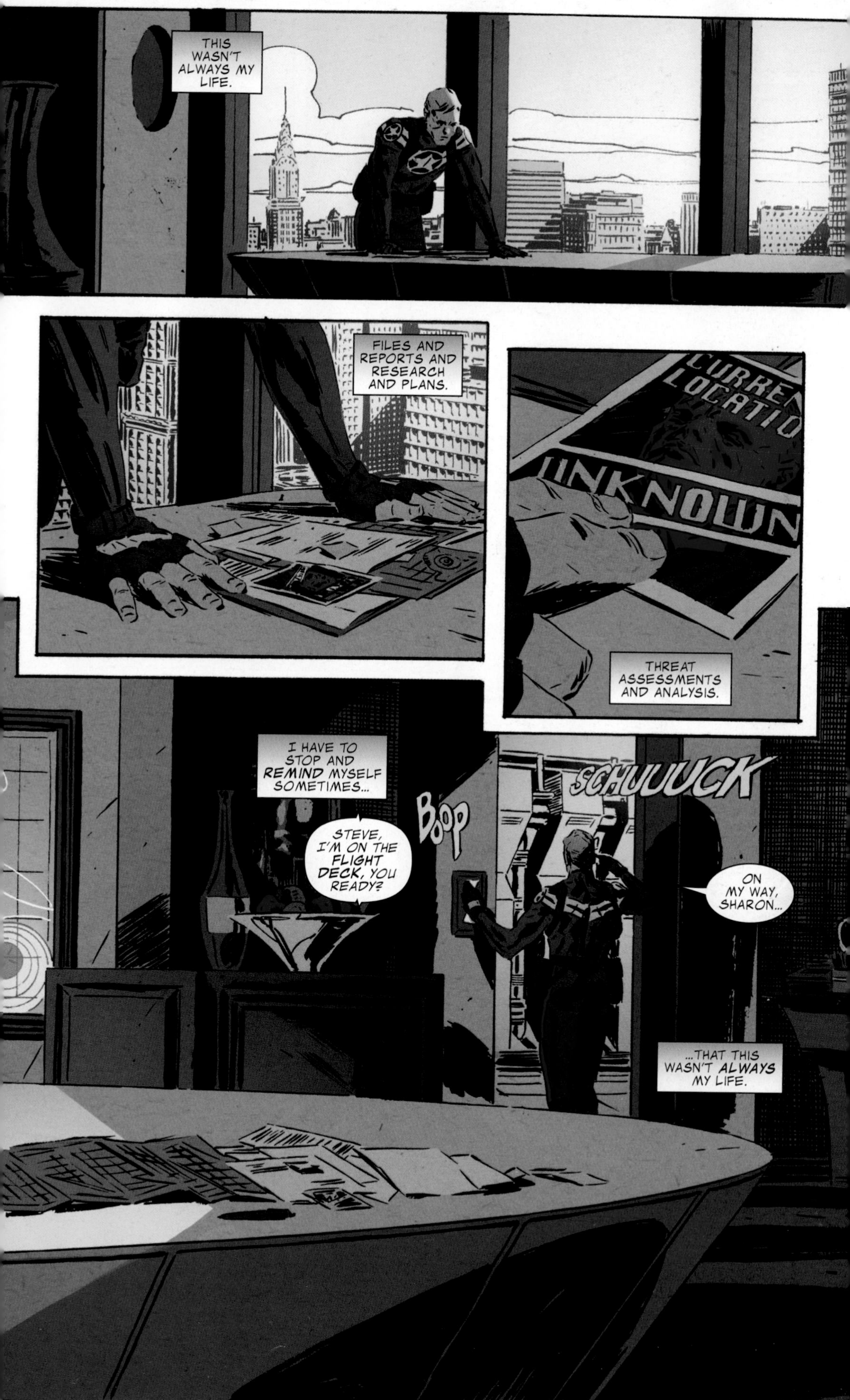
THIS WASN'T ALWAYS MY LIFE.
FILES AND REPORTS AND RESEARCH AND PLANS.
CURRENT LOCATIO
UNKNOWN
THREAT ASSESSMENTS AND ANALYSIS.
I HAVE TO STOP AND REMIND MYSELF SOMETIMES...
STEVE, I'M ON THE FLIGHT DECK, YOU READY?
BOOP
SCHUUUCK
ON MY WAY, SHARON...
...THAT THIS WASN'T ALWAYS MY LIFE.

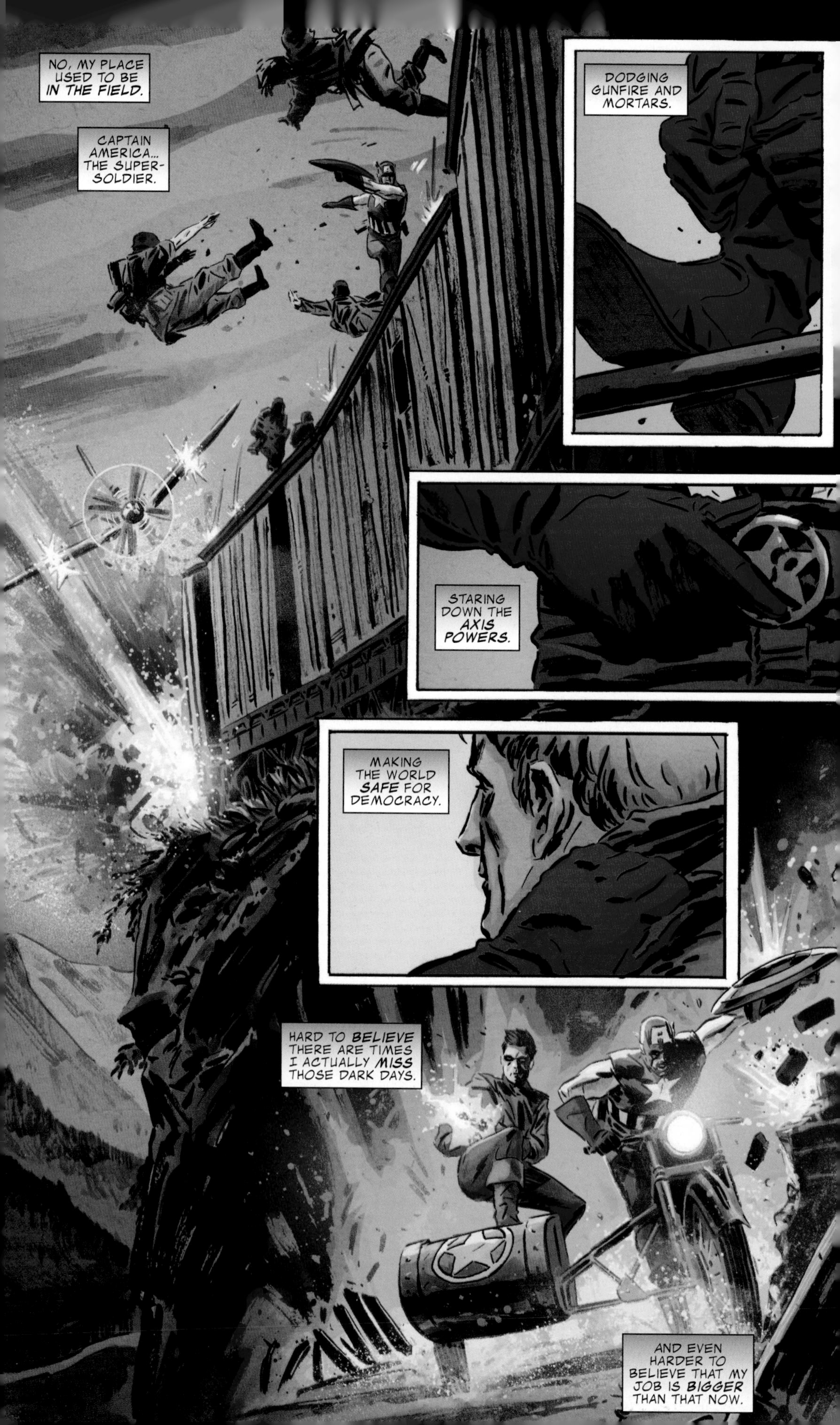
NO, MY PLACE USED TO BE IN THE FIELD.
CAPTAIN AMERICA... THE SUPER-SOLDIER.
DODGING GUNFIRE AND MORTARS.
STARING DOWN THE AXIS POWERS.
MAKING THE WORLD SAFE FOR DEMOCRACY.
HARD TO BELIEVE THERE ARE TIMES I ACTUALLY MISS THOSE DARK DAYS.
AND EVEN HARDER TO BELIEVE THAT MY JOB IS BIGGER THAN THAT NOW.

How are his **stats** looking, Malus?

Excellent. I think this one might actually be a **worthy** candidate. The procedure went **perfectly...**

...as you can see for yourself.

Impressive. And he's as strong as **the real thing?**

WHMP

THNK

"Stronger... and probably **twice as fast.**"

DDABUDDABUDDABUDDABUDDABUDDABUDDABUDDABUDDAB

"**Good,** that's **exactly** what we need."

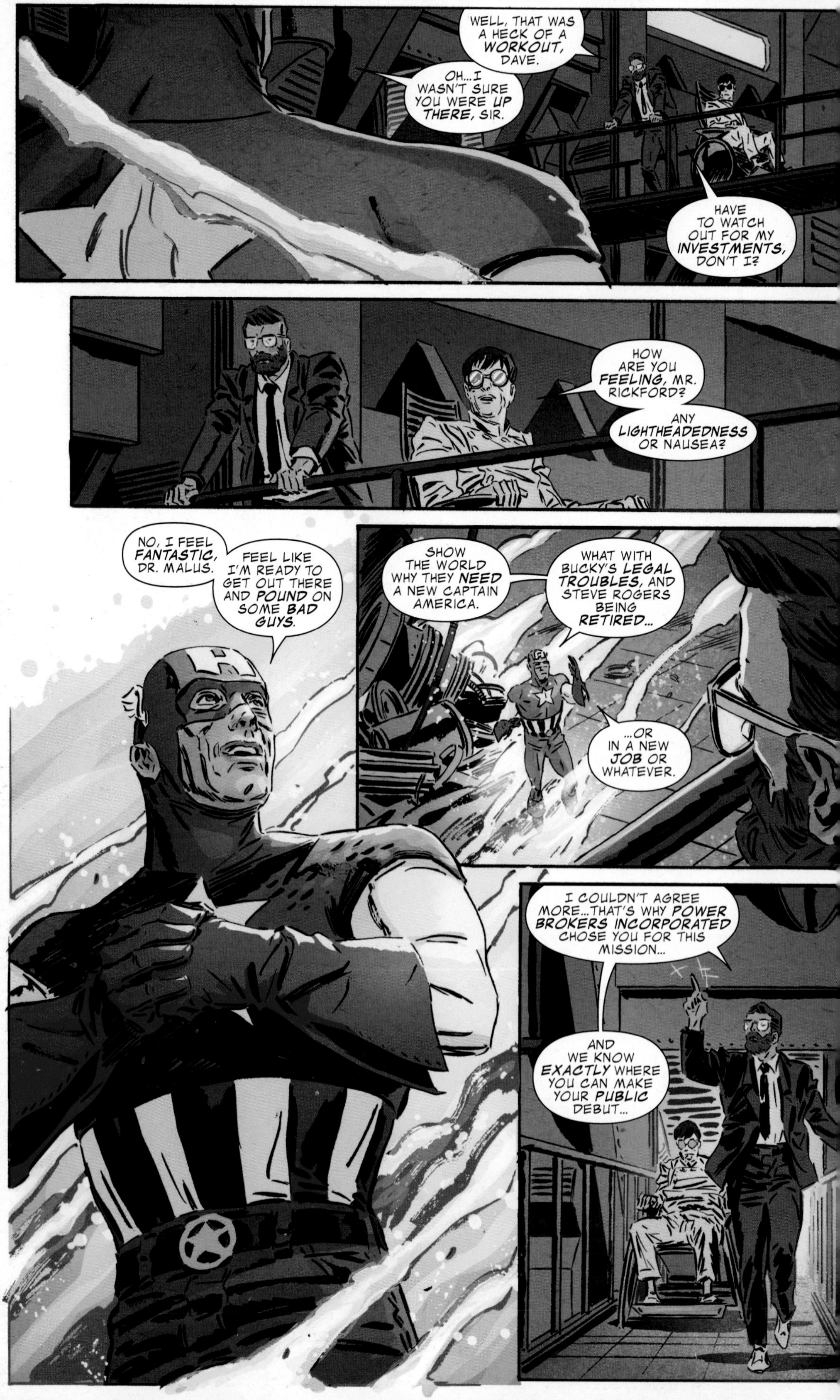

WELL, THAT WAS A HECK OF A WORKOUT, DAVE.
OH...I WASN'T SURE YOU WERE UP THERE, SIR.
HAVE TO WATCH OUT FOR MY INVESTMENTS, DON'T I?
HOW ARE YOU FEELING, MR. RICKFORD?
ANY LIGHTHEADEDNESS OR NAUSEA?
NO, I FEEL FANTASTIC, DR. MALUS.
FEEL LIKE I'M READY TO GET OUT THERE AND POUND ON SOME BAD GUYS.
SHOW THE WORLD WHY THEY NEED A NEW CAPTAIN AMERICA.
WHAT WITH BUCKY'S LEGAL TROUBLES, AND STEVE ROGERS BEING RETIRED...
...OR IN A NEW JOB OR WHATEVER.
I COULDN'T AGREE MORE...THAT'S WHY POWER BROKERS INCORPORATED CHOSE YOU FOR THIS MISSION...
AND WE KNOW EXACTLY WHERE YOU CAN MAKE YOUR PUBLIC DEBUT...

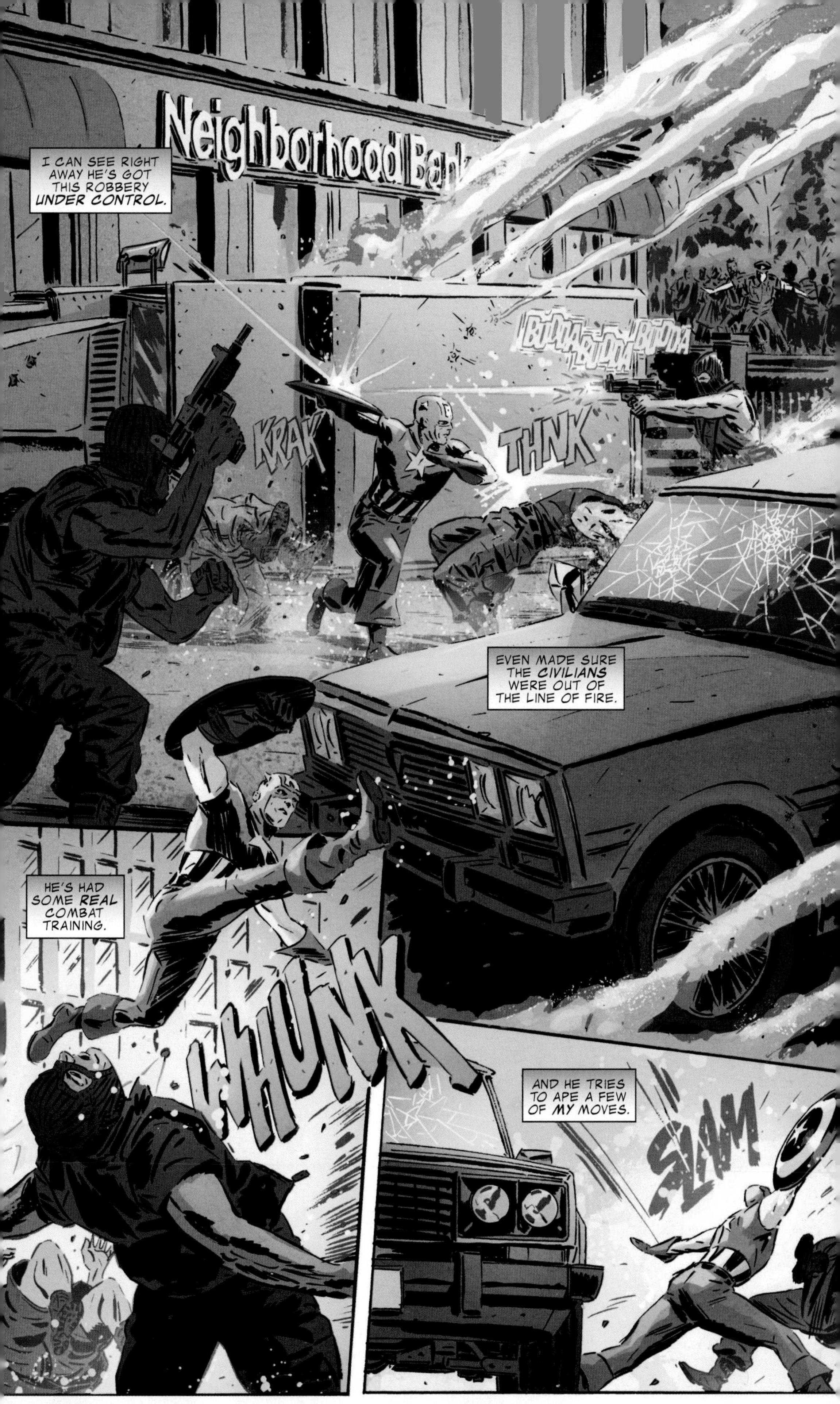
Neighborhood Bank
I CAN SEE RIGHT AWAY HE'S GOT THIS ROBBERY UNDER CONTROL.
BUDDABUDDA BUDDA
KRAK
THNK
EVEN MADE SURE THE CIVILIANS WERE OUT OF THE LINE OF FIRE.
HE'S HAD SOME REAL COMBAT TRAINING.
WHUNK
AND HE TRIES TO APE A FEW OF MY MOVES.
SLAM

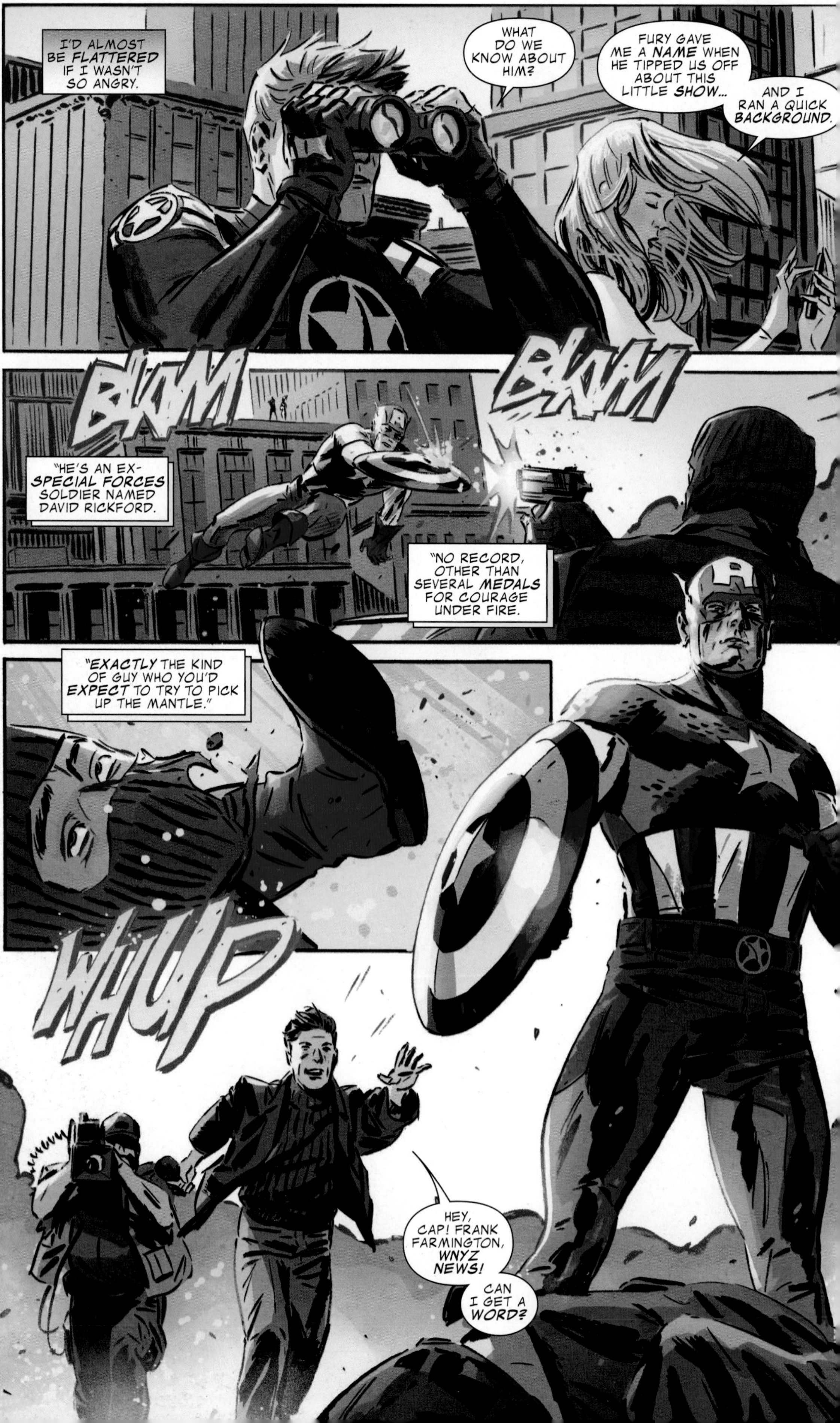
I'D ALMOST BE FLATTERED IF I WASN'T SO ANGRY.
WHAT DO WE KNOW ABOUT HIM?
FURY GAVE ME A NAME WHEN HE TIPPED US OFF ABOUT THIS LITTLE SHOW...
AND I RAN A QUICK BACKGROUND.
BLAM
BLAM
"HE'S AN EX-SPECIAL FORCES SOLDIER NAMED DAVID RICKFORD.
"NO RECORD, OTHER THAN SEVERAL MEDALS FOR COURAGE UNDER FIRE.
"EXACTLY THE KIND OF GUY WHO YOU'D EXPECT TO TRY TO PICK UP THE MANTLE."
WHUP
HEY, CAP! FRANK FARMINGTON, WNYZ NEWS!
CAN I GET A WORD?

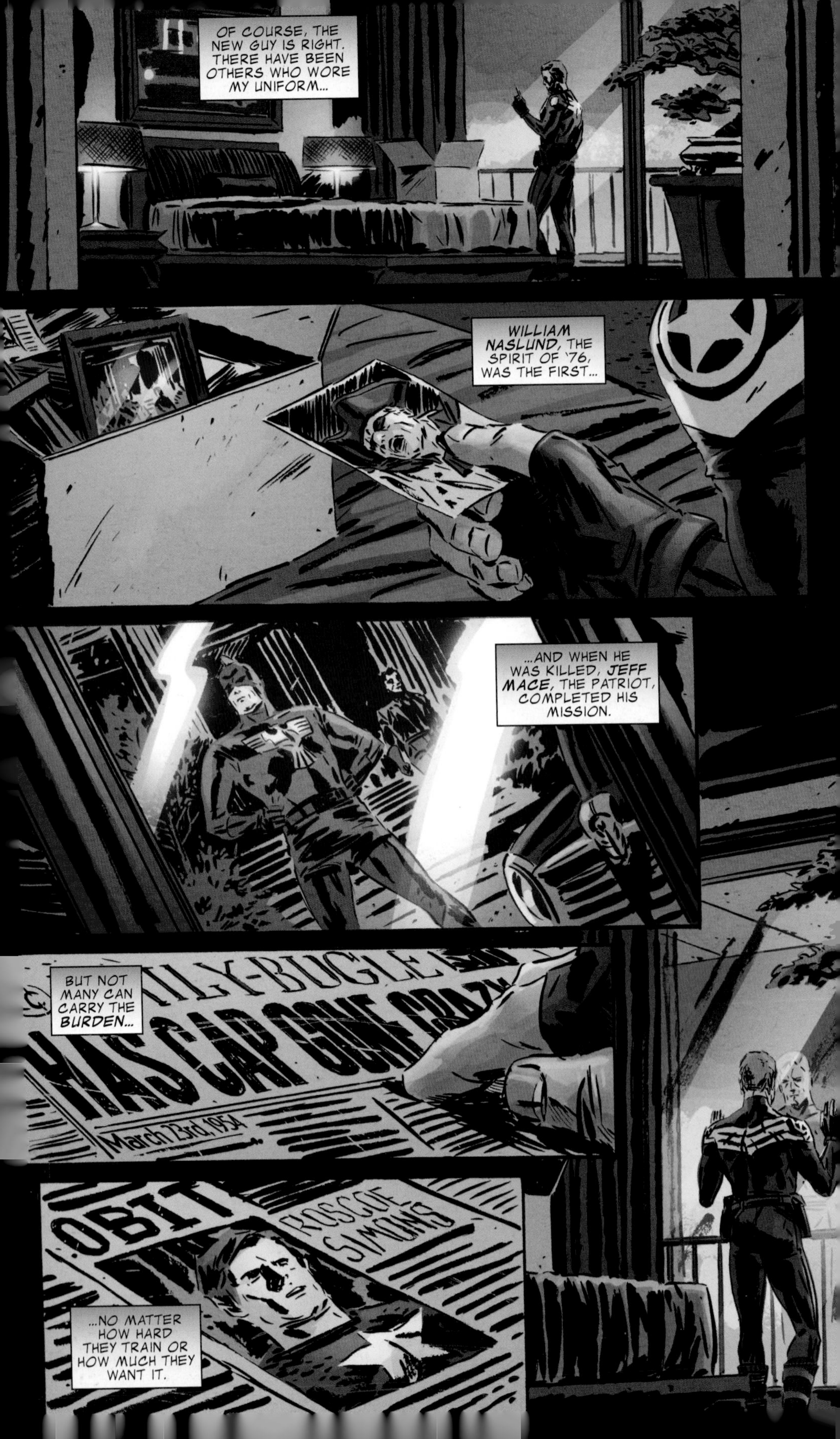

OF COURSE, THE NEW GUY IS RIGHT. THERE HAVE BEEN OTHERS WHO WORE MY UNIFORM...
WILLIAM NASLUND, THE SPIRIT OF '76, WAS THE FIRST...
...AND WHEN HE WAS KILLED, JEFF MACE, THE PATRIOT, COMPLETED HIS MISSION.
BUT NOT MANY CAN CARRY THE BURDEN...
ILY-BUGLE
HAS CAP GONE CRAZY
March 23rd, 1954
OBIT
ROSCOE SIMONS
...NO MATTER HOW HARD THEY TRAIN OR HOW MUCH THEY WANT IT.

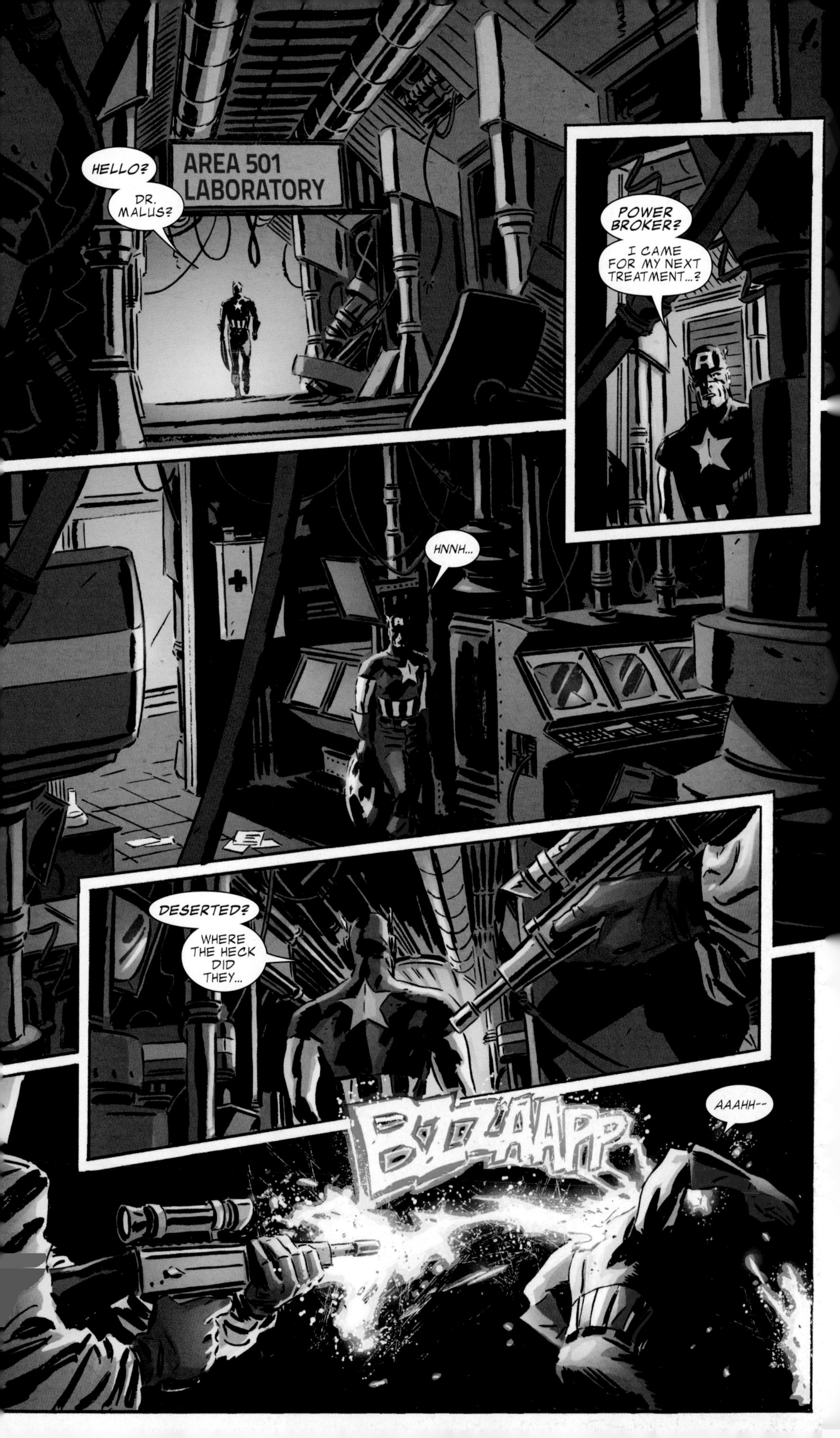
AREA 501
LABORATORY
HELLO?
DR. MALUS?
POWER BROKER?
I CAME FOR MY NEXT TREATMENT...?
HNNH...
DESERTED?
WHERE THE HECK DID THEY...
BZZAAPP
AAAHH--

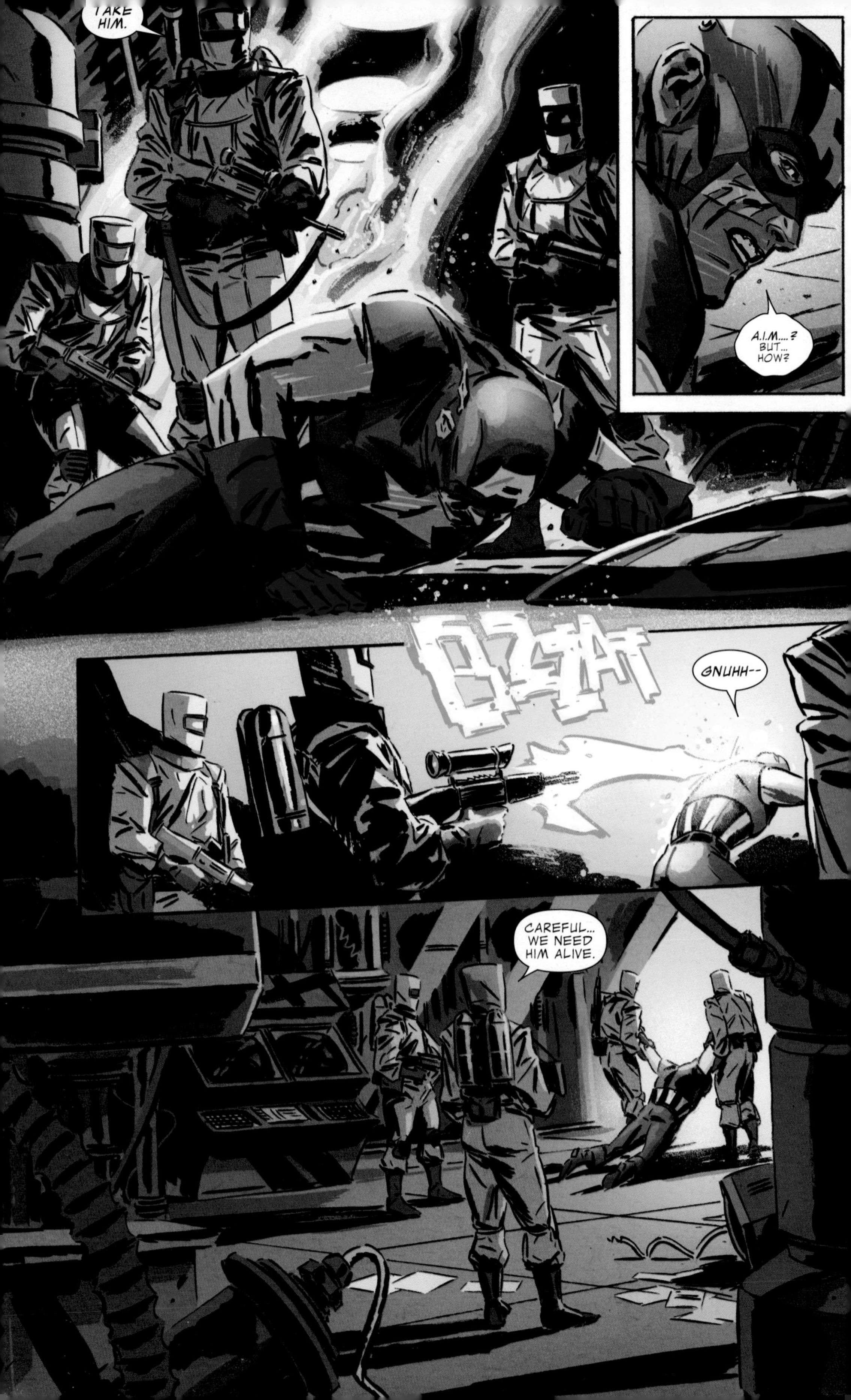
TAKE HIM.
A.I.M....? BUT... HOW?
BZZAT
GNUHH--
CAREFUL... WE NEED HIM ALIVE.

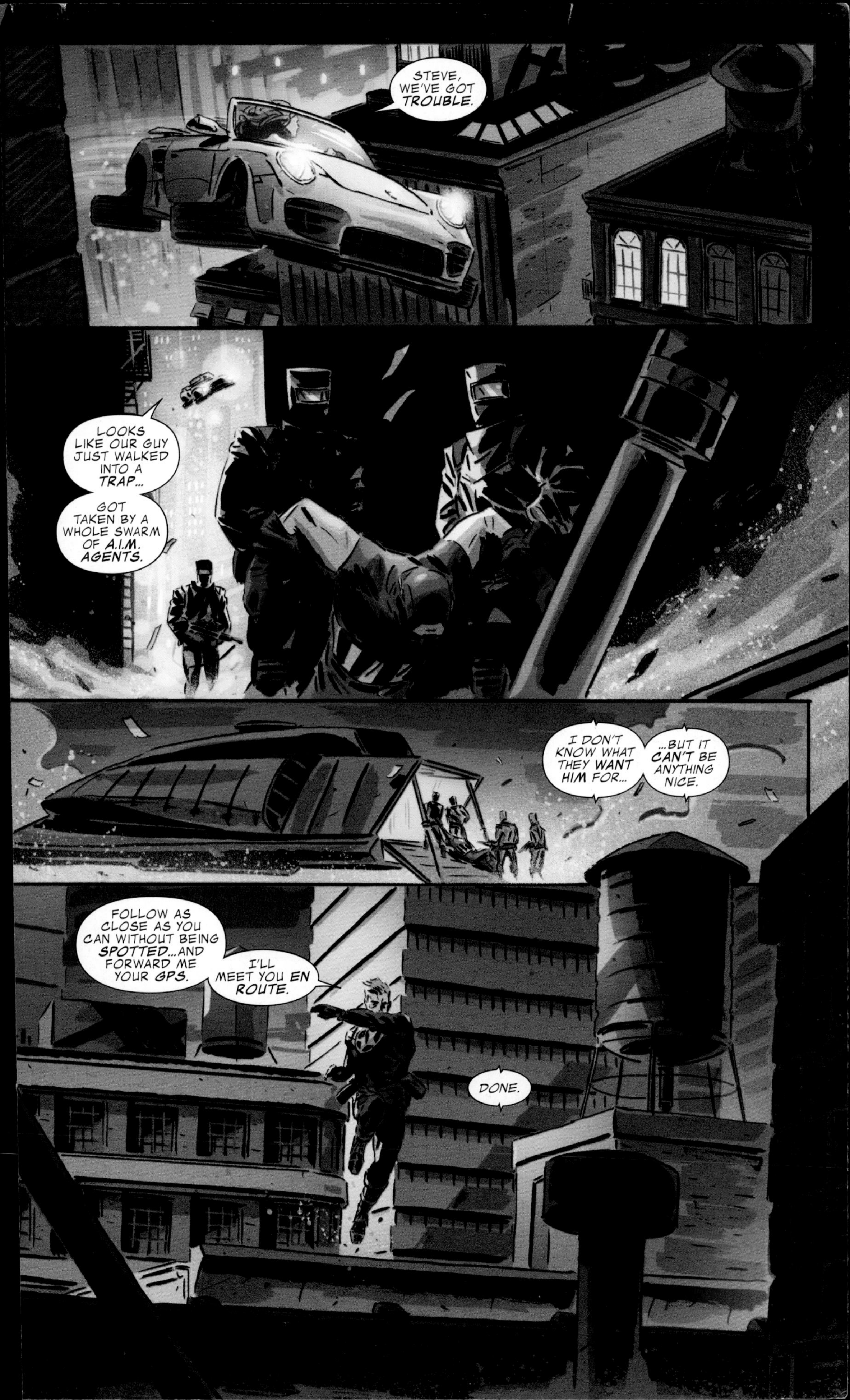
STEVE, WE'VE GOT TROUBLE.
LOOKS LIKE OUR GUY JUST WALKED INTO A TRAP...
GOT TAKEN BY A WHOLE SWARM OF A.I.M. AGENTS.
I DON'T KNOW WHAT THEY WANT HIM FOR...
...BUT IT CAN'T BE ANYTHING NICE.
FOLLOW AS CLOSE AS YOU CAN WITHOUT BEING SPOTTED...AND FORWARD ME YOUR GPS.
I'LL MEET YOU EN ROUTE.
DONE.

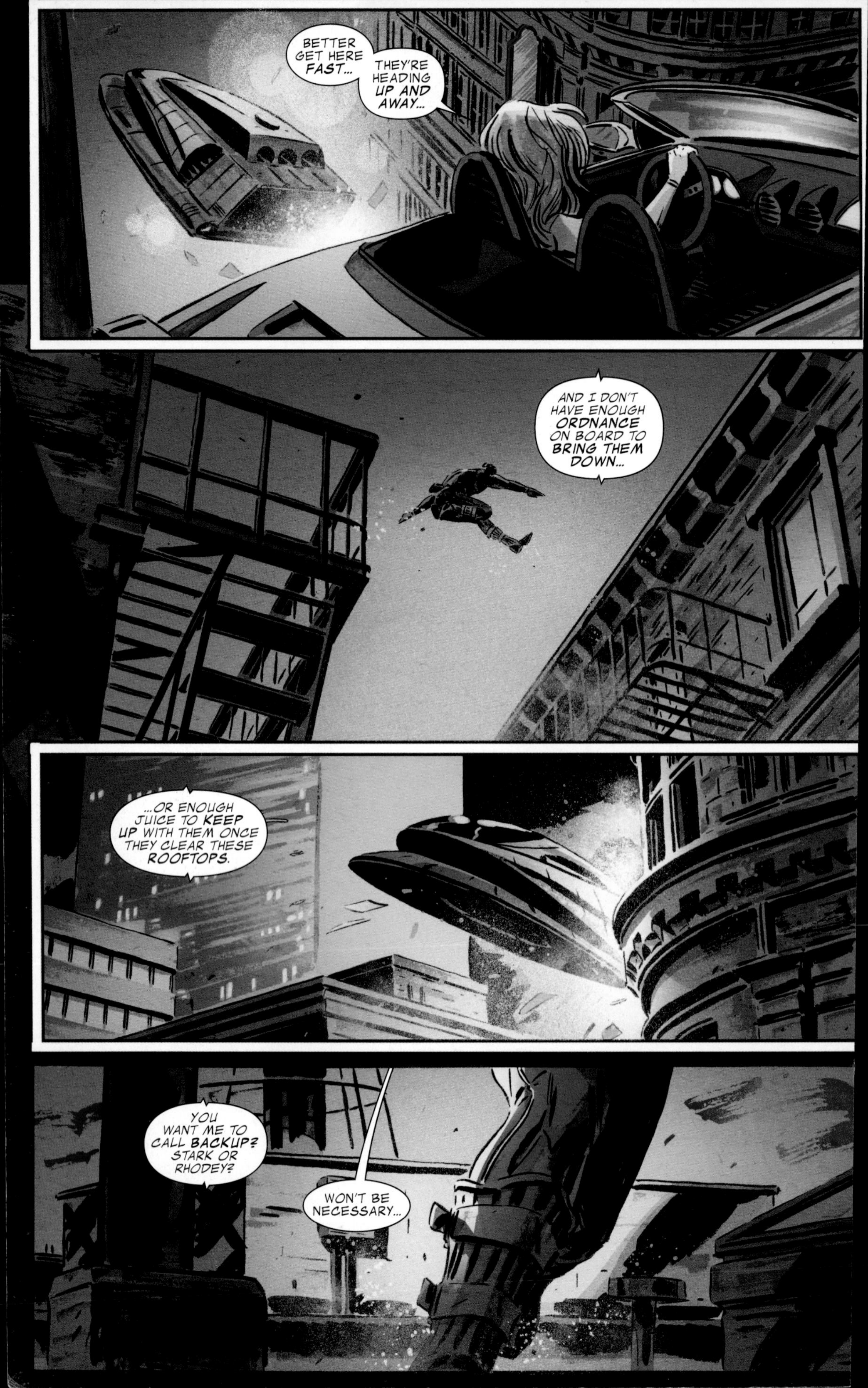
BETTER GET HERE FAST...
THEY'RE HEADING UP AND AWAY...
AND I DON'T HAVE ENOUGH ORDNANCE ON BOARD TO BRING THEM DOWN...
...OR ENOUGH JUICE TO KEEP UP WITH THEM ONCE THEY CLEAR THESE ROOFTOPS.
YOU WANT ME TO CALL BACKUP? STARK OR RHODEY?
WON'T BE NECESSARY...

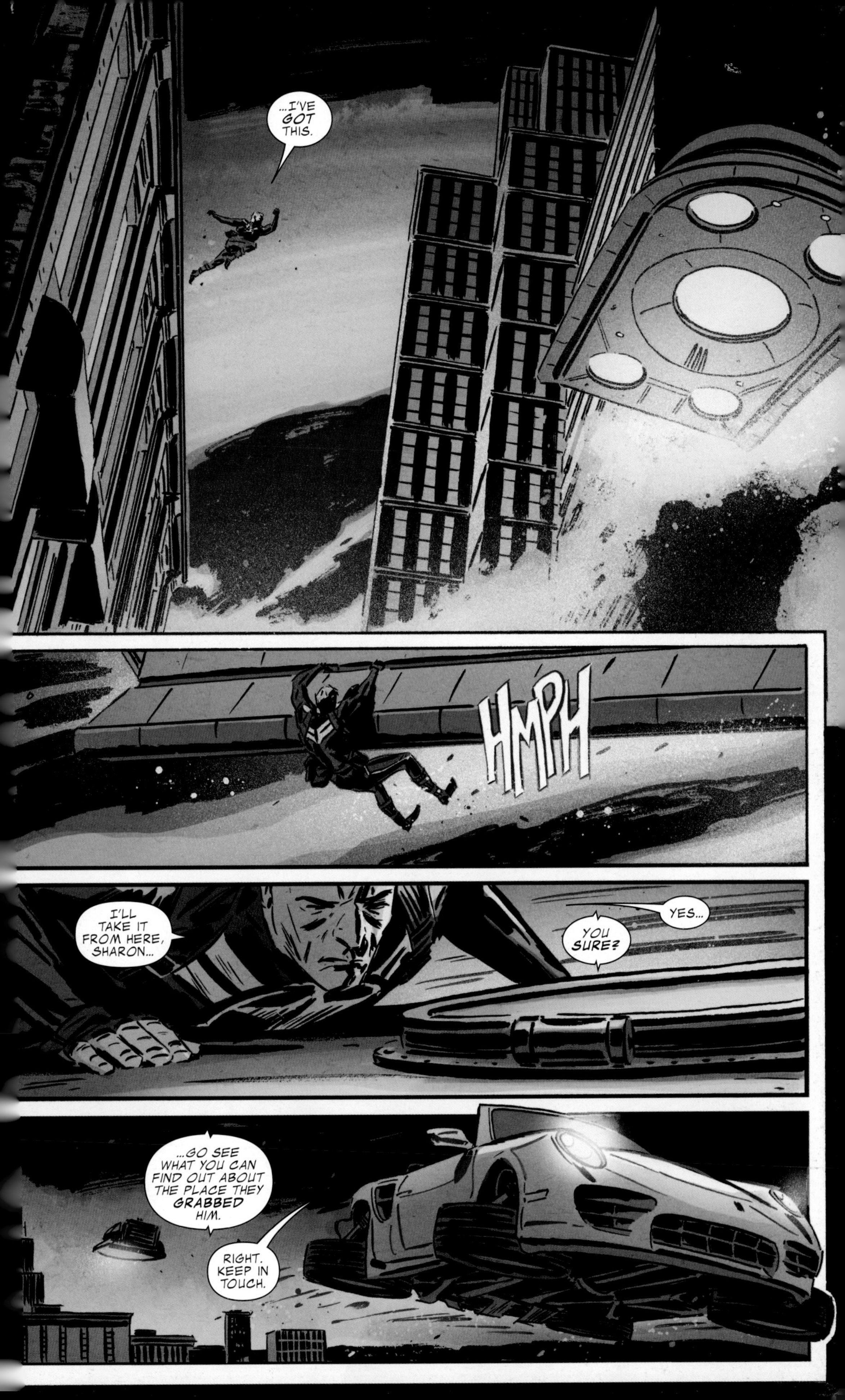
...I'VE GOT THIS.
HMPH
I'LL TAKE IT FROM HERE, SHARON...
YES...
YOU SURE?
...GO SEE WHAT YOU CAN FIND OUT ABOUT THE PLACE THEY GRABBED HIM.
RIGHT. KEEP IN TOUCH.

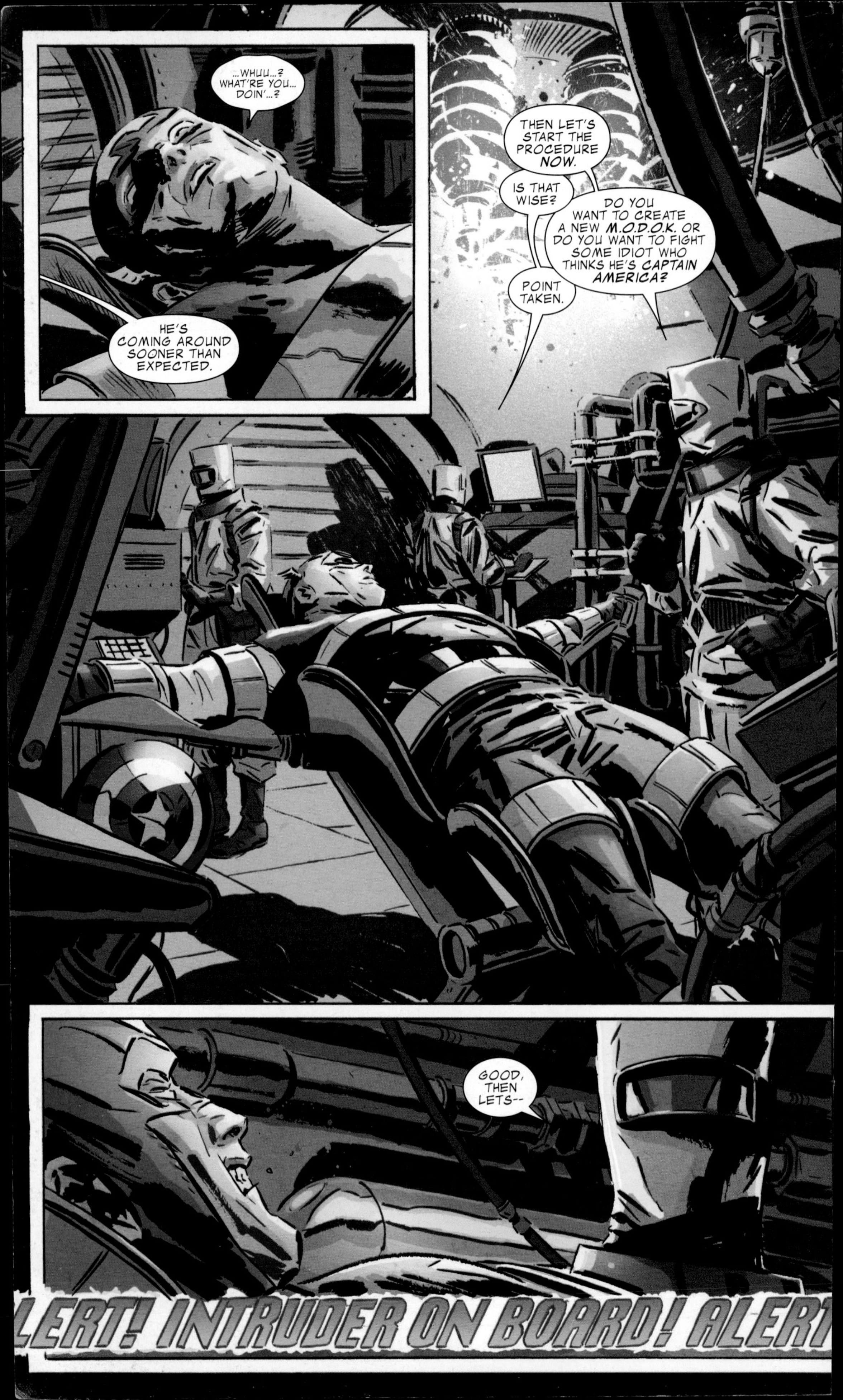

...WHUU...? WHAT'RE YOU... DOIN'...?
HE'S COMING AROUND SOONER THAN EXPECTED.
THEN LET'S START THE PROCEDURE NOW.
IS THAT WISE?
DO YOU WANT TO CREATE A NEW M.O.D.O.K. OR DO YOU WANT TO FIGHT SOME IDIOT WHO THINKS HE'S CAPTAIN AMERICA?
POINT TAKEN.
GOOD, THEN LETS--
LERT! INTRUDER ON BOARD! ALERT

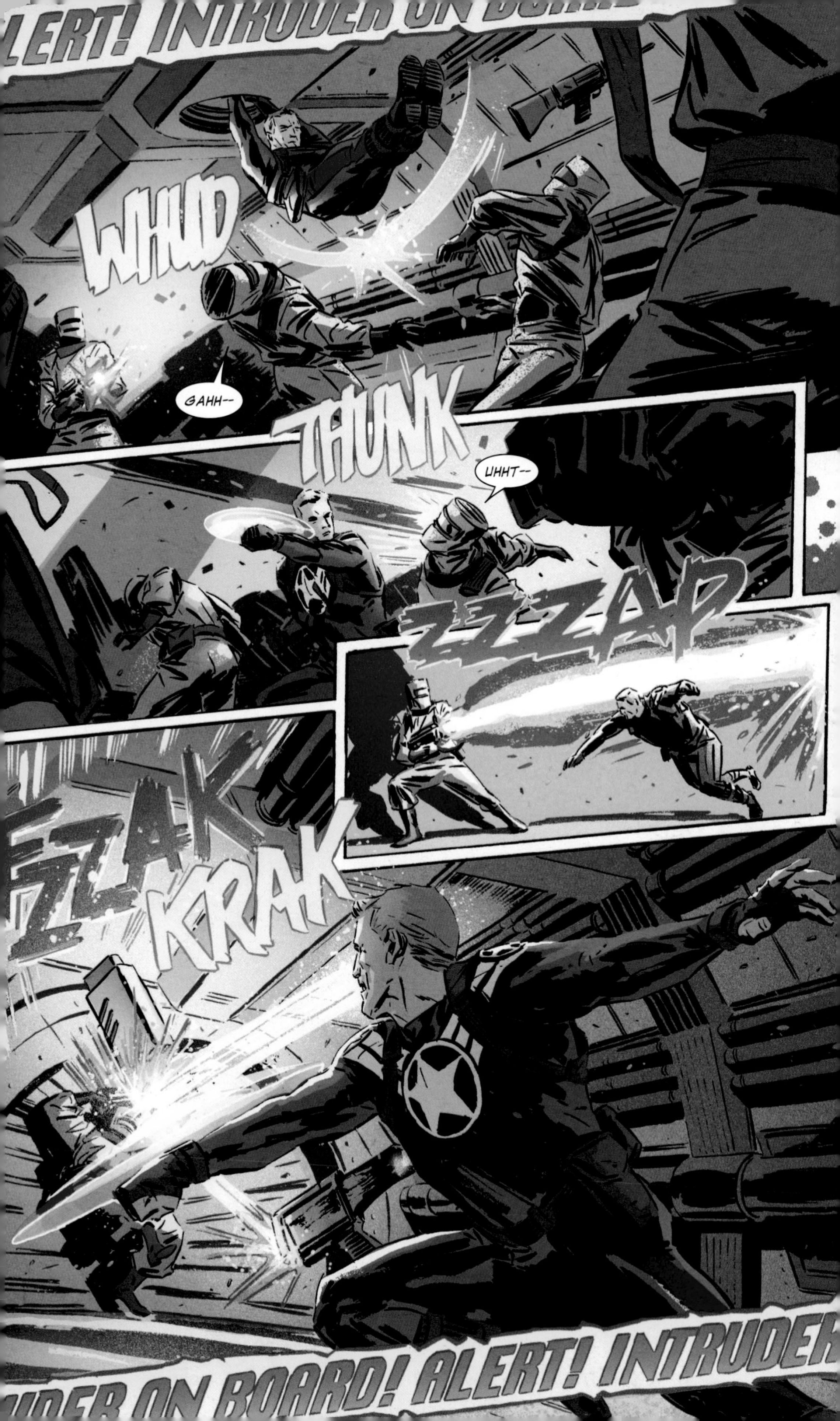

LERT! INTRUDER ON BOA
WHUD
GAHH--
THUNK
UHHT--
ZZZAP
ZZAK
KRAK
UDER ON BOARD! ALERT! INTRUDER

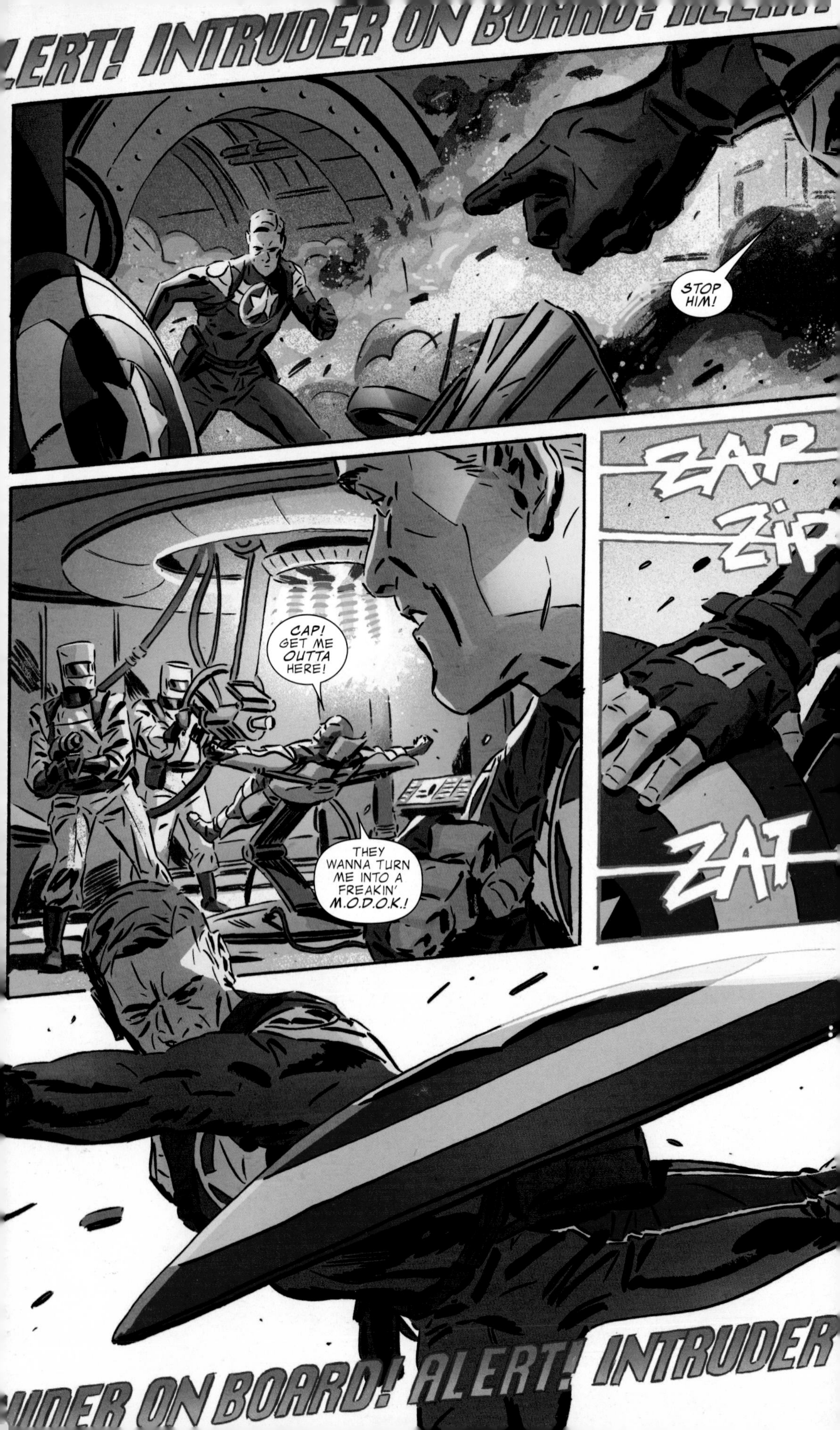
ALERT! INTRUDER ON BOARD! ALERT!
STOP HIM!
CAP! GET ME OUTTA HERE!
THEY WANNA TURN ME INTO A FREAKIN' M.O.D.O.K.!
ZAP
ZIP
ZAT
UDER ON BOARD! ALERT! INTRUDER

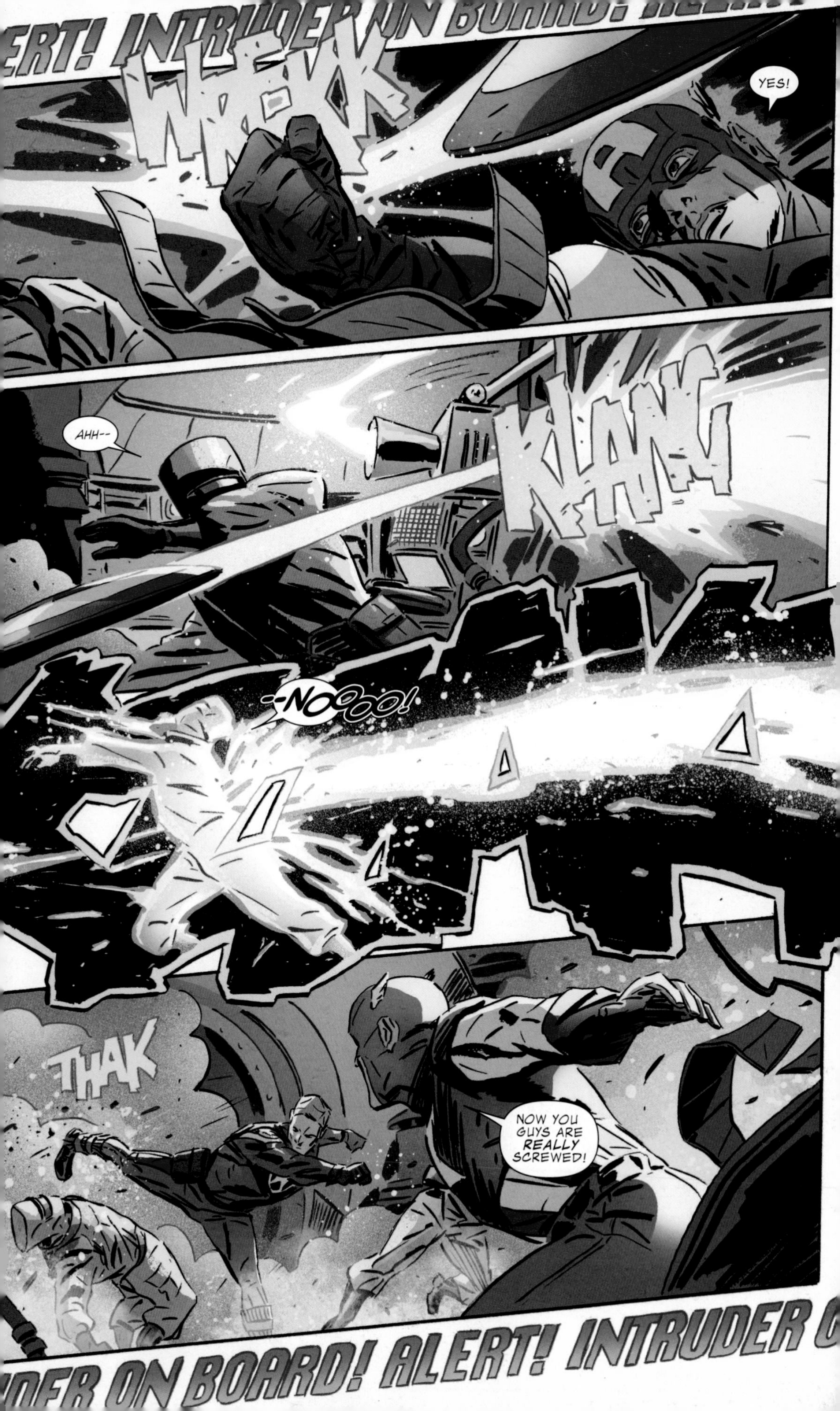

ERT! INTRUDER ON BOARD!
WRECK
YES!
AHH--
KLANG
--NOOOOO!
THAK
NOW YOU GUYS ARE REALLY SCREWED!
DER ON BOARD! ALERT! INTRUDER

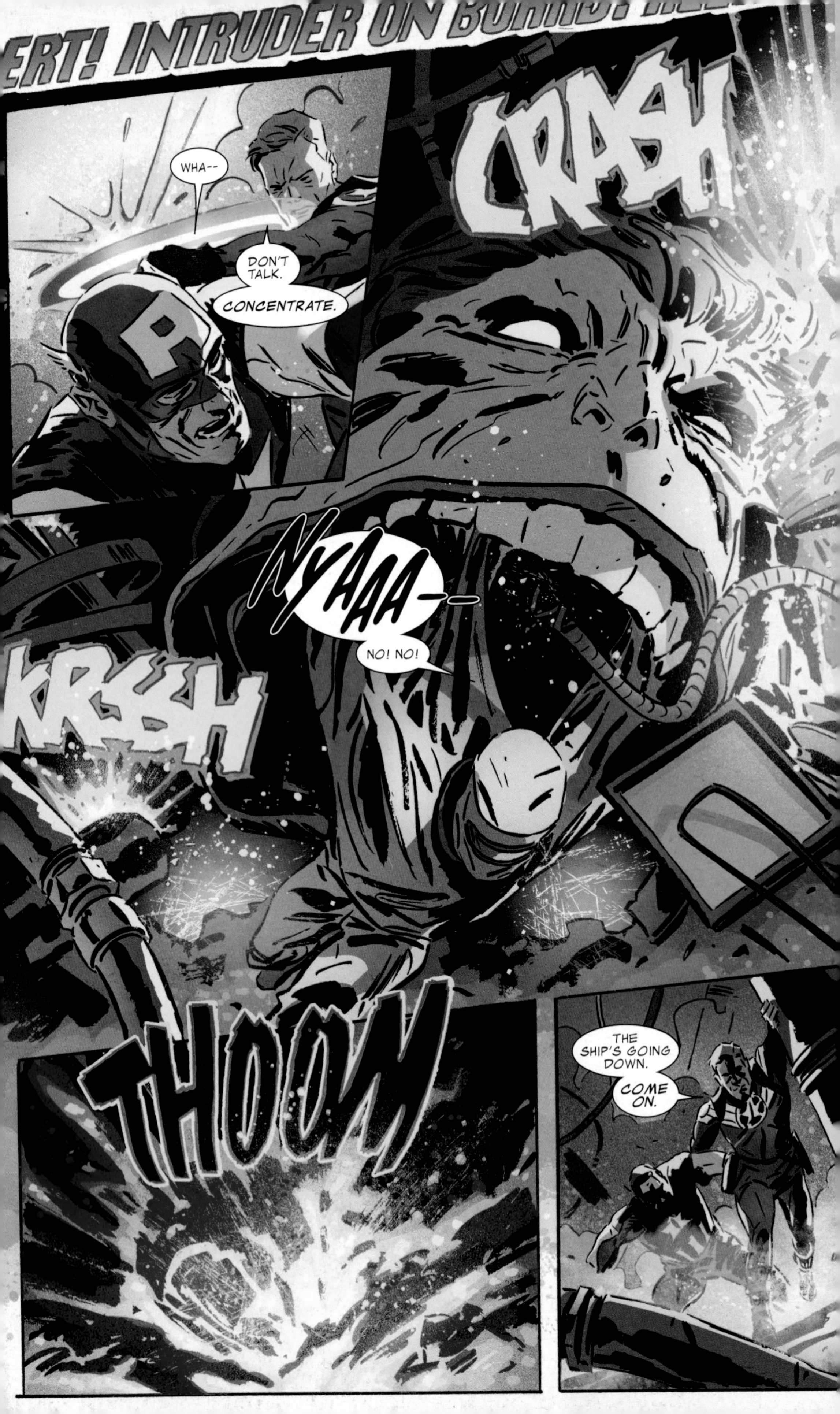
ERT! INTRUDER ON BOARD!
WHA--
DON'T TALK.
CONCENTRATE.
CRASH
NYAAA--
NO! NO!
KRASH
THOOM
THE SHIP'S GOING DOWN.
COME ON.

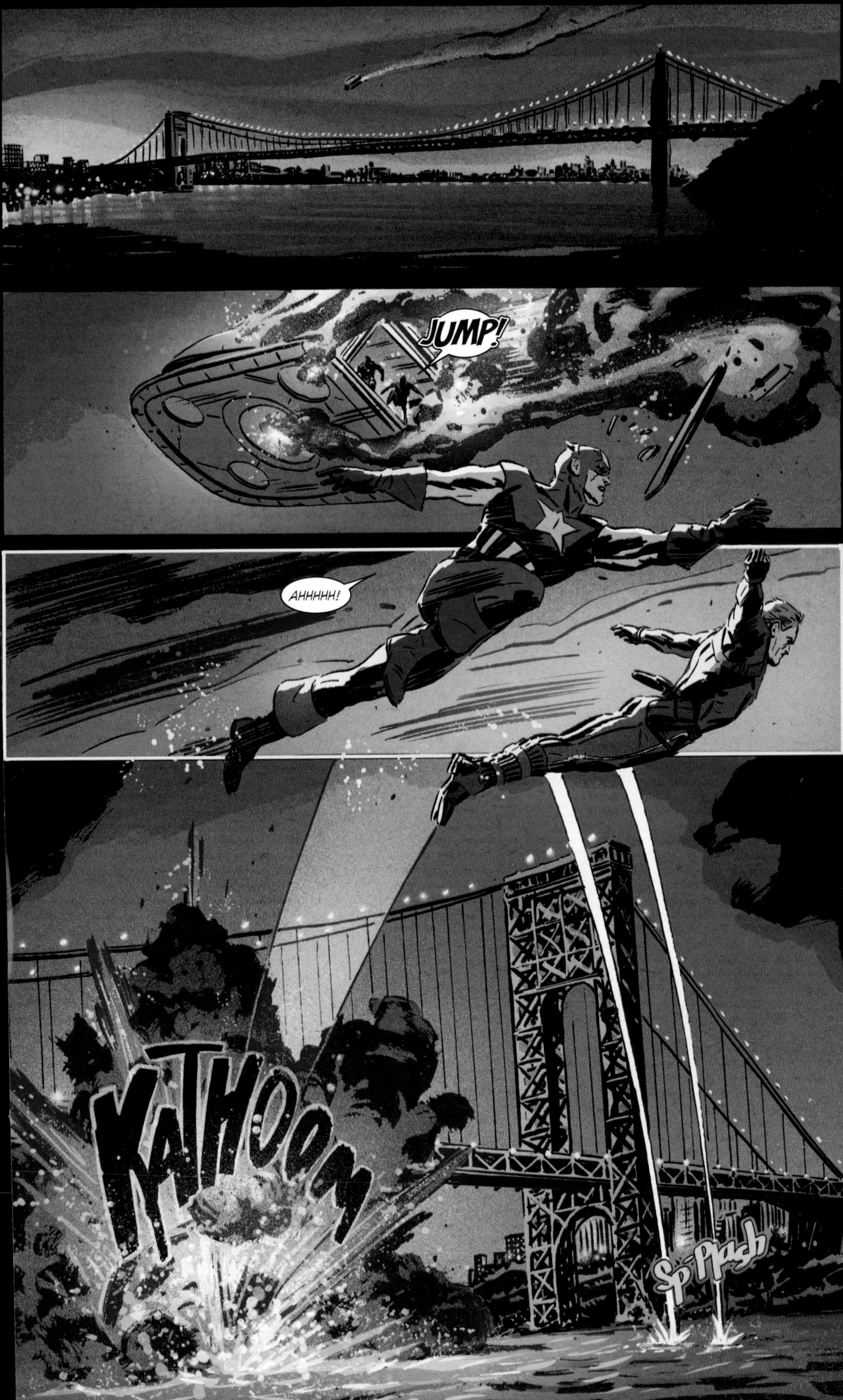
JUMP!
AHHHHH!
KATHOOM
SP-PLASH

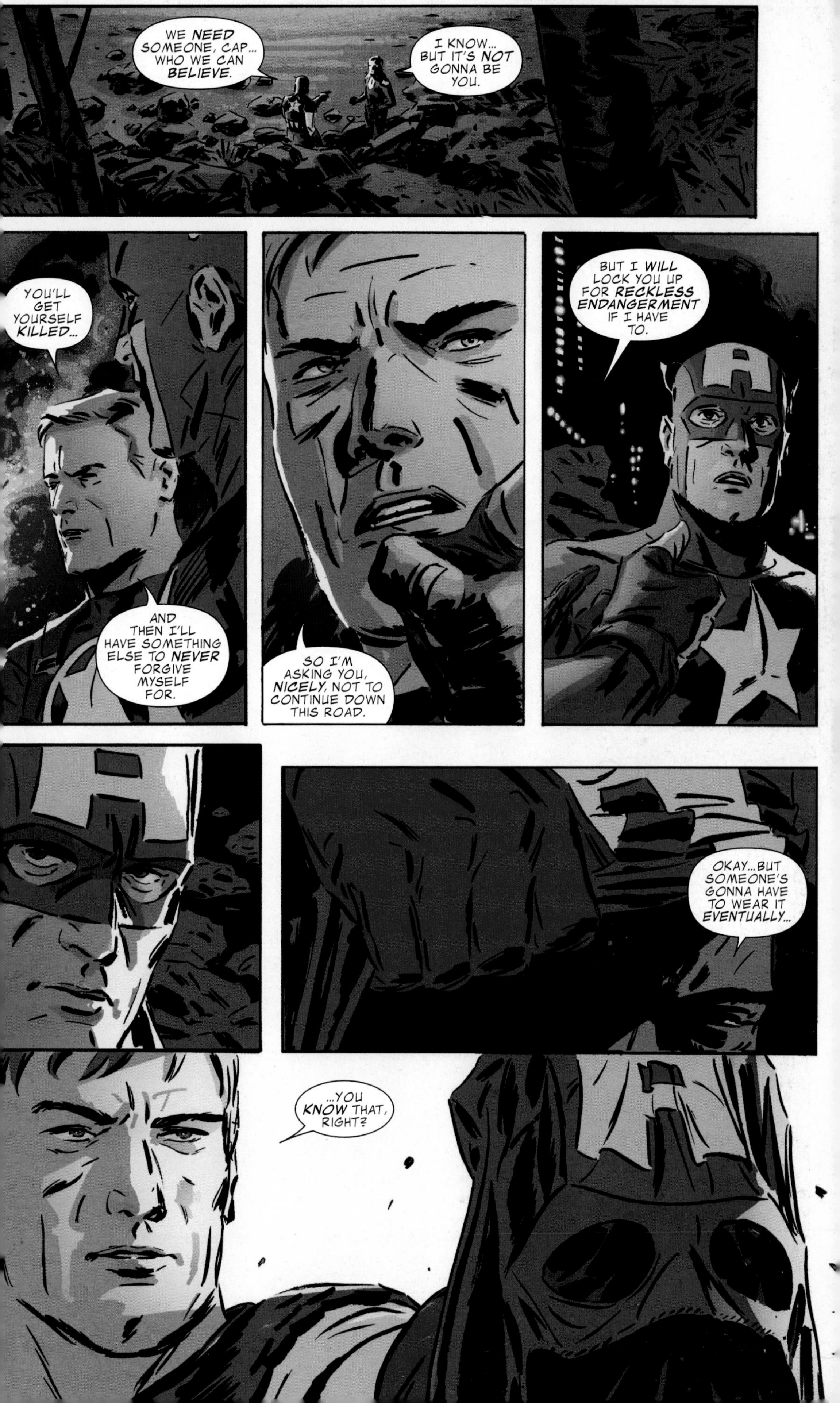
WE NEED SOMEONE, CAP... WHO WE CAN BELIEVE.
I KNOW... BUT IT'S NOT GONNA BE YOU.
YOU'LL GET YOURSELF KILLED...
AND THEN I'LL HAVE SOMETHING ELSE TO NEVER FORGIVE MYSELF FOR.
SO I'M ASKING YOU, NICELY, NOT TO CONTINUE DOWN THIS ROAD.
BUT I WILL LOCK YOU UP FOR RECKLESS ENDANGERMENT IF I HAVE TO.
OKAY...BUT SOMEONE'S GONNA HAVE TO WEAR IT EVENTUALLY...
...YOU KNOW THAT, RIGHT?

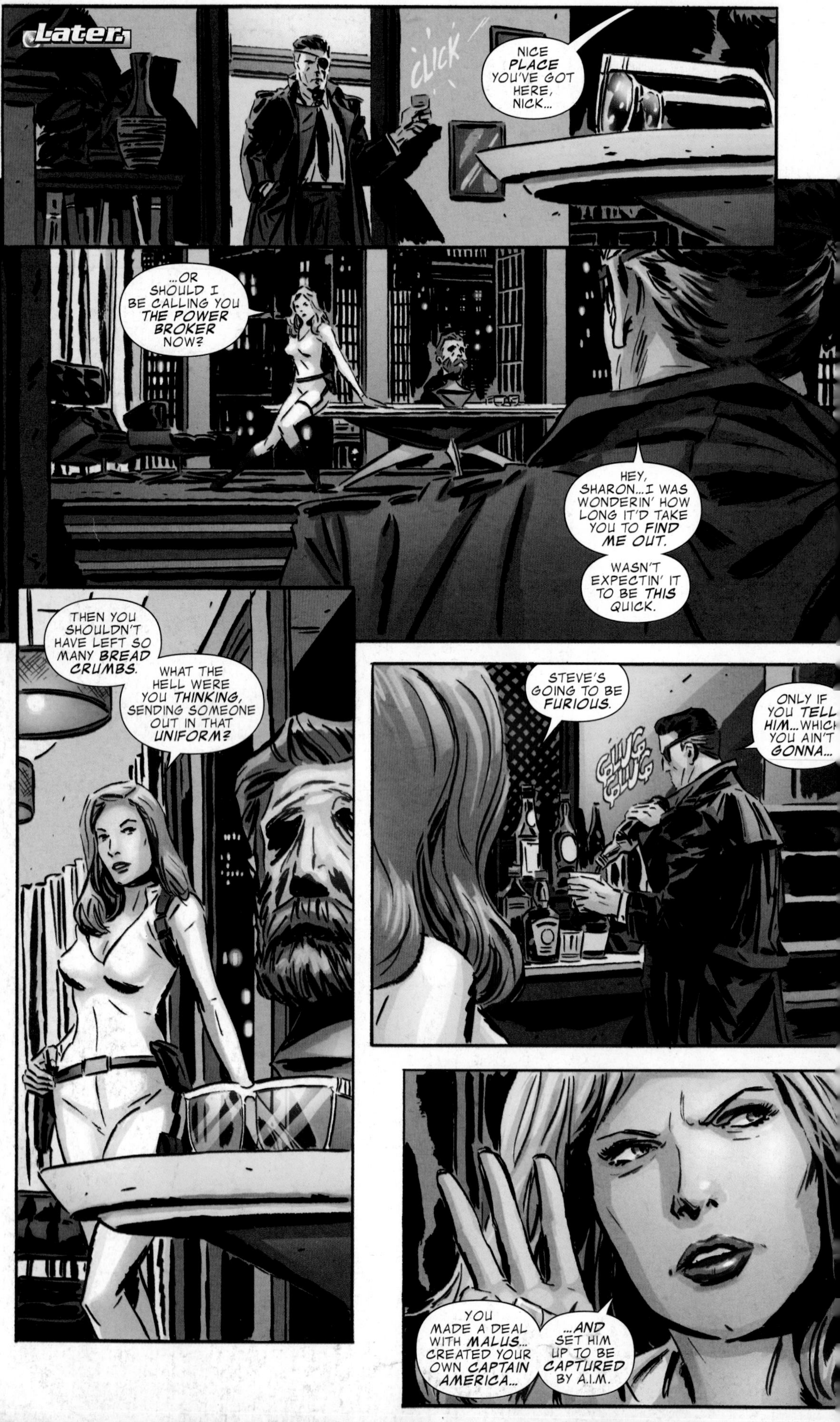
Later.
CLICK
NICE PLACE YOU'VE GOT HERE, NICK...
...OR SHOULD I BE CALLING YOU THE POWER BROKER NOW?
HEY, SHARON...I WAS WONDERIN' HOW LONG IT'D TAKE YOU TO FIND ME OUT.
WASN'T EXPECTIN' IT TO BE THIS QUICK.
THEN YOU SHOULDN'T HAVE LEFT SO MANY BREAD CRUMBS.
WHAT THE HELL WERE YOU THINKING, SENDING SOMEONE OUT IN THAT UNIFORM?
STEVE'S GOING TO BE FURIOUS.
ONLY IF YOU TELL HIM...WHICH YOU AIN'T GONNA...
GLUG GLUG
YOU MADE A DEAL WITH MALUS... CREATED YOUR OWN CAPTAIN AMERICA...
...AND SET HIM UP TO BE CAPTURED BY A.I.M.

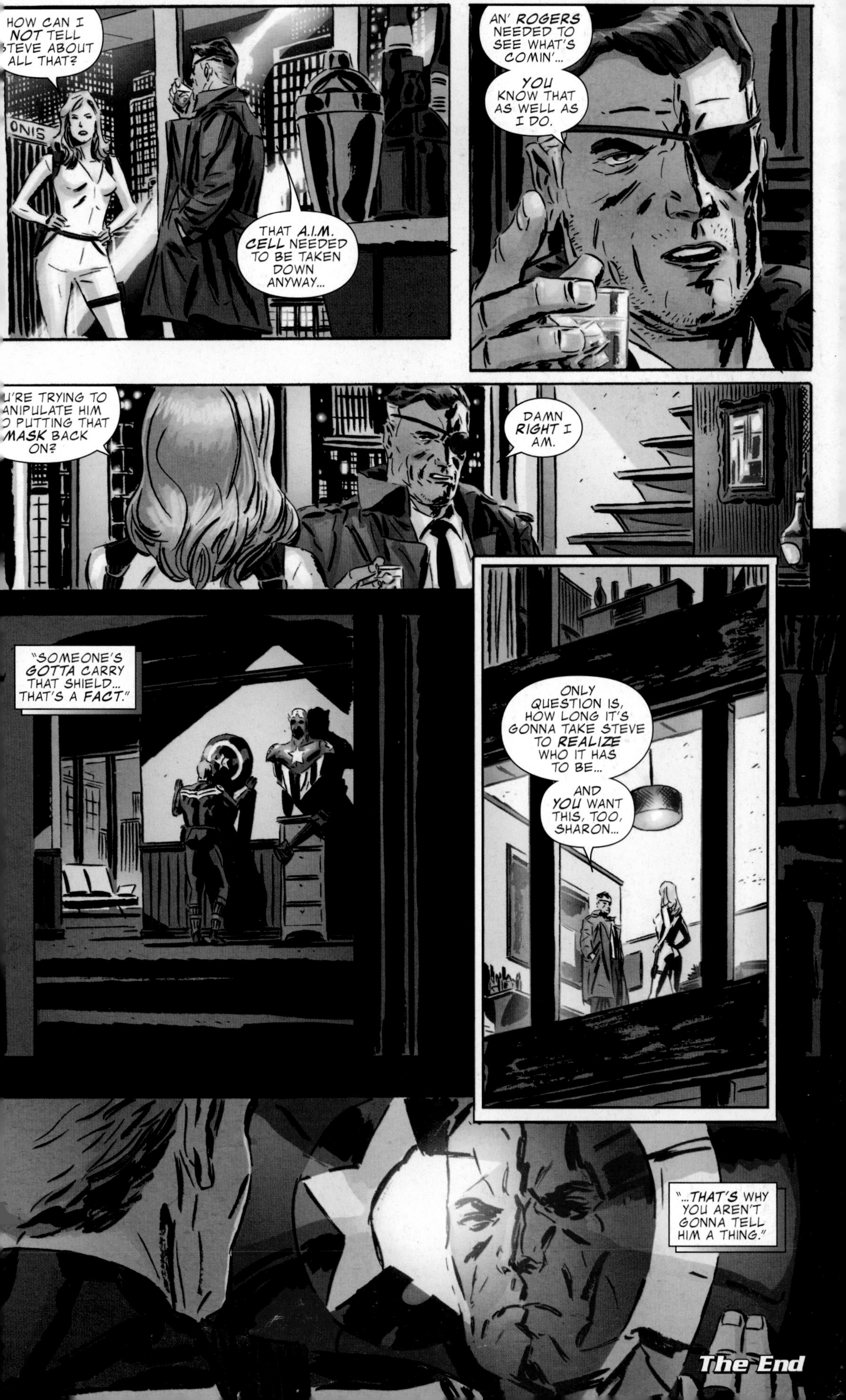
HOW CAN I NOT TELL STEVE ABOUT ALL THAT?
ONIS
THAT A.I.M. CELL NEEDED TO BE TAKEN DOWN ANYWAY...
AN' ROGERS NEEDED TO SEE WHAT'S COMIN'...
YOU KNOW THAT AS WELL AS I DO.
U'RE TRYING TO ANIPULATE HIM O PUTTING THAT MASK BACK ON?
DAMN RIGHT I AM.
"SOMEONE'S GOTTA CARRY THAT SHIELD... THAT'S A FACT."
ONLY QUESTION IS, HOW LONG IT'S GONNA TAKE STEVE TO REALIZE WHO IT HAS TO BE...
AND YOU WANT THIS, TOO, SHARON...
"...THAT'S WHY YOU AREN'T GONNA TELL HIM A THING."
The End

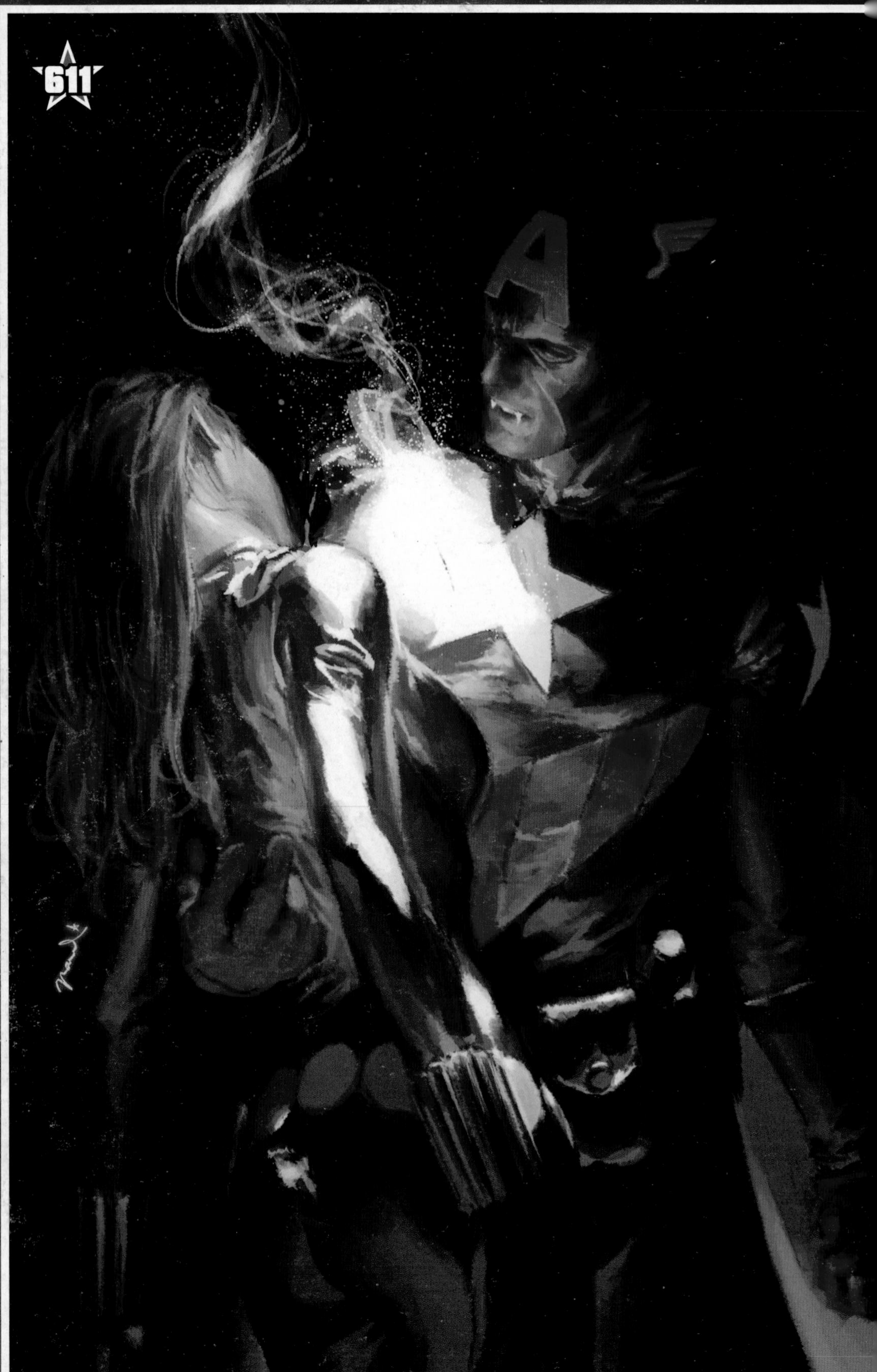
611

VAMPIRE VARIANT BY GERALD PAREL